Political Protest and Undocumented Immigrant Youth

What does it mean to be a young undocumented immigrant? Current public debate on undocumented immigration provokes discussion worldwide, and it is estimated that there are more than 11.1 million undocumented immigrants in the United States, yet what it really means to be an undocumented immigrant appears less explicitly delineated in the debate.

This interdisciplinary volume applies theories from Media, Cultural, and Literary Studies to investigate how undocumented immigrant youth in the United States have claimed a public voice by publishing their video narratives on YouTube. Case studies show how political protest significantly shapes these videos as activists narrate and perform their 'dispossession', redefining their understanding of the mechanisms of immigration in the Americas, and of home, belonging, and identity. The impact of the videos is explored as the activists connect them to Congressional bills and present their activities as a continuation of the legacy of the civil rights movements of the 1960s and 1970s.

This book will be of interest to a wide range of scholars and students involved in debates on migration, communication, new media, culture, protest movements, and political lobbying.

Stefanie Quakernack is a postdoctoral researcher and project manager at Ruhr-University Bochum. Her fields of research are immigration, education, and language. Up until 2017, Stefanie Quakernack was a lecturer and doctoral research fellow in the American Studies department at Bielefeld University, where she studied fields of U.S. immigration at the intersections of Media, Political, Literary, and Cultural Studies. Much of the research presented in this book originates in the field research that she carried out in Chicago, Illinois in spring 2014.

InterAmerican Research: Contact, Communication, Conflict

Series Editors: Olaf Kaltmeier, Josef Raab, Wilfried Raussert, and Sebastian Thies

The Americas are shaped by a multitude of dynamics that have extensive, conflictive, and, at times, contradictory consequences for society, culture, politics, and the environment. These processes are embedded within a history of interdependence and mutual observation between North and South, which originates in the conquest and simultaneous 'invention' of America by European colonial powers.

The series will challenge the ways we think about the Americas, in particular, and the concept of area studies, in general. Put simply, the series perceives the Americas as transversally related, chronotopically entangled, and multiply interconnected. In its critical positioning at the crossroads of area studies and cultural studies, the series aims to push further the post-colonial, post-national, and cross-border turns in recent studies of the Americas toward a model of horizontal dialogue between cultures, areas, and disciplines.

The series pursues the goal to 'think the Americas different' and to explore these phenomena from transregional as well as interdisciplinary perspectives.

Entangled Heritages
Postcolonial Perspectives on the Uses of the Past in Latin America
Edited by Olaf Kaltmeier, and Mario Rufer

Mobile and Entangled America(s)
Edited by Maryemma Graham and Wilfried Raussert

Practices of Resistance
Narratives, Politics, and Aesthetics across the Caribbean and its Diasporas
Edited by Wiebke Beushausen, Miriam Brandel, Joseph Farquharson, Marius Littschwager, Annika McPherson and Julia Roth

Political Protest and Undocumented Immigrant Youth
(Re) Framing *Testimonio*
Stefanie Quakernack

For more information about this series, please visit https://www.routledge.com/InterAmerican-Research-Contact-Communication-Conflict/book-series/ASHSER-1426.

Political Protest and Undocumented Immigrant Youth

(Re) Framing *Testimonio*

Stefanie Quakernack

Routledge
Taylor & Francis Group
LONDON AND NEW YORK

First published 2018
by Routledge
4 Park Square, Milton Park, Abingdon, Oxon OX14 4RN
605 Third Avenue, New York, NY 10017

Routledge is an imprint of the Taylor & Francis Group, an informa business

British Library Cataloguing-in-Publication Data
A catalogue record for this book is available from the British Library

Library of Congress Cataloging-in-Publication Data
Names: Quakernack, Stefanie, author.
Title: Political protest and undocumented immigrant youth: (re-)framing testimonio / Stefanie Quakernack.
Description: Abingdon, Oxon; New York, NY: Routledge, 2018. | Series: InterAmerican research: contact, communication, conflict | Includes bibliographical references and index.
Identifiers: LCCN 2018001255 | ISBN 9780815378525 (hbk) | ISBN 9781351232234 (ebk)
Subjects: LCSH: Illegal aliens—Political activity—United States. | Immigrant youth—Political activity—United States. | Children of illegal aliens—Political activity—United States. | YouTube (Electronic resource)—Social aspects—United States.
Classification: LCC JV6477 .Q34 2018 | DDC 305.235086/9120973—dc23
LC record available at https://lccn.loc.gov/2018001255

ISBN: 978-0-8153-7852-5 (hbk)
ISBN: 978-1-351-23223-4 (ebk)

Typeset in Times New Roman
by codeMantra

Figure 0.1 (Dis-)possessing America – Scene During Protest by Stefanie Quakernack

Contents

Figures and Tables

Figures

Tables

Preface

DREAMers Conference, Illinois Institute of Technology, Chicago, 22 March 2014

Joining a panel on 'community outreach' at a College DREAMers Conference, an 'undocumented student resource fair' in Chicago in spring 2014, and running a little late, I squeeze myself into the circle of chairs in order to listen to some of the students' 'coming out' stories. Luckily, there is some room for the chair I grab next to a young man, who helps me integrate into the circle. As the meeting proceeds, I cannot help but stare at the man's profile. It seems incredibly familiar to me. At the sound of his voice, deep and distinct, I know it: I'm sitting next to Carlos Roa, the undocumented student from Miami; the activist who walked all the way from Miami to Washington D.C. on the 'Trail of Dreams'; that student, who, if he could, would have proudly joined the U.S. army and would probably be fighting battles for the United States – the country that doesn't want his help – somewhere overseas by now. [...] Carlos Roa's digital *testimonio* on YouTube is one of the eight digital narratives that I analyzed for this study. By the day of the conference, I had watched his video clip a few dozen times; I knew his biography by heart; I knew how he pronounced his words and formed his gestures, and how tears looked in his eyes.

When approaching him after the panel, I am amazed to see that the person whose narrative I analyzed for so many hours, whose face, voice, and body I studied under the powerful influence of coffee and sugar, was actually a real human being.

His discomfort at my knowledge about him, my many questions, and my excitement grow steadily. Obviously, Carlos had not only changed visually: wearing glasses, less tan, and looking a bit older. He also deferred what his digital *testimonio* depicted as his eternal dream: joining the military. By contrast, Carlos now attends the Illinois Institute of Technology, majoring in architecture – all made possible through the Illinois DREAM Act and the Deferred Action for Childhood Arrivals.

What I realized that day at the conference was that – no matter how permanent and desperate things seem – there is always room for transformation. Indeed, Carlos Roa had changed. His post on the Internet, his video clip on YouTube, his *testimonio* to the world, however, had not.

Acknowledgements

I would like to express my sincere gratitude to my advisor Prof. Wilfried Raussert for the continuous support of my PhD study and related research, for his advice, immense knowledge, confidence, and positivity. My sincere thanks also goes to Prof. Joachim Michael.

My research stay in Chicago in spring 2014 was a very valuable experience. I would sincerely like to thank the *Immigrant Youth Justice League*, who provided me with the opportunity to join their team, and who gave me access to their meetings, workshops, and political activities. Thank you, Antonio Gutiérrez, Marcela Hernandez, Uriel Sánchez, and Gabriela Benítez, among many others, for sharing your thoughts with me.

I owe my deepest gratitude also to Judith Hiltner and Jim Walker, who made me feel so incredibly welcome in their home in Chicago, and for their help, interest, and inspiration. And to Libby Broadwell, Larry Gulde, and Anna Broadwell-Gulde, who have introduced me to so much good in life already.

I thank my colleagues at Bielefeld University for the stimulating discussions, encouragement, and for all the fun we have had during these four years. In particular, I am grateful to Dr. Luz Angélica Kirschner and Dr. Julia Andres for being such vivid and smart women, who have always provided me with great advice and warm encouragement. C4 – I loved being part of you!

I would also like to thank all my friends, whom I can always count on, and all my girls especially…! (Schlaeppis, you are wonderful…!) Be daring, dashing, and powerful!

I am indebted to my family, who never ceased believing in me, encouraging me, and being proud! I particularly would like to thank my parents, Gabi and Herbert, who have made this possible, and my two sisters, Katharina and Verena.

Finally, I would like to thank the love of my life, Matthias, who has been a constant source of comfort, joy, and support.

Acknowledgements

1 Introduction

Digital narratives of undocumented immigrant youth

1. On being 'unauthorized'

Today, more than ever, the public debate on undocumented immigration fuels countless discussions all over the world. While opinions are easily formed, statements quickly made, what it really *means* to be an undocumented immigrant appears less explicitly delineated in the debate. Manuel et al., editors of a film project about the lives of undocumented youth in the U.S., summarize the implications that the immigration status holds for children growing up as undocumented as follows:

> Approximately two million undocumented children live in the United States [...]. Sixty-five thousand undocumented youth graduate from high school every year [...] without 'papers.' In most states, they can't get a driver's license or state ID and in most cases it is against the law to work. It is difficult, if not impossible in some states, to attend college. [...] Universities have varying policies about whether they accept undocumented students. If they are accepted, undocumented students are not eligible for federal financial aid.
>
> (iv–v)

The list of impediments does not end here. Far from worries about higher education are more immediate problems: discrimination, criminalization, poverty, and fear of deportation, enforcing a life in the shadows.

In December 2005, the 'Sensenbrenner Bill', officially named the Border Protection, Anti-Terrorism, and Illegal Immigration Control Act (H.R. 4437), was ratified by the U.S. House of Representatives, turning undocumented immigrants and those who helped them into felons (cf. Mauk and Oakland 73). That following spring, the Immigrant Rights Movement experienced a revival that successfully staged mega-marches and massive public protest against the introduction of the Sensenbrenner Bill. It was young people, in particular, who formed "identified undocumented student groups and statewide networks" in ever-growing numbers to speak out against this act of legislative criminalization (Pérez 83). Nevertheless, this development has been missing in current research despite its urgency, Pérez notes (69). In particular, "the debate has largely ignored the civic engagement of immigrant youth", he adds (ibid).

Who, then, are 'undocumented youth'? As of 2015, there were approximately 11.1 million undocumented immigrants in the United States. Of those, roughly 65,000 undocumented students get their high school degree each year, now seeking college opportunities (cf. Rusin 3). Further, "many of these children came here during the population boom in the 1990s" (2). Anguiano employs the term '1.5 generation' to describe a generation that is stuck between the parental generation who grew up in the home country and their younger brothers and sisters who are U.S. citizens (cf. 6). By means of this definition, she highlights the identity conflict of this generation, an aspect that gains more attention when discussing the intersections of identities in the following chapters. These youths literally grow up "in-between" two cultures (4). These struggles, in addition to the impediments that undocumented status entails, would seem to defeat even the most determined attempt to find a political voice in U.S. society that speaks against the criminalization of a whole population. Or maybe not? Is it possible for undocumented immigrant youth to participate in U.S. society while 'officially' not being a part of the whole?

Seeking alternative ways to engage, Bendit observes that "even if formal participation of young people in existing political structures and institutions is decreasing in almost all societies everywhere", they nevertheless "play an important – sometimes even central – role in social movements aiming at societal change and transformation", often "based on voluntary work and informal participation" (37). But how so? When I asked an undocumented youth leader from Chicago how he relates his political participation to his 'unauthorized', undocumented status, his response was the following:

> It's saying like 'I'm not *allowed* to do something'. And that's how I see that word [...]. I feel like I can do whatever I want, because I'm still here and I'm still human. [...] We don't have to be citizens in this nation to have that right of ... be able to speak and be able to organize ourselves and be able to wish for a better treatment. And I think when you're saying 'unauthorized', it's like putting you into this conversation, this box, of like, 'you're not allowed to do certain things' and I truly don't believe that.
>
> (Gutiérrez, personal interview)

It is in this underlying conviction of the basic right to improve one's personal situation through personal activism by all means in which undocumented youth frequently ground their basic understanding of immigrant rights activism, as this extract from the interview shows. Personal activism underlies a movement that steps beyond the sphere of action that the human is assigned to act within and which authorizes the individual to adhere to social and cultural norms (and matrices) (cf. Butler, *Dispossession* 21).

Both aspects – the wish to improve one's situation and activism outside of the assigned sphere – are not innovative but defining characteristics of any movement and/or activism. It is a particularly thought-provoking fact that "despite the dangers involved in speaking out publicly, many students [...] are finding strength and courage in numbers" to 'out' themselves as undocumented in public (Pérez 84). What is more, many of these 'coming out' narratives can also be found online, on platforms such as YouTube – the platform that this project uses as a source for accessing narratives of undocumented youth. Three crucial factors explain this move. First, YouTube essentially has "its roots in youth culture" (Kavoori 4). Second, YouTube further serves as an excellent example of the observation that "that storytelling is at the heart of all media" (2). Third, while YouTube is widely famous for its role in entertainment culture, Jenkins stresses that "shifts in technical infrastructure, including the emergence of YouTube, have dramatically expanded the [...] capacity to respond to human rights abuses" (121). Thus, in video clips posted on YouTube, undocumented youth come out as undocumented, refraining from any anonymity to protect their identity other than the enormous vastness of Web 2.0. They tell *their* stories of a life with undocumented status, connecting it to their undocumented peers, family, and community; ethnic and gender identity; and personal acts of resistance within the frame of a developing Immigrant Rights Movement. As Pérez has documented, "in efforts to claim rights and a political voice", undocumented youth have actively spoken to the public during conferences or public events (83). Further, undocumented youth meet with officials from almost any institution that touches their lives, in the schools themselves and also in the community in order to "increase awareness of policies like in-state tuition laws" and improve their options for the future (ibid).

Having spent two months in such an organization, the Immigrant Youth Justice League (IYJL), in Chicago in spring 2014, I witnessed determined youth activism, manifested in, for instance, organization meetings and conferences, various acts of civil disobedience, emotional outbursts in personal interviews, and, most importantly, the National Coming Out of the Shadows Day that IYJL created. This unique event consisted of public speeches delivered annually by undocumented immigrants on Chicago's federal plaza and in various other cities across the nation on March 10.

This act showed a different side of the undocumented population to the public and encouraged further people to participate (cf. Pallares, *Family Activism* 113). Being a witness to such events, I can legitimately affirm that the Movement[1] has gained momentum through its use of new media that is unprecedented in the history of immigrant civil rights struggles.

From an interdisciplinary perspective, intertwining insights from cultural, media, and literary studies, this study addresses Kellner and Hammer's request to "overcome divisions" in the field of media and cultural studies (xxxiv) by providing perspectives on "an open-ended project" that takes seriously "the ways that different forms or examples of media and culture function in our society and can be read to provide enlightenment and insight about the society" (xxxv). Mediatization theory will be used for these purposes. In addition to that, the (political) context of the Immigrant Rights Movement since 2006 is the main referent to interpret the narrative's political messages in eight digital narratives of undocumented youth published on YouTube. This approach to understanding the narratives reduces, in part, the risk that videos "get decontextualized as they enter this hybrid media space" on YouTube and, thus, bear "progressive potential" when recontextualized, as Jenkins emphasizes (122). Likewise, while the space to do so is limited, by applying theory on new media narrative and narratology, such as 'intermediality' and 'multimodality', this study will address Punday's concern that "cybertexts [...] are like some new species recently discovered", lacking in "cybertext theory", which consists of adequate categories and terms "that are fair to this new medium" (19). The Latin American narrative genre of the *testimonio* serves as a connection between media and cultural studies in the analysis of the narratives.

2. Waking the 'sleeping giant': the Immigrant Rights Movement in 2006

In early 2006, different immigrant organizations and institutions came together to plan a 'National Day of Action' on March 10 of that year (cf. Flores-González and Gutiérrez 5). Consequently, large marches took place in roughly 250 cities across the United States throughout the months of March and April. These protested against the 'Sensenbrenner Bill' – a bill that was considered "draconian" by the immigrant and (non-immigrant) population (Pallares and Flores-González xv). Especially in Chicago, the march became a (literally) huge success, as one hundred thousand people marched together toward the city center (cf. Flores-González and Gutiérrez 5). Consequently, the spring of 2006 became known as the 'Spring of the Immigrant', which counted among "the largest immigrant rights activities in U.S. history" (Pallares and Flores-González xv).

This study focuses geographically upon events in Chicago, Illinois in order to define the development of the Immigrant Rights Movement. Next to the fact that the many personal conversations with activists[2] and leaders of IYJL during my research stay in Chicago heavily informed my understanding of the Movement, the choice of this city as a 'base' has multiple other empirical advantages: The focus on this city, according to Pallares and Flores-González, sheds light on the "different types of organizations, institutions, and social actors that have shaped the contemporary immigrant rights movement" (xxi). Further, Pallares and Flores-González stress the city's "complex history of immigrant activism" (ibid). Not only has the city hosted the largest Coming Out of the Shadows event in 2010, it could also be described as the "ground zero for the first day of actions" (Anguiano 152).

With regard to its immigration history, the city not only counts as the "second-largest Mexican community (after Los Angeles)" (Anguiano 152), it can also safely be called a 'city of immigrants' (cf. Misra n.pag.). Naturally, Latino activism has been a vital part of the city's culture and politics since the 1920s (cf. Pallares, *The Chicago Context* 38). Insights gained in more recently emerging Chicago immigrant youth activism thus serves as a rich basis for analyzing narratives of undocumented youth.

In multiple attempts, the Comprehensive Immigration Reform Act failed in summer 2007, causing "great disappointment" among immigration activists (Pallares, *Family Activism* 41). However, the protests clearly articulated Comprehensive Immigration Reform as their general objective, as well as the halt of the deportations of undocumented immigrants (cf. Pallares, *Family Activism* 96 and 112–113). In this mobilization for Comprehensive Immigration Reform, the marches became the "movement's main muscle" (Pallares, *The Chicago Context* 54). In particular, in these gatherings, new networks and coalitions were formed, "essentially consolidating the immigrant rights efforts that emerged after the 1986 reform" (5) and demonstrating a political power that had been underestimated by all (cf. Flores-González and Gutiérrez 7): Now, and for all, the metaphor that compares the Latin@ population of the United States to the body of a sleeping giant has been exposed as inadequate (cf. Pallares, *The Chicago Context* 58). Most importantly, the resurgence of the Movement expressed that undocumented immigrants need to claim their "rights to have rights" (ibid).

Focusing upon strategies for publicity and an agenda as a means for defining politics, this study opens the discussion for the affordances and challenges that the new media sphere brings upon young activists. The analysis of the eight narratives of undocumented youth, produced between 2006 and 2013, places the political message that these narratives produce in the context of the Immigrant Rights Movement since its revival in 2006.

3. Mediatizing politics: testimonial storytelling online

A concept useful for grasping the changes in *testimonios* through new media is 'mediatization', a theoretical perspective that "refers to the meta process by which everyday practices and social relations are historically shaped by mediating technologies and media organizations" (Livingstone x). The basis for mediatization is the observation of "the increasing presence and importance of the media in all parts of social and political life" (Schulz 9). Nowadays, according to Hjarvard, the media "organize public and private communication in ways that are adjusted to the individual medium's logic and market considerations" (17), which results in a (political) society that becomes increasingly dependent on media (cf. Lundby, *Introduction: Mediatization* 12). As the key to the public sphere, media not only 'mediate' (political) content but actively *form* public opinion (cf. Esser and Strömback 4). But which processes are actually at work?

Because we lack a detailed conceptualization, Esser and Strömbäck have described four dimensions of the mediatization of politics (cf. 7): The first dimension understands media as a source of information about politics and society. The second dimension emphasizes the growing autonomy of media as an (or many) institution(s). Both of these dimensions have been well-known and researched.

The third and fourth dimensions point to the "degree to which media content and the coverage of politics and current affairs is guided by media logic or political logic" and how political actors and organizations are "guided" by these logics (Esser and Strömbäck 7). These latter two dimensions serve as the basis for understanding online narratives of undocumented youth in this study. For our purposes, we need to understand, in particular, the media logic of social media because this logic serves as the 'engine' of mediatization processes and, ultimately, influences social movements, political institutions, and individual actors. These realize that "in order to influence the media, and through the media the public, they will have to adapt to the media and the media's logic" (7–8).

Media logic, however, should not be understood as 'logic' per se but as "terms as agreement", "reasoning", and "necessity" (Lundby, *Media Logic* 114). Altheide and Snow further understand media logic as "the process through which media present and transmit information", embracing "various media and the formats used by these media" to communicate, including "how material is organized, the style in which it is presented, the focus or emphasis on particular characteristics of behavior, and the grammar of media communication" (10). It follows that through media logic, we may actually 'see' and interpret social and cultural phenomena (cf. 9), which we perceive as "normalized" at first glance (12).[3]

In the mediatization of politics, the 'political logic' is "about collective and authoritative decision-making" and their "implementation" (Esser and Strömbäck 14). It embraces the "public face" that is closely related to "tactics and strategies for winning support and publicity, image projections and branding" (Esser and Strömbäck 15). Thus, it includes "the presentational side of politics" as well as the implementation and distribution of political power connected to that (ibid). Naturally, the intertwinement of media logic and political logic are connected ongoing social processes and prone to change under different agendas and, thus, never fixed (cf. Schrott 58).

A significant aspect of media logic is the 'affordances' of a particular medium, that is the "socio-technological format" that shapes the content in the production processes of that medium (Esser and Strömbäck 18) – pressing a content into a particular format, one could say. Television, for instance, reinforces visuals, while digital media emphasize "interactivity and instantaneousness" (ibid). A social medium such as YouTube, on the other hand, affords "networking, time-shifting, sharing content, co-creating media products, and mashing-up messages" (Schulz 62). New media, most importantly, often serve multiple logics, blending different modes and media.[4]

The information deduced from the interviews with undocumented youth from Chicago is consistent with Esser and Strömbäck's construct in crucial respects. The Immigrant Rights Movement positions new media, in particular, as its major source of information and device for communication. Due to the fact that "social movement media represent a dizzying variety of formats and experiences, far greater than mainstream commercial, public, or state media" (Downing xxv), YouTube has become an interesting field of research for investigating the mediatization of politics and will therefore serve as a platform to gather digital narratives of undocumented youth for this study. As Kavoori stresses, YouTube is "much more than a website – it is a key element in the way we think about our online experience and (shared) digital culture" (3). What is most relevant for our purposes is the extent to which "it becomes more important for political actors and institutions to use the media to reach out to larger groups in society" (Esser and Strömbäck 7). The central questions resulting from this elaboration on the mediatization of politics in the context of the Immigrant Rights Movement are, in particular:

- Which political messages do the narratives of undocumented youth on YouTube produce, and how do they relate to the Immigrant Rights Movement?
- How do undocumented youth activists embed the medium's logic (YouTube) into their videos, and how does this shape their content and form?

4. (Digital) *testimonio* – a literature of combat

As early as in 1996, Gugelberger prognosticated that

> the end of this century and years into the next will be characterized by migrations unforeseen in the past [...]. It might be proper to ask how this scenario bears on literature and theory, not so much how it is reflected in literature but rather how literature and theory can function in a responsible and perhaps even rehumanizing way.
>
> (7)

In this quote, Gugelberger highlights the role of literature in the questions of humanity that (im)migration poses for our culture. By bringing to life their stories, undocumented youth people might have a chance at persuading "the American public to care about them and think about this situation in a more nuanced and compassionate manner", Galisky hypothesizes (x). Testimonials, interviews, and family histories, in particular, possess the power to reflect the human plight of undocumented youth and their families (cf. Mathay xiii).

The fact that testimonials have gained publicity is not a coincidence. While narratives have always been understood as a "central mode of human thought and as a vehicle of meaning making" (Erstad and Wertsch 28), the 'narrative turn' emphasizes *personal* stories as subjective accounts of reality. The *grand narratives*, on the other hand, have "lost their force" (Polletta 2). Consequently, the narrative turn unleashed a myriad of "biographical methods or the renewal of interest in autobiography" in the humanities (Chamberlain 142).

For social movements, in general, it is stressed that "storytelling sustains groups as they fight for reform, helping them build new collective identities, link current actions to heroic pasts and glorious futures, and restyle setbacks as way stations to victory" (Polletta 3). However, next to the positive qualities attributed to personal stories, storytelling can also be limiting, as the cultural frame that stories are created in also shapes the 'structural conditions' of these stories, which can be potentially limiting (cf. 4). Therefore, movements instrumentalize cultural norms in their stories: "Once movements are underway, activists have a real stake in using culture strategically, embracing dominant beliefs and conventions of representation where it serves them and refusing them where it does not", Polletta observes (5). It follows that throughout different phases of a social movement, some stories can become "canonical" for a movement, affecting the political logic of the movement, while, at the same time, always being subject to change (7). Here, storytelling becomes a "cultural performance" (Madison and Hamera xvii) that can potentially cause change. By this, narratives produced within a social movement become 'counter-discursive' – acts of power that challenge the dominant, "socially constructed knowledges of (some aspect of reality)" (Kress and Van Leeuwen 4) that are "delivered and circulated by all kinds of modes of communications" (Abrams 110).

In the narratives produced in the context of the Immigrant Rights Movement, undocumented status intersects with issues in the family and community, as well as ethnic identity, gender, and mental health. When listing these fields of focus, we need to emphasize that due to the fluid and intersecting character of identities, the latter cannot be analyzed independently from each other. Rather, from an intersectional perspective, different identities serve as trajectories for "addressing the interlacing of different relations of dominance" (Kallenberg et al. 21), such as those evoked by the lack of 'papers' in the lives of undocumented youth.

Detecting compliant thematic and formal structures, narrative strategies, visual techniques, and a dominant political message, this study demonstrates that the narratives of undocumented youth selected are similar to a particular genre, the *testimonio*. Difficult to define, *testimonios* finds themselves "at the crossroads of all the discourses of institutional battles in recent years" (Gugelberger 7). One basic trait of the *testimonio*, however, is that the narrator "gives his or her personal testimony 'directly,' addressing a specific interlocutor" (Yúdice 42), depicting a significant life experience. At the same time, the narrator connects his/her story to a particular political struggle (oftentimes a liberation movement) (cf. Zimmerman 107), intending to effect change (cf. Roth 178), or "at least [to] raise consciousness" (Gugelberger 4).

'Consciousness', hence, counts as a form of political power. In an interview, community organizer Marcela Hernandez argues that "it has really meant for a way to fight for my own rights. [...] to realize my dreams and also, to know that I could change the situation I was in, and it wasn't hopeless, so hopeless" (Hernandez). Likewise, according to Cedillo, undocumented students coming out of the shadows attempt to change the "hateful rhetoric" that is part of the public discourse on immigration (Manuel et al. viii). Power, thus, can simply mean 'breaking silences', crossing imaginary and real borders.

Locating the political messages of the narratives of undocumented youth in their performance of 'marginalized' or dispossessed identities, this study highlights the ways that these youths 'resist their oppression'. Connecting narrated life experience in *testimonio* to Judith Butler and Athena Athanasiou's recent work on 'dispossession' and resistance through the performative of the body and the speech act of the narrator offers a normative understanding of the hardships that undocumented youth experience. Understanding dispossession as 'the performative in the political', Butler and Athanasiou connect performance studies that demonstrate the potential to "interrogate and enrich our basic understanding of history, identity, community, nation, and politics" (Madison and Hamera xii). This perspective investigates "multiple operations of performance (performativity and the performative) within a written text, a life world, and in domains of cognitive and imaginary expressions" (xxiv). Performativity, a term coined by Butler, points to identity constructions as 'speech acts' that reiterate identity constructions through repetitive utterances and behavior and, thus, inhabit the potential to create a "moment of a counter-mobilization" (*Excitable Speech* 163). Undocumented youth narrate and perform this moment of 'dispossession' that they experience, which serves as a paradigm interconnecting the stories. The range of tragic stories of dispossession in the core of the digital narratives is vast: from having to work three jobs, not being able to attend university, to experiencing severe discrimination and dehumanization, suffering from depression, and even suicidal thoughts, to name just a few. But what is the reason for and the effect of publishing such intimate detail in form of a digital testimonial narrative on YouTube with regard to the politics of the Immigrant Rights Movement?

Clearly, analyzing narratives of undocumented youth published online in the context of the 'traditional' testimonial genre requires a modified approach to narrative. Here, the 'digital *testimonio*' proves of use. According to Rina Benmayor, who coined the term, the digital *testimonio* incorporates two practices: the traditional *testimonio* and multimedia devices for storytelling (cf. 507) – a practice which provides the *testimonio* with new creative power (cf. 508).

This 'mediatization' of the storytelling tradition includes different categories of storytelling devices: multimedia storytelling (a combination of different media systems), intermedial storytelling (using media combination, transfer, and references), as well as multimodal storytelling (a combination of modes within the same media system).

Shaping content with a combination of modes, "multimodality" is an important affordance of social media and to the narratives of undocumented youth. The combination of modes points to "the actions, materials and artefacts people communicate with" (Jewitt, *Introduction to Multimodality* 16). Ventola et al. stress that serving as a 'language' for storytelling, "multimodality and multimediality, when seen as combinations of writing, speaking, visualisation, sounds, music, etc., have always been omnipresent in most of the communicative contexts in which humans engaged" (1). However, they point out that

> it is relatively recent that the developments of the various possibilities of combining communication modes in the 'new' media, like the computer and the Internet, have forced scholars to think about the particular characteristics of these modes and the way they semiotically function and combine in the modern discourse worlds.
>
> (ibid)

Investigating digital *testimonios* of undocumented youth, hence, as mediatized *testimonios* offers a new perspective upon this 'new language' that new media platforms such as YouTube utilize. Integrating into the media logic on YouTube, however, the narratives need to negotiate their own, political logic that the genre of the *testimonio* as a form of political communication in and for the purposes of the Immigrant Rights Movement inhabits. In order to understand the latter's politics, this study, hence, sets out to explore the negotiation of the respective media logic(s) with the political logic(s) of the narrators in the digital narratives. We need to think more critically about whether media merely reproduce or perhaps *reframe* the *testimonio* in its digital form online and, in this way, shape the content, form, and political message of digital *testimonios* of undocumented youth.

5. Research questions and outline of study

In 2006, undocumented youth demonstrated the potential for actively resisting impending criminalizing legislative changes. That year, activists and allies, undocumented and 'legal' immigrants, in the United States formed political resistance that presented "an attractive alternative to the frustrating impediments of legal marginality", as Pérez observes (78). Is it possible, then, to argue that testimonial 'storytelling' online illustrates a mediatization of the *testimonio* that connects the logic of the medium with their political message and, hence, forms an inherently new type of political protest, responding to media changes? In short, do undocumented youth with their digital *testimonios* online serve as an example of the mediatization of politics that triggers major political protest?

The following chapter introduces, in detail, the politics of the revived Immigrant Rights Movement since the mega-marches in 2006, including a definition for the use of 'politics' in this study. To provide a focus, this study investigates the Movement within the frame of the legislative period of the Obama regime. Significant aspects are the historical developments of the Movement with regard to its current public agenda, leadership, and communication. The chapter further presents personal interview data that reveal the significance of (new) media for the Movement from the perspective of four undocumented immigrant activists from Chicago. The chapter also introduces media logic on YouTube and presents the selection of the corpus of digital narratives of undocumented youth for this investigation.

Chapter 3 introduces the narratological toolbox for analysis in this study. It provides an understanding of 'narrative' and elaborates on the *testimonio* as a counter-discursive genre with inherent political significance that has frequently been debated. Narrowing down the definition of *testimonio* as far as possible, it introduces the digital *testimonio* proposed by Benmayor in contrast both to the tradition of the *testimonio* and to digital storytelling on YouTube. Offering this framework, however, raises issues for understanding digital narratives on YouTube as *testimonios* due to the socio-technological format of the website – an inherent aspect of the latter's media logic. The focus, as traced from the interviews, shall lie on the participation, personalization, and performance of the political communication in the narratives. Further, the chapter narrows down which affordances and their semiotic resources[5] the selecteddigital narratives choose.

As a chapter that both introduces a theoretical approach and applies it subsequently, Chapter 4 narrows down the content of the digital *testimonios* as stories of dispossession, with reference to Butler and Athanasiou's theory and introduces the concept of the performative in dispossession as political protest. The chapter also introduces the basic content of each digital *testimonio* with regard to the narrator's 'dispossession'.

Answering the basic question of how these narrators *perform* their dispossession in their digital *testimonios* by means of multimodal storytelling that the YouTube video affords in order to shape their political meaning, the final chapters are devoted to the analysis of the narratives. The chapters are structured according to different modes, as the overview in Chapter 4 suggests, and interpret the different narratives interchangeably according to the different categories of that mode. According to the logic on YouTube, Chapter 5 begins with the most literal type of performance – the corporeal performance – a performance which, in the digital *testimonios*, is mediatized as a motion image, filmed by a camera, and 'starring' the narrator of each of the eight *testimonios*. As all analysis chapters, Chapter 5 first introduces the basic categories for analysis that the analysis features. The chapter thus narrows down the virtual corporeal, face-to-face performance of the narrator in moving image to the effect of gestures, facial expressions, space, and movement. It further introduces the use of an 'other narrator' through film editing – cutting and zoom, in particular, and the interplay between verbal spoken narrative and the visual moving image.

Chapter 6 investigates the use of voice, noises, and music in the narratives. It lays particular emphasis on the tradition of the *testimonio* as a form of oral storytelling (that is then transcribed by an interlocutor and edited into written text). Thus, the introduction of the narratives, in particular, bears close resemblance to *testimonios* such as that of Rigoberta Menchú, most famously. The chapter further connects this tradition to performativity as materialized performances and speech acts in which one can locate inherent insurgent qualities to counter dispossession. Paraverbal features such as speech tempo, loudness, and pitch, as well as the use of dramatic silences, acoustic space, and, finally, instrumental background music, reveal the richness of sound in the digital *testimonios* that this chapter sheds light upon.

Finally, Chapter 7 explores the use of written language, static images, and props as significant markers of space in the videos. The use of captions, in particular, illustrates new filmmaking techniques that the videos adapts to and makes its own in the creation of meaning. Photos add another visual level that reestablishes the connection of the digital *testimonio* to its offline context: actions of protest and photo evidence of the immigration background upon which undocumented youth base their stories.

Shifting the current focus on entertainment "to citizenship", according to White and Whyn, the narratives chosen "place the emphasis on the ways in which these technologies contribute to and shape community, belonging, and engagement with society" (212). As the focus on mediatization highlights, instead of simply accepting, we should *question* "the uses of YouTube by real people as part of everyday life" (Burgess and Green 8). If we indulge in this thought, indeed, digital narratives of undocumented youth enter spheres that might fulfill their *testimonio*'s promise to put "spoken word to social action" and transform an "oral narrative of personal experience as a source of knowledge, empowerment, and political strategy for claiming rights and bringing about social change" (Benmayor et al. 153).

Notes

1 Throughout this study, I capitalized (the) "Movement" whenever I refer to the contemporary Immigrant Rights Movement that this study investigates.

2 In line with Elliott, the definition for 'activism' in this study connotes a broad understanding of activists as "those in a political group who want to take active steps towards the objectives of the group rather than merely to proclaim a programme" (7). Bradbury adds that an activist is usually "a volunteer", in a sense "enjoy[ing] political activity for its own sake, or they have off-medium views", "pull[ing] the party or interest group towards the position they favour, rather than the position it would take to maximize its vote or influence" (1–2). With regard to the potentially endangering consequences that public activism of undocumented youth entails, I argue that a personal 'passion' for the cause is vital.

3 It needs to be noted here that the 'normality' we associate with new media technologies in the 'Digital Age' is a solely Western perspective. Ginsburg argues that "this naturalization seems even more remarkable given certain realities: only 12 percent of the world is currently wired [...] and only sixteen people in every one hundred of the world's population are serviced with telephone land lines" (129).

4 The term 'mode' could be described as a small unit *within* a system (=the medium). For some, medium and mode are synonymous in that they both "refer to the manner and the means by which textual material is presented and conducted" (Doloughan 6).

5 Semiotic resources can broadly be defined as "the actions, materials and artefacts people communicate with" (Jewitt 16).

References

Abrams, Lynn. *Oral History Theory*. London: Routledge, 2010.

Anguiano, Claudia A. "Undocumented, Unapologetic, and Unafraid: Discursive Strategies of the Immigrant Youth Dream Social Movement." Diss. U. of New Mexico, 2011. Web. 15 May 2013.

Bendit, René. "Growing Up in the Context of Globalization and Social Change: Present and Future of Youth and Challenges for Youth Research and Youth Policies." *Youth Transitions: Processes of Social Inclusion and Patterns of Vulnerability in a Globalised World*. Ed. René Bendit and Marina Hahn-Bleibtreu. Leverkusen, Germany: Barbara Budrich Publishers, 2008. 27–40.

Benmayor, Rina. "Digital 'Testimonio' as a Signature Pedagogy for Latin@ Studies." *Equity & Excellence in Education: University of Massachusetts School of Education* 45.3. (2012): 507–524.

Benmayor, Rina, Rosa M. Torruellas, and Ana L. Juarbe. "Claiming Cultural Citizenship in East Harlem: 'Si Esto Puede Ayudar a la Communidad Mía...'." *Latino Cultural Citizenship: Claiming Identity, Space, and Rights*. Ed. William V. Flores and Rina Benmayor. Boston, MA: Beacon Press, 1997. 152–209.

Bradbury, Jonathan. "Activist." *Oxford Concise Dictionary of Politics*. Ed. Iain McLean and Alistair McMillan. 2nd ed. Oxford: Oxford University Press, 2003. 1–2.

Burgess, Jean, and Joshua Green. *YouTube: Online Video and Participatory Culture*. Digital Media and Society Series. Cambridge: Polity Press, 2009.

Butler, Judith. *Excitable Speech: A Politics of the Performative*. New York: Routledge, 1997.

Butler, Judith, and Athena Athanasiou. *Dispossession: The Performative in the Political*. Cambridge: Polity Press, 2013.

Doloughan, Fiona J. *Contemporary Narrative: Textual Production, Multimodality and Multiliteracies*. London: Continuum, 2011.

Downing, John D. H., ed. Introduction. *Encyclopedia of Social Movement Media*. Los Angeles, CA: SAGE, 2011. xxv–xxviii.

Elliott, Florence. *A Dictionary of Politics*. 7th ed. Hardmondsworth, UK: Penguin Books Ltd., 1973.

Erstad, Ola, and James V. Wertsch. "Tales of Mediation: Narrative and Digital Media as Cultural Tools." *Digital Storytelling, Mediatized Stories: Self-Representations in New Media*. Ed. Knut Lundby. New York: Peter Lang, 2008. 21–40.

Esser, Frank, and Jesper Strömbäck, eds. "Mediatization of Politics: Towards a Theoretical Framework." *Mediatization of Politics: Understanding the Transformation of Western Democracies.* New York: Palgrave Macmillan: 2014. 3–28.

Flores-González, Nilda, and Elena R. Gutiérrez. "Taking the Public Square: The National Struggle for Immigrant Rights." *Marcha! Latino Chicago and the Immigrant Rights Movement.* Ed. Amalia Pallares and Nilda Flores-González. Urbana: University of Illinois Press, 2010. 3–36.

Galisky, Anne. Introduction. *PAPERS: Stories by Undocumented Youth.* Ed. José Manuel et al. Portland, OR: Graham Street Productions, 2012. viii–xiii.

Ginsburg, Faye. "Rethinking Documentary in the Digital Age." *Cinema Journal* 46.1 (2006): 128–133.

Gugelberger, Georg M., ed. "Introduction: Institutionalization of Transgression: Testimonial Discourse and Beyond." *The Real Thing: Testimonial Discourse and Latin America.* Durham, NC: Duke University Press, 1996. 1–19.

Gutiérrez, Antonio. Personal interview. 25 March 2014.

Hernandez, Marcela. Personal interview. 27 March 2014.

Hjarvard, Stig, ed. "The Mediatization of Religion: A Theory of the Media as Agents of Religious Change". *Northern Lights Film and Media Studies Yearbook.* Vol. 8. Bristol: Intellect, 2008. 9–26.

Jenkins, Henry. "What Happened Before YouTube." *YouTube: Online Video and Participatory Culture.* By Jean Burgess and Joshua Green. Digital Media and Society Ser. Cambridge: Polity Press, 2009. 109–125.

Jewitt, Carey, ed. "An Introduction to Multimodality." *The Routledge Handbook of Multimodal Analysis.* London: Routledge, 2009. 14–27.

Kallenberg, Vera, Johanna M. Müller, and Jennifer Meyer, eds. "Introduction: Intersectionality as a Critical Perspective for Humanities." *Intersectionality und Kritik: Neue Perspektiven für alte Fragen.* Wiesbaden: Springer, 2013. 15–35.

Kavoori, Anandam. *Reading YouTube: The Critical Viewers Guide.* New York: Peter Lang, 2011.

Kellner, Douglas, and Rhonda Hammer, eds. "From Communications and Media Studies through Cultural Studies: An Introduction and Overview." *Media/Cultural Studies: Critical Approaches.* New York: Peter Lang, 2009. ix–xvii.

Kress, Gunther, and Theo van Leeuwen. *Multimodal Discourse: The Modes and Media of Contemporary Communication.* London: Hodder Education, 2001.

Livingstone, Sonia. "Foreword: Coming to Terms with Mediatization." *Mediatization: Concept, Changes, Consequences.* Ed. Knut Lundby. New York: Peter Lang, 2009. ix–xiii.

Lundby, Knut, ed. "Introduction: Mediatization as Key." *Mediatization: Concept, Changes, Consequences.* New York: Peter Lang, 2009. 1–20.

———. "Media Logic: Looking FOR Social Interaction." *Mediatization: Concept, Changes, Consequences.* New York: Peter Lang, 2009. 101–119.

Madison, D. Soyini, and Judith Hamera. "Introduction: Performance Studies at the Intersections." *The SAGE Handbook of Performance Studies.* Ed. D. Soyini Madison and Judith Hamera. Thousand Oaks, CA: SAGE, 2006. xi–xxv.

Manuel, José, et al., eds. Foreword. *PAPERS: Stories by Undocumented Youth.* Portland, OR: Graham Street Productions, 2012. iv–vii.

Mathay, Angelo A. Preface. *Underground Undergrads: UCLA Undocumented Immigrant Students Speak Out.* Ed. Gabriela Madera et al. Los Angeles, CA: UCLA Center for Labor Research and Education, 2008. xii–xiii.

Mauk, David, and John Oakland. *American Civilization: An Introduction*. 5th ed. New York: Routledge, 2009.

Misra, Tanvi. "Why Chicago Is Still the No. 2 U.S. City for Mexican Immigrants." *The Atlantic*. 9 Oct. 2014. *Citylab*. Web. 17 Aug. 2015.

Pallares, Amalia. *Family Activism: Immigrant Struggles and the Politics of Noncitizenship*. New Brunswick, Canada: Rutgers University Press, 2015.

Pallares, Amalia, and Nilda Flores-González, eds. "Introduction." *Marcha! Latino Chicago and the Immigrant Rights Movement*. Urbana: University of Illinois Press, 2010. xv–xxix.

———. "The Chicago Context." *Marcha! Latino Chicago and the Immigrant Rights Movement*. Ed. Amalia Pallares and Nilda Flores-González. Urbana, Chicago, and Springfield: University of Illinois Press, 2010. 37–61.

Pérez, William. *Americans by Heart: Undocumented Latino Students and the Promise of Higher Education*. New York: Teachers College Press, 2012.

Polletta, Francesca. *It was Like a Fever: Storytelling in Protest and Politics*. Chicago, IL: Chicago University Press, 2006.

Punday, Daniel. "From Synthesia to Multimedia: How to Talk about New Media Narrative." *New Narratives: Stories and Storytelling in the Digital Age*. Ed. Ruth Page and Bronwen Thomas. Lincoln: University of Nebraska Press, 2011. 19–34.

Roth, Julia. *Occidental Readings, Decolonial Practices: A Selection on Gender, Genre, and Coloniality in the Americas*. Inter-American Studies 10. Trier: Wissenschaftlicher Verlag Trier, 2014.

Rusin, Sylvia. "Addressing the Elephant in the Room: Understanding the Daily Life of Undocumented Latino High School Youth." *Honors Projects 41*. n.p.: Illinois Wesleyan University, 2013. Web. 8 July 2013.

Schrott, Andrea. "Dimensions: Catch-All Label or Technical Term." *Mediatization: Concept, Changes, Consequences*. Ed. Knut Lundby. New York: Peter Lang, 2009. 41–61.

Schulz, Winfried. "Mediatization and New Media." *Mediatization of Politics: Understanding the Transformation of Western Democracies*. Ed. Frank Esser and Jesper Strömbäck. New York: Palgrave Macmillan, 2014. 57–73.

Ventola, Eija, Cassily Charles, and Martin Kaltenbacher, eds. Introduction. *Perspectives on Multimodality*. Document Design Companion Series 6. Amsterdam: John Benjamins Publishing Company, 2004. 1–6.

White, Rob, and Johanna Wyn. *Youth & Society: Exploring the Social Dynamics of Youth Experience*. 2nd ed. Oxford: Oxford University Press, 2008.

Yúdice, George. "*Testimonio* and Postmodernism." *The Real Thing: Testimonial Discourse and Latin America*. Ed. Georg M. Gugelberger. Durham, NC: Duke University Press, 1996. 42–57.

Zimmerman, Marc. "*Testimonio* in Guatemala: Payeras, Rigoberta, and Beyond." *The Real Thing: Testimonial Discourse and Latin America*. Ed. Georg M. Gugelberger. Durham, NC: Duke University Press, 1996. 101–129.

2 The movement, politics, and media logic in YouTube narratives of undocumented youth

1. Politics of the Immigrant Rights Movement since 2006

1.1. Social movement, contention, and public sphere(s)

In Tilly and Tarrow's triad of contentious politics, where contention, collective action, and politics converge (cf. 7), social movements reveal common characteristics: They systematically build "sustained campaign[s] of claim making, using repeated [public] performances that advertise that claim, based on organizations, networks, traditions, and solidarities that sustain these activities" (8). Here, 'claims' form the basis for contention as they typically "bear on someone else's interests" (4). The role and rights of immigrants in the United States has been discussed for centuries, with different parties and groups having very different agendas in mind. Yet, while social movements are commonly "based on common purposes and social solidarities" (Tarrow, *Contentious Politics* 4), the condition that claims for change are made *collectively* is not naturally a given among members of a social movement.

Therefore, the understanding of the collective identities[1] does not indicate complete unity in agenda-setting and goal-making. A more general understanding of collectivity, as the spring marches since 2006 have shown, is the essential element in a political 'struggle'. In his survey of the Movement's history, Ramírez, for instance, points to collectivity as "the most powerful weapon that could be wielded by the oppressed against dominant social forces, especially to challenge institutional mechanisms of state control" (*Social Action* 178). Just as any other type of identity, collective identities, however, also remain fluid. While in the U.S. civil rights movements, for example, "collective identities were assumed and understood to be determined by one's race, gender, and/or class", after the 1990s, social movement scholarship understood collective identities as a source for mobilizing resources and challenging "the state to make legal and political changes" (Desai 422).

In so-called 'new' social movements, it is the accomplishment of collective identities that takes place "via self-reflexive processes of articulation" that is regarded as 'novel', while 'traditional' social movements were seen as "strategic and instrumental" (ibid; cf. Munck 27). Originating roughly after World War II, when "movements would start anew and create a new society that rejected both consumer capitalism and bureaucratic socialism", social movements typically rejected "all forms of subordination" (Munck 25). They included issues such as gender, sexual politics, race and ethnicity, war and peace, and environmental issues. They further returned to "protest on material issues of social justice", according to Fenton (197–198).

One of the greatest legacies of the diverse 20th-century civil rights movements and their intersections, as also the Chican@ Movement (CM) exemplifies, is an erection of "self-image, instilling pride and a sense of common racial identity" (Bigler 111) – a "common spirit" that "acknowledges and supersedes the regional differences" across the United States (Zamarripa 104). Diverse and national activism now puts the rights of immigrants at the forefront, as well as encourages Latin@ culture, art, and study programs at universities (cf. Bigler 111). With reference to academia, Kymlicka, however, critically notes that

> although the Anglo-American world has witnessed a much-celebrated 'rebirth' of normative political philosophy in the 1970s and 1980s – including important new theories of justice, freedom, rights, community, and democracy – the sorts of issues raised by minority cultures have rarely entered these discussions.
>
> (*The Rights of Minority Cultures* 1)

Therefore, it is no surprise that many different social movements originated this discrepancy in the public debate. Likewise changing is a movement's "repertoires of claim-making routines" (Tilly and Tarrow 16). These 'repertoires of contention', as Tilly coined the term, vary from occasion to occasion. Thus, "when people make collective claims, they innovate *within* limits set by the repertoire already established" (16, *emphasis added*). Nowadays, "the rise of new technologies, and new communicative networks" has become a central aspect in the growth of "these new movements" (Gilroy 405). Likewise, the study of the Immigrant Rights Movement implies that a strong focus shall lie on the development of 'new' concerns and respective 'new' strategies for entering the public debate. As the study will show, digital narratives published on YouTube shall serve as an example for the latter.

The fact that "movements are created when political opportunities open up for social actors who usually lack them" explains the enhanced sense of agency that undocumented youth assume in the Immigrant Rights Movement (Tarrow, *Power* 1). Undocumented youth are not only marginalized due to their status; they do not even possess basic civil and even human rights, leaving them 'dispossessed' (see: Butler and Athanasiou) by the rules of the state. These technically exclude them from any type of access to political organization and activism (as from any other form of civic engagement) due to the agents' undocumented status. The 'political opportunities' that Tarrow further ascribes to such agents imply a public dimension of the term 'political'. While the terms 'political' and 'politics' can be broadly defined, the analysis of YouTube videos as means of political expression requires a definition for 'the political' that stresses the public face of the Movement because activists in the Immigrant Rights Movement since 2006 have gained greater media coverage than ever before (cf. Pérez 69).

This aspect changed the Movement drastically. The public face of movements is now frequently mediated through *new media*, resulting in new uses and products (cf. Bennett and Entman 1). Esser and Strömbäck correlate the public face of a movement to public support. They claim that politics necessarily has a "public face" as it focuses on a variety of tasks in the public sphere, such as "tactics and strategies for winning public support and publicity, symbolic politics, image projections and branding, and on the presentational side of politics" (15). These processes of garnering support, in sum, have the ultimate goal to "increase public or political support in different processes of problem definition and framing, agenda-setting, policy formation and political negotiations" (ibid).

The most important aspect included in this definition of the political is the notion of a 'public sphere' as a negotiating space for "power- and publicity-gaining presentational politics", which Esser and Strömbäck propose (16). Habermas' original[2] coining of the term stresses that political communication is grounded in a public sphere, which is an ideal space between the state and the private, where public opinions are discussed and formed and where citizens can participate on an equal basis (see, i.e. Bennett and Entman 3; Edgar 124; Hands 99). He argues, in particular, that the private and the public are negotiated in the public sphere (cf. Habermas 12).[3] Further, derived from inter alia Greek mythology, Habermas describes active communication in the public sphere as follows: In the 'exchange among equals', which he pictures an ideal dialogue, only the 'best' may win and gain credit for their superiority in the argument.[4] Moreover, Habermas stresses the appreciation that the public sphere can grant its participants.[5] Habermas echoes Esser and Strömbäck's emphasis of publicity and presentation of the political, further highlighting, however, the aspect of 'power', which Habermas seems to exclude in an attempt to make all his agents in the sphere equal (he talks of 'Ruhm' – glory – but not directly of 'power' that one interlocutor has over the other in the public sphere). To what extent do narratives of undocumented youth, in the tradition of the *testimonio*, hold a claim to political (or personal) empowerment, if any?

It is further crucial to mention the ideal character of Habermas' normative notion of the public space. Bennett and Entman, for instance, critically note that "in this sphere, individuals have the freedom to judge the quality of their governmental decisions independently of censorship" (2) – an ideal that "has never been achieved, and [...] probably never will", they argue (3). However, through this ideal model, the scholars also expound Habermas' public sphere as "a construct against which different real-world approximations can be evaluated" (ibid). For their purposes, they define it as "*any and all locations, physical or virtual, where ideas and feelings relevant to politics are transmitted or exchanged openly*" (2–3, *emphasis given*). In a similarly open way, Edgar claims that "public sphere" denotes "those social institutions that allow for open and rational debate between citizens in order to form public opinion" (124), stressing the various forms of communication that can take place between the citizens. Not being citizens, undocumented youth are theoretically excluded from Habermas' concept, which directs attention to the precise uses that undocumented youth make of this public sphere. The major question that comes up from both definitions is whether the platform YouTube, which serves as the *space* where undocumented youth make their narratives *public* – where they *communicate* – serves as such a public space for political processes as those defined above. This suggests the reformulation of existing ideas through the very presence of their otherwise undocumented, non-existing personhood: Undocumented youth publish their digital narratives in a public sphere that might not live up to Habermas' ideal realm of equal citizens but that still can be defined as a space for political communication. Through their participation in the political discourse about immigration on YouTube, they not only redefine the public sphere according to their purposes – those of an *undocumented* person, and *not* a citizen – they also actively claim a belonging to the public sphere and, in broader terms, the U.S. public. Applying these thoughts, the following sections document the activism that undocumented youth have initiated outside of YouTube, as well as the historical foundations for their activism, in order to claim the aforementioned public sphere in other public spaces such as YouTube.

1.2. Historical legacy and politics of the Movement

The heterogeneity of the Immigrant Rights Movement points to the historical – not at all universal – character as one of the few features common to *all* social movements (cf. Tilly and Tarrow 8). The Immigrant Rights Movement, too, consists of a network of traditional and new community, grassroots, and policy organizations (cf. Pallares, *The Chicago Context* 52–53). This strong diversity among activists, of course, also entails different repertoires of contention – different "visions, goals, strategies, and tactics" (Pallares and Flores-González xxv). Most notably, older generations of the Movement carry the legacy of what is known as the CM, an immediate predecessor and solid historical base of the Immigrant Rights Movement:

The term 'Chican@'[6], first of all, relates to "persons of Mexican ancestry residing in the U.S." (hence, *Meshicano*; short form *Shicano*) (Gutiérrez 25). Mexican-Americans frequently identified as 'Chican@' in the 1950s–1980s, the time that the "social movement [...] occurred in the United States with increased activity in the southwest and midwest" (ibid; see also Curry 101).

Further, the choice of the name 'Chican@' for Mexican-Americans denotes a "sensibility" that connects an inherently re-evaluated understanding of socio-historic and cultural identity to a concrete geographical space, Curry explains: The term 'Chican@' connects the "focus on the rights of the poor and working-class members of the community" with a "specific geographic and historic space, the U.S.-Mexico borderlands" (101). Texan Chicano Activist Reis López Tijerina highlighted the "force, violence, and repression" that "had much to do with the making of colonial Mexico" (Gómez-Quiñones ix), a legacy carried far beyond Mexican independence from Spain on 16 September 1810. Colonial violence found its immediate expression in the fact that "the United States border moved toward Mexico and incorporated not only land mass but also Mexican people" on as much as "three occasions" between 1836 – after the Texas revolt for independence from Mexico – and a real estate deal called the "Gadsden Purchase" in 1853 (Gutiérrez 25). Most significantly, "the United States acquired parts of what was then northern Mexico in 1848, through the Treaty of Guadalupe Hidalgo, which ended the Mexican-American War" (Bigler 109). The movement around Tijerina therefore reflects 'cultural pride' in indigenous roots by connecting it to the historical and graphical space for Mexican-Americans whose demands at the time literally stepped out of the assigned sphere.

Counting as a major achievement of the CM in the Southwest of the 1960s and 1970s, a newly organized Mexican-American labor force successfully protested against inhumane working conditions in the fields. Inspired by Gandhi and Martin Luther King, leader of the farmworkers and founder of the National Farm Workers Association (NFWA) in California, César Chávez, among others, "utilized nonviolent tactics" and, according to Bigler, "made particularly effective use of a nationwide boycott of produce to press growers for union recognition" (110).

As the farm workers' strikes spread across the nation, urban Chican@ youth, however, became increasingly "frustrated by the slow pace of change" (Bigler 110). They "took to the streets to protest educational conditions in their high schools and universities" (ibid), organized by the Mexican-American Youth Organization, in particular (Gutiérrez 25). While they also used "the nonviolent weapons" such as "school boycotts, strikes, walkouts, and demonstrations" (ibid), "the later 1960s saw an increasing radicalization of urban Chicano youth and a greater willingness to confront directly the institutions that oppressed them", according to Bigler (110). Immediate results of the African-American liberation struggle for civil rights, such as the passage of the Civil Rights Act[7] in 1964, further necessitated reforms such as the Immigration Act of 1965. The bill changed immigration to the United States "dramatically" (Briggs 61), as it "abolished longstanding national-origin quotas on immigration" (Baca 21). Not only did migration then become a possibility to many previously excluded Latin Americans and Asians, "over the course of the 1970s, the rise of dictatorial governments in Argentina, Brazil, Chile, Peru, El Salvador, and Guatemala motivated waves of immigrants seeking political asylum", de Baca explains (ibid).

An example that highlights the intersectionality of the struggle particularly well is the formation of the Brown Berets that not only "supported UFW labor struggles" but also "allied" with the Black Panthers in the African American community against racism while maintaining their 'high-profile protest' against the Vietnam War (Baca 22). Great unity during the conventions and marches, however, was not a matter of cause. Urban riots led by Chican@ and Latin@s of other national origins and riots in cities such as Chicago or New York, de Baca stresses, in particular, "reflected a larger problem": the "lack of community togetherness", which eventually "resulted in the establishment of several grassroots organizations" in the 1970s (Baca 21). Along the same lines, internal struggles in the CM involved female resistance to sexism and *machismo* that even "threatened to undermine Chicano culture and El Movimiento" (Curry 101). Here, again, other movements such as 'Anglo' feminism served as an inspiration while it was generally rejected by Chican@s (cf. 102).

The changing migration pattern after 1965 made Mexico the country that supplied most immigrants, along with the Philippine Islands (cf. Briggs 79). A consistent number of illegal immigration, also mostly from Mexico, turned into "an especially controversial political and social topic in recent years as the foreign-born population of the United States increases and large Latin@ communities have emerged in areas where they previously did not exist" (García 249). In order to solve the problem, in 1986, the Immigration Reform and Control Act passed and legalized many undocumented immigrants (cf. Yoshikawa 32). The reform represented a basic success for immigrant communities. However, it remained ineffective in the restriction of (illegal) immigration, and in addition made "it a crime for employers to hire undocumented workers" (García 250).

Legal amendments that followed the Immigration Reform and Control Act were kindled by "restrictionist and nativist sentiments [...] at the state and national levels during the early 1990s" (Flores-González and Gutiérrez 8). The Illegal Immigration Reform and Immigrant Responsibility Act from 1996, for instance, restricted the availability of legalization processes (cf. Yoshikawa 34) and facilitated more stringent immigration laws pertaining to admission and deportation, mostly executed by Border Patrol. In consequence, immigrant communities and organizations such as the Illinois Coalition for Immigrant and Refugee Rights shifted their agenda from "amnesty assistance to other kinds of support and integration services for the immigrant population" and later also mobilized "against national and local restrictive immigration bill proposals" (Flores-González and Gutiérrez 8). Organized Communities against Deportation, a recent state-based network that "focuses on Illinois cases working with immigrants of all ages", focusing on the separation of families through deportation, in particular (Pallares, *Family Activism* 124).

Throughout the 1990s, restrictive 'operations' carried out by Border Patrol had also unraveled large protests in larger immigrant-populated cities such as Los Angeles, Houston, Chicago, New York, Philadelphia, and Detroit. Incited by restrictions and racism, local and national organizations split into different local groups (cf. Flores-González and Gutiérrez 16), although generally again embracing a "broader civil and human rights agenda" (13) and working toward immigrant rights in the "increasingly restrictive environment" after September 11 (16). This aspect also emerges as one of the central aspects on the agenda of the Immigrant Rights Movement since 2006.

Remarkable is also the shared cause that undocumented youth activists of the current Movement perceive with regard to the civil rights movements from the 1960s and 1970s (cf. Pérez 85). In the Immigrant Rights Movement, civil rights struggles gain an intersectional dimension, as the immigrant community also bears that fight. These parallels will also find their way into the 'narratives of dispossession' in this study. What is more, the contemporary Immigrant Rights Movement, in contrast to earlier movements, is now "characterized by an agenda that centers on immigrant rights, civil rights, and workers' rights that concern most Latinos and all working-class communities of color", yet positions immigrant rights on the "central platform" (Pallares and Flores-González xxii). The shift away from *primarily* civil and human rights to *immigrant* rights with a focus on civil and human rights thus signals the importance of the Movement's activism and rights movements in immigrant communities.

What is also striking about the association with civil rights movements and, in particular, the black Civil Rights Movement in the United States is not only the implicit fight against discrimination on the basis of the color of the skin – racism – but also the change in definition that this latter movement brought about in the 1970s. As Munck reports, "prior to the 1960s, the dominant approach to social movements stressed their anomalous, practically irrational character" (20). But, he observes,

> these attitudes were to change in the 1960s, particularly in North America, 'when for the first time in history large numbers of privileged people … had considerable sympathy for the efforts of those at the bottom of society to demand freedoms and material improvements'.
>
> (Goodwin and Jasper in Munck 21)

Association with this Movement, hence, is not only a cry for the cause of the revived Immigrant Rights Movement but also a cry for widespread acceptance of the Movement *itself*. It seems less striking then that issues concerning race in immigrant communities (such as racial profiling) are central in the political agenda of the Movement but also part of a set of strategies against worst-case scenarios such as deportation due to prior racial profiling (cf. Pallares, *The Chicago Context* 56).

Different is also the attention that *undocumented* immigration has gained within the Movement. In contrast, earlier immigrant rights movements had largely separated themselves "from any association with undocumented immigrants" by "emphasizing 'Americanness'" in order to gain sympathy and become more effective (Pallares and Flores-González xxii). The degree to which 'Americanness' again hits the top of the agenda, especially in the 'early' years of the Movement, will be a central question when contextualizing the digital narratives of undocumented youth selected for this study.

The term 'undocumented', at this point, also requires further definition. While there are many other terms describing and naming people who are in the country without legal permission either by immigrating into the country or by overstaying a visa, for example, the term 'undocumented' remains the most-widely accepted one. Along with the 'illegal', the two terms present migration categories that have "a long history in the United States" even prior to official birth of the terms in the 1920s (Abrego 215). The term 'illegal' originates in the category of the 'illegal alien', which was established through "laws excluding Chinese laborers and other marginalized groups" (ibid). More recently, it has undergone several phases of explicit political attack because it criminalizes and dehumanizes immigrants without making any further distinctions (cf. Rusin 3). The protest finally manifested itself in the 'Drop I-Word'-campaign, launched by Colorlines.com in 2010, which succeeded in getting the Associated Press to drop the compound noun 'illegal immigrant' from its stylebook (Rivas n.pag.). In a personal interview, Antonio Gutiérrez explains the background of the campaign against the term 'illegal' as follows:

> Overall, we haven't done anything wrong; we haven't done any big crime, I mean, I know that, practically, or in a legal sense, yes, being here undocumented is an illegal form of being here, just because we *entered* 'illegally' or we stayed here 'illegally' and based on *their* laws, but overall, as human beings we haven't done anything criminal, as far as I know, because we came here with the reason of bettering ourselves, of bettering our families. So, yeah, I mean, the term 'illegal' just doesn't make any sense to me and I feel like the 'Drop I-Word', which was a campaign for dropping the word 'illegal', it did a very good sense of that; of, like, we're a community that is not a *criminal* community; we're just here to make a better life. And so we shouldn't be named or represented with that word.
>
> (personal interview)

In another interview, Gabriela Benítez further connects the campaign to the black civil rights movement from the 1960s and 1970s:

> To respect the African-American community I wouldn't want to say that but I do say that it's a [...] derogatory term that the community has

> really pushed against in a way that we have seen some sort of progress. But even in that, there's a conversation around in the Movement around, instead of not using the term to 'owning' the term. (*laughs*) But I feel like I wouldn't wanna own a term that makes me cringe, you know?
>
> (personal interview)

As we can see from both statements, undocumented youth activists see the word indeed as derogatory; however, at least the term does provide an opportunity for activism against the status of being undocumented. Summing up, while the term does not have a history of discrimination as does the n-word for African-Americans, as Gabriela Benítez says, its offending meaning is discussed within the Movement and the issues of discrimination and racism appear in many of the public narratives. Which terms are chosen to describe 'undocumented immigrants' in the narratives thus provides clues for the time in which the narrative was published in addition to the political standing of the individual narrator.

It is crucial to recognize the central focus of 'undocumented' immigration in this revived Immigrant Rights Movement. Orner, for instance, challenges the word 'undocumented' altogether: "An undocumented person is not undocumented at all. Of course they [undocumented immigrants] have documents: family photos, diplomas, driver's licenses, love letters, emails, credit card bills, tax forms, homework, child's drawings" (12). And yet "the only thing that truly links them together is their lack of federal immigration status – in other words, certain pieces of paper" (ibid).

Being an undocumented immigrant, however, embraces many more facades that are ultimately connected to the state of being 'dispossessed' in Butler's sense. Orner stresses that it is not only citizenship rights that the undocumented are lacking in their attempts to exercise from the underground but also the most basic human rights.[8] "The lack of legal protection afforded to undocumented immigrants – as well as the capricious enforcement of laws", he argues, "has led to serious human rights abuses, both by the government and by those private individuals who would exploit the vulnerability of undocumented people" (10). Consequently, they are petrified by "the fear of deportation, of being separated from one's family, of losing one's job", which "frequently overrides any wish to go to authorities" (ibid).

Given these intimidating circumstances, it may seem paradoxical that undocumented youth are 'coming out of the shadows'. However, fear can also be examined as a motivating agent generating *testimonios*, which are a well-known strategy to overcome psychological constraints, frequently used in psychological therapies. The initiative for 'coming out of the shadows', we should mention at this point, relates to the 'Coming out of the Shadows' – campaigns led by homosexuals within the greater civil rights movements of the 1960s, 1970s, and 1980s (cf. White 990). This association is not accidental. Many leading activists are also openly 'homosexual' and call themselves 'Undocu-queers': These activists acknowledge a shared history of discrimination and have moved from a single-issue struggle toward a Movement that often unites the struggle against both types of discrimination and oppression (the sexual and the undocumented) (ibid). Antonio Gutiérrez reports:

> I came out as a homosexual to my friends and family when I was a senior in high school and it was a very, also very fearful time for me and I was very afraid that I wasn't gonna be accepted by my family [...]. But at the end of the day I decided to do it and I had the best reaction that I could have thought of. They were very accepting. If anything, I became closer to them because now, I was able to have this other side of me be able to be shown to them. Unfortunately it wasn't the same thing for me coming out as being undocumented. I didn't come out as being undocumented maybe until I was a junior in college [...]. Coming out as being undocumented, it was even more nerve-wracking than coming out as being gay. I just remember being so afraid of getting myself into trouble and getting my family into trouble and I think it feels, just having both – being gay and also being undocumented – is double the oppression in individuals. And I know a lot of people that have to deal with that. But it just really adds on.
>
> (personal interview)

As Gutiérrez explains, the struggle "adds on"; he teaches us that the line cannot be drawn neatly when it comes to who is included and who sees him-/herself as included in the Movement.

1.3. The public face: leadership in the Movement

Gabriela Benítez formulates the origins of the Movement as follows:

> It was the first, sort of core group of folks – and I remember we had this legislative training and all of the staff, and it was ... I met *so* many other people that were going through the same thing that I was going through and it just became like the support system I didn't have. It was more than that [...]. It was with students like me, right? And students from other states, students from Massachusetts, students from just all over the place, Florida, New York, and yeah, so I continued to organize, I continued to do that.
>
> (personal interview)

As diverse as the origins of the different foci for the Movement might seem, just as many different interests are represented and united in the contemporary Immigrant Rights Movement. Like the difficulty of delineation associated with the concept of 'Americanness', and with undocumented identity, the Movement is similarly characterized by ambiguity when it comes to the notion of leadership. Yet, because there are so many networks and organizing styles, just as many different voices are included (cf. Pallares and Flores-González xxv–xxvi; see also: *The Chicago Context* 54). In particular, the political and economic interests of the different campaigns in the various organizations differently emphasize the discourse on (undocumented) immigrants. Here, Pallares makes an essential differentiation between the grassroots versus the institutional organizations of undocumented immigrants, expressing an "institutional/grassroots divide": "Grassroots' organizations lesser resources and access to national-level policymakers have led some activists to [...] express a desire to play a more active role in policy creation (*The Chicago Context* 57). As a consequence, "many local and regional organizations are already working with national organizations [...] to affect the immigration debate in Congress" (ibid). The possible transfer of these continuing differences to the sector of new media – and mediatization – is now an interesting component for the analysis of the Immigrant Rights Movement in the United States since 2006.

There is also disagreement regarding the eventual 'goal' or wish for 'outcome' of the Movement. As stated earlier, Comprehensive Immigration Reform (CIR) represents the basis for common goals, yet details of it are debated among individuals in the community. The only point of agreement for all is that the immigration system is 'broken'. Gabriela Benítez, one of the long-term activists I interviewed in spring 2014, expresses her frustration with the particular details in the CIR Bill proposed by Obama and passed in the Senate:

> Especially after the Senate Bill was proposed [...] it's a joke! It's compromising so much of our community in order to pass this and relief to so little of it. Border militarization, and drones and just so many requirements and fines and lack of accessibility to our community, it's a joke! *I* don't want it to pass, I don't want it to pass.
>
> (personal interview)

Yet, what seem to be evident boundaries separating activists also unite them into a hybrid Movement. Pallares and Flores-González have found "this movement [to be] a hybrid one, in which the principal actors are both legal and undocumented"; the citizens "struggle for equal citizenship", the undocumented "struggle for formal citizenship", and, finally, these two struggles turn out to be "deeply intertwined" (xxiii). Topics such as 'family separation' become more important to all activists as the Movement evolves with the years (cf. Pallares, *Family Activism* 1), and as deportation numbers increase to unprecedented levels (cf. Preston n.pag.). Within families, the boundaries between undocumented and legal immigrants slowly dissolve as "many naturalized Latinos have undocumented immigrants in their immediate or extended families", regarding it as their "responsibility to serve as the voice for those not recognized as legitimate spokespersons" for the causes of the undocumented (Pallares and Flores-González xxiii). In fact, the topic of family has gained increasing importance during the most current phase of the Movement: As Pallares argues, 'the family' has "become politicized in new ways" (Pallares, *Representing 'La Familia'* 215). Mixed-status families, for instance, have become one focus, challenging "the notion of individual rights, arguing that the deportation of parents violates the right of citizen children to be raised by their parents in their country of birth" (219). With regard to the current focus on 're-entry'-campaigns (against the system that marks immigrants with a previous deportation as a 'high-priority' case for a renewed deportation), the issue of 'family (re-)union' therefore also gains central importance (cf. 220). The issue of 'family' and 'family' unity will be a focal point in the analysis of the earliest narrative, Stephanie's, and the latest narrative, that of Luis, yet with quite different outcomes.

According to Gabriel Benítez, additional divisions within the Movement spring from disparate economic necessities, resulting in different strategies and goals, as well as emotionally charged fights over the particular goals that activists aspired to reach. She begins with her own experience in the Movement as it developed in Tennessee and ends by referring to current strategies and focus of the Movement:

> But at the same time [...] a Movement, I wouldn't say 'split' but it 'grew'. *United We Dream*, which was the big organization, sort of leading it, had *NIYA* formed, the National Immigrant Youth Alliance. I wasn't fully part of all of that, because in Tennessee we didn't have all the resources to be fully involved and so wherever we could fundraise to go to, but at that point I was like, it was sort of depressing but at the same time, as time went through, I saw that it's a good way because we were providing off-voice in different strategies – even now you see with the 'Bring Them Home'-campaign, it's been very controversial but at the same time it has gardened a lot of support. That goes again to the big question of not just supporting the 'Dream Act' but supporting something bigger. The Comprehensive Immigration Reform, CIR, conversation isn't there anymore as much, I would say, it's not the only topic discussed on dinner tables and immigrant communities and meetings, now it's deportations. And that has been part of lots and lots of work. I was saying 'We're *tired* of *being tired* of fighting for this thing that's never gonna pass'.
>
> (personal interview)

In her account, Gabriela Benítez references the two key campaigns, the national DREAM Act[9] as well as CIR. As both legislation proposals have been debated frequently but never passed, Gabriela Benítez voices her frustrations with the system and a shift in focus: With the numbers of annual deportations as high as ever, she argues that fighting deportations is more important than the actual legislative component of the Immigrant Rights Movement – the CIR. Her statement shows that different strategies within the Movement are inextricably connected to personal aspirations, family situations and, also, the success of the previous strategies for a particular cause. Further, whenever we analyze personal narratives within the context of a social movement, we should be aware of the personal background and resulting subjectivity and frame the individual political stance in the Movement itself. Because of this, the situations of dispossession will be closely examined with a focus upon the connections between 'the personal' and 'the political' in Chapter 4.

Further, glancing back at the history of the Immigrant Rights Movement, we see differences in opinions and political strategies evolving among activists united by the cause. While its historical roots are portrayed above as a consolidated basis for the revived Immigrant Rights Movement since 2006, the movement of the 1960s and 1970s was indeed diverse and split into different, smaller interests. Ramírez recounts:

> At the onset of the Movement, there was greater unity. Even when differences arose, it was often necessary to work in alliance with others in order to make progress. There was a moment when the powerful effects of racism and class marginalization created strong bonds of solidarity. Initially, the them-against-us perspective tied activists to one another despite political differences, personalities, and organizational allegiances.
>
> (*Preface* xiii)

This postcolonial mission to fight a form of oppression unifies the Movement despite its internal differences. When investigating undocumented youth and their personal narratives within the Immigrant Rights Movement, we must recognize that different interests and tensions exist between the many ideas, activists and non-activists, organizations, political, and discursive trends all over the nation. In this sense, the revived Immigrant Rights Movement is not new but incorporates new dimensions, including its cultural output online. Further, these collisions of different viewpoints are processes in social movements that, as Ramírez shows, are "not solely a question of personalities, ambitions, or a general tendency for all social movements to splinter and disintegrate over time" (*Preface* xiv). Rather, the ever-existing fractions in social movements should also be seen within their historical contexts:

> Understanding the nature of divisions that arose during the 1960s and 1970s is important for contemporary political mobilization. Massive protests in support of immigrant rights in the first decade of the 21st century and the subsequent differences and rivalries that surfaced within the ranks of the immigrant-rights leadership are reminders of the continuous need to identity, clarify, and understand the roots of tension among leaders.
>
> (xiii)

As Pallares reminds us, while we analyze the digital narratives of undocumented youth in the context of the Immigrant Rights Movement since 2006, we need to bear in mind the differences within one and the same Movement (cf. *The Chicago Context* 52). "Moreover", she argues, "most of the differences visible in Chicago are faced by immigrant activists throughout the country" (ibid), which is an essential condition for the interpretation of the political message, legislation requests, and organizational backgrounds of the narrators, producers, and distributors of the digital narratives. Naturally, these different goals also evoke the creation of different strategies, as the following quote shows:

> 'Coming Out of the Shadows' came out in March, or at least what we know of it, in March of 2010 and 'Shout it Out' was in October of 2009. And I think if you saw a 'Coming Out', a lot of those discussions that we had were free-ranging; they were from, like, writing just something on the Internet, and spreading that out, or having something a little bit more private to actually having the whole full-on civil disobedience action in federal buildings. [...] So I think, while having that discussion of those different kinds of ideas for 'Coming Out' meant that there were different people with different ideas and there were in the Movement or in the political sense of, like, where they were and personally at different stages. So not everybody was necessarily ready to do a civil disobedience action; not everybody wanted to just do like a little private event or online thing. People wanted to do *different* things.
>
> (Sánchez, personal interview)

As the quote shows, Uriel Sánchez defines 'Coming Out of the Shadows' events as deliberate strategies of the Movement that, however, are not embraced equally by all activists in the Movement.

2. Online repertoires of contention: political uses of the Internet in the *Immigrant Youth Justice League*

Positioning the digital narratives of undocumented youth in the context of the Immigrant Rights Movement involves multiple processes that are subsumed under the term of 'mediatization'. Before displaying interview data from my investigations at the Immigrant Youth Justice League, it needs to be stressed that there is a two-sided debate on the role of new media and the Internet in activism: Cyber-optimists and cyber-skeptics. An optimistic interpretation understands the significance of the Internet as a device for activists and a tool to change legislation. For undocumented youth, for instance, social media and networking has become "a powerful tool" to sustain the Movement and "promote legislations" such as the DREAM Act or the Deferred Act for Childhood Arrivals (DACA) (Pérez 83).

Like Pérez, numerous studies have argued that "digital communication technologies provide a medium through which dispossessed or marginalised groups of young people [...] construct political identities and a sense of belonging" (White and Wyn 217; see also: Ginsburg 131). Further, in an optimistic interpretation, traditional repertoires of contention are extended to and enriched by innovations based on new digital possibilities and then "rapidly and globally" shared "through the process of cyber-diffusion" (cf. Rolfe 72). They are thus seen as essentially fostering political organization and actions, enabling especially young people to engage in "a horizon of dissent, resistance and rebellion" (Hands 18).

Cyber-skeptics, on the other hand, point to the nature of the political output by such young movements. Inherently shaped by the technical affordances of social media communication, activism is apparently less effective, as it is prone to focus on the self-expression of an individual through, for example, "hashtag solidarity, postings of updates and images, datafied emotions and relations" (Dencik and Leistert 4–5). Cyber-skeptics claim that social media do not actually sustain a movement like the contentious repertoires of grassroots organizations would (cf. 3). This is partly caused by a focus on the Internet as an actual tool for engaging and motivating people, which Gladwell rejects vehemently. He argues that the strongest motivation for people to become involved in a movement is close ties to other people who are affected by a cause that inherently challenges the status quo. Gladwell strongly criticizes social media as tools for activism because ties on the web are oftentimes not as strong as real-life ties, and hence, cannot lead to a strong intrinsic motivation to become involved in activism. 'Friends' on social media are acquaintances that may serve as a good source of information and inspiration but do not trigger the motivation necessary to become involved in serious or 'high-risk' activism such as that during the civil rights movement 1960s and 1970s (cf. Gladwell n.pag.). Further, questions of censorship on the Web and the use of technologies for economic development, control, and repression have fueled the discussion. Free and equal access, too, is yet a problem to solve. Ginsburg, for instance, stresses the drastic persistence of the 'digital divide' (cf. 129). She strongly questions the equality of the worldwide distribution and access to computers and/or the Internet.

An important socio-technological condition on YouTube is the difficulty of ascertaining the extent to which the video was created professionally and who/how many people were involved in the production process, if not explicitly noted.[10] Publishing on YouTube certainly requires a minimum degree of 'new media literacy'[11], which implies that authors are not only able to produce their own videos but also "comprehend the way YouTube works as a set of technologies and as a social network" (Burgess and Green 72). As this understanding underlies a learning process and youth cannot simply be dismissed as 'digital natives'[12], YouTube creates 'participation gaps' (cf. Jenkins 258), "which often exhibit familiar socio-cultural inequities based on sex, gender, ethnicity, and class" (Lange 12). This discussion indicates that we need to question the producer (and narrator) of the digital *testimonio* on YouTube, as the latter demand a new understanding of participation, personalization, and performance that seems incommensurate, at first glance, with testimonial narratives. Those narrators who are not 'literate' in this sense of the word would not appear, or require somebody to publish their narrative *for* them. The group of undocumented youth might have one day the chance to be considered elite, well aware of the fact that with every step, they are moving further and further away from the *actual* subaltern group.

In the interviews carried out for this study, I asked four young undocumented youth from Chicago about the role of new media in and for the current Immigrant Rights Movement in spring 2014. As the data will show, approaching the changes that new media triggered for the politics of the Immigrant Rights Movement from critical perspective was not an easy task. The answers that I gathered in the interviews mostly stress the positive effects of the changes that new media and the Internet have had for political participation inside and outside the Movement.

One of my interviewees, Uriel Sánchez, for instance, emphasizes the importance of new media, and particularly, the Internet for the Movement as a means for organizing, because the Internet is "free, accessible" and exhibits no "preference for socio-economic standard" (personal interview). He further highlights the speed and multiple applications that accelerate communication, which, according to him, helps a great deal to "keep this Movement going" (ibid). Uriel also connects new media and the Internet to the Movement's gain in power, claiming that

> information is power, now you don't have only power holders that are monopolizing over that power which existed with traditional media. Now you have a new medium; people doing their own thing and being able to have autonomy with what they choose to spread.
>
> (ibid)

What he stresses, in particular, is the choice and power that undocumented immigrants have over the content that is published on them, since they can choose to publish something *themselves*. His statement also makes clear that media has always been a topic for (undocumented) immigrants in the United States, clearly linking current media developments in the Movement and statuses of marginalization and criminalization within its history.

Marcela Hernandez's answer to my question is very similar to Uriel's, while she also stresses the role of undocumented youth as major agents in the new media sphere:

> And now, that we found this tool, called news stream, we were actually able to produce our media and record our own Movement. And put it out there to anybody in the nation or the world that wanted to watch it. So, it has really allowed us to produce a, you know, to really record our

> own voices and put it out there, even if mainstream media is not gonna cover all of it. So, I think that has been one of the most valuable things that we have used in recent, you know, in the last probably three, four years. That power of not relying on mainstream media and now creating our own media and put in our own stories out there.
>
> (personal interview)

Marcela Hernandez further includes in the description of the role of new media for the Movement the 'stories' that activists in the revived Immigrant Rights Movement produce. Her word choice with regard to the output published in new media is interesting, insofar as she does not explicitly refer to it as 'information' – like Uriel Sánchez did – but as 'stories'. Thereby, she includes a degree of fictionality and subjectivity in the output, which apparently does not make a difference with regard to the representation of the Movement in the media. Choosing the words 'stories' and 'own voices', Marcela Hernandez further highlights personal aspects (such as biographical elements, for instance) that flow into the production of the Movement's output in new media. Clearly, she validates a shared background and community. Marcela Hernandez further argues that connecting with other activists via the Internet "let us know that we are not alone [...]. I mean, there was a bigger network of people who are working on this issue" (personal interview). To Marcela Hernandez, it does not seem to matter that this community exists, first and foremost, virtually, connecting real, personal feelings such as a boost in confidence to the virtual space. On the contrary, Uriel Sánchez also stresses that undocumented immigrant activism on new media such as YouTube does not necessarily need to be connected to organizations that also exist offline. He argues that

> that's how a lot of people started organizing. And still, in a sense, organize. Or at least share their opinion on the issue is by not necessarily being affiliated with a group or an organization but just doing their own thing. I think that's just as powerful because now you're showing, again, contrary to – and, you know, it could be any global place, it could be somebody something very pro-immigrants, somebody posting something very anti-immigrant.
>
> (personal interview)

Thus, YouTube, in Uriel's view, is a basis for organizing via either personal or organizational means, but, in any case, highly subjective.

To this list of positive attributes and uses of new media for the Movement, Antonio Gutiérrez adds the ease with which the Movement can reach its desired 'audience' to call for support. He argues that new media on the Internet not only "help [...] communicate the movement", in other words, represent it but they also provide activists with "the opportunity to reach people" and "to approach people to really care about the subject" (personal interview). In this statement, Antonio hints at the usage of communicative strategies in order to address people effectively and *convince* them of the necessity for their supporting the Movement. Clearly, Antonio Gutiérrez refers to the prominence of new media for the publicity and support gaining activities of the Movement, one prominent aspect of the definition of 'politics' used in this study. He elaborates this thought in the following quote, rating the Movement political strategies as generally successful:

> We're very good at messaging and knowing how to approach people to really care about the subject. [...] And we are reaching all of these audiences, the ones that are really visual or the ones that are a little more about *reading* and getting all the information or the ones that just really want to have it on their *IPhone* and they just wanna click one button and say 'Yes, I support!'.
>
> (personal interview)

Also emphasized here are the different media and modes that the Movement's producers of output *know how to use* in order to communicate their messages to as many different and diverse people as possible in order to gain support.

Antonio's conviction that his Movement is 'very good' at producing political strategies is also confirmed by Marcela Hernandez. She reports that the prominence of new media has also proven to be helpful insofar as "you can share resources so it made us stronger, because we can share our strategies across states". What was explicitly broached in the interviews is the complexity that this type of communication has assumed via the use of *social* media. Of my four interviewees, Uriel Sánchez and Marcela Hernandez, in particular, emphasize the merit of interaction with the audience and the consequential, immediate feedback that the Movement receives for its activism transmitted via social media through activities such as comments on websites or the act of 'liking' something on Facebook. Uriel Sánchez further connects interaction to the "participatory" character of the Movement's media usage, while he describes 'old media' to be "one-way". According to Antonio Gutiérrez, it is possible to "use [...] social media to really get to push our audiences and the people that support us". Highlighted in this statement is the particular prominence of the political agenda in forms of new media.

One of my interviewees explicitly names YouTube as a website which provides video content that *shows* offline organized activities such as civil disobediences or the annual *Coming Out of the Shadows* event in Chicago.

> Actions that have happened and new types of, like, YouTube is from 2006. The marches happened in 2006. That's, like, I think that's huge! You know, what if YouTube wouldn't have existed? Would have been like an, I don't know, what existed before that? Videos or something like that? Like little videos. I mean, I don't think little videos existed yet. But

> *something* existed. Pretty sure. But it wouldn't have been the same, you know. In organizing, keeping that momentum going.
>
> (Sánchez, personal interview)

As Uriel's example shows, the power for the Movement that lies in YouTube resides in the virtual performance of political activism for a potentially unlimited audience and the never-ending persistence of the event so long as the video is not removed. Thus, the action virtually 'takes place' over and over again. The 'visual' channel of the video, hence, serves as 'evidence' for offline political activism that, in turn, empowers the Movement in spheres far from the digital.

Yet another aspect that the undocumented youth activists from Chicago stress is the personalization of the content published online by the Movement. Personal voices, often in the form of personal stories that incorporate intimate biographical events, render political output subjective and potentially even fictional. However, this subjectivity potentially raises the debate about what a 'personal story' connotes. The emphasis on the personal aspect extends the debate about authenticity and truth in online political texts and contexts. In turn, personal stories from 'ordinary' participants who may not even be involved in the 'offline' Movement, add another level of meaning to the stories that might be dismissed as 'merely personal, too subjective', and therefore, politically useless. In addition to that, the interaction with an audience is an important trigger for audience-generated political output and feedback for the Movement. Also user-friendly is the storage of data on platforms online that offer the audience the possibility to revisit activism online independently and frequently.

These generic observations call for a more detailed investigation of the specific uses that undocumented youth make of the Internet in order to communicate their politics. Due to the broadness of this endeavor, this study focuses upon the use of personal stories, one form of communication that integrates many of the features the interviewees mention. Personal stories published online are not only a form of political participation on the Web, they also illuminate issues of personalization and the positioning of the narrator in the offline Movement. Moreover, the narrators use new media forms of multimedia/multimodal communication that the medium offers through its technological affordances to tell their stories, shaping their content through the use of a specific medium.

This study employs a set of narratives published on YouTube, a channel that the Movement's activists explicitly refer to. The following section displays the grounds for selection of those narratives that will serve as case studies for the use of the new media for the Movement's purposes.

3. Storytelling format on YouTube: media logic as grounds for selection

Navigating the difficulty of finding a coherent corpus on YouTube is the only nascent research on it. In the meantime, YouTube has not only managed to survive despite the Internet's fast-moving nature, but it has also grown quite mature for its age. In the past ten years, the platform www.youtube.com has developed as a steady component of the "mainstream media landscape" (Burgess and Green vii).

YouTube videos contain "radically reduced timeframes" and "allow [...] everyone to perform" their stories themselves, showing "what a 'bottom-up' [...] model" of contributions "might look like in a technologically enabled culture" (Hartley 132–133). What is more, YouTube videos "share an architectural similarity" (Kavoori 7). They are "short, readily accessible, and, most importantly, part of the *same* visual experience – appearing alongside the main video, but exchanging places with it should the viewer click on any of them" (ibid). Similarly, Jenkins, Ford, and Green observe that "spreadability emphasizes producing content in easy-to-share formats, such as the embed codes that YouTube provides, which make it easier to spread videos across the Internet, and encouraging access points to that content in a variety of places" (6). Likewise, Hands identifies YouTube as a space for "the proliferation of user-created content", "for sharing information", and "for social networking" (79). All of these features of YouTube reinforce its democratic potential. Equality of access is reinforced not only in 'user-friendly' distribution and reception processes, but, more significantly, in the processes of 'output' production. Namely, digital configurations use multiple modes and media of expression and communication in their videos and on the website which, as Kress points out, is "made easy, usual, 'natural' by these technologies" (5). Here, Kress affirms Altheide and Snow's understanding of our unconscious adaptation to the media in our everyday lives (cf. 9), which we simply perceive as "normalized" (12). But it is precisely this diverse format, the multimodality applied to produce the video clips and the forms of communication on the website itself, which "may foster changes in practices that are part of mediatization processes" (Lundby 13).

In view of mediatization processes, any selection of narratives for critical analysis requires a closer look at YouTube's 'grammar'. Certainly, YouTube is characterized by dynamic changes in content, service, and form. According to Kavoori, the website is "inherently polysemic in its textuality", as it ranges across different genres and formats of authorship (10). Because YouTube is so 'polysemic', the process of selecting narratives for analysis requires a definition of narrative that is characterized by use of multiple media and modes – different textualities attached to the text – in the narration of the story. It should be noted, at this point, that stories in different media inhabit different forms of narrativity, mediality, and structures. If follows that meaning is added to the text by the meaning *traditionally* attached to (multi-)modal choices of a text, in addition to interpretive processes – the 'experientiality' – of a text (cf. Reinfandt 17–18). The *narration* of a story – "the process by which narrative is conveyed" – involves "complex combinations of cues in different channels (visual, auditory, tactile, etc.)" inherent to the structure of the text, Herman adds (279). On the basis of this, one could propose that as a "mental representation", a story does not rely on a particular medium to be told in (Ryan 26). Herman further proposes a broad definition of narrative that is open for different media and modes, claiming that narrative is "a basic human strategy for coming to terms with time, process, and change" (3).

Recognizing the polysemic nature of the narratives of undocumented youth as a given, I propose a definition of 'narrative', which is inherently connected to the 'story' and the practice of 'storytelling' that one can find on YouTube, on which I ground the search of YouTube narratives of undocumented youth:

> Narrative is a representation of (i) a structured time-course of particularized events that (ii) introduces conflict (disruption or disequilibrium) into a storyworld (whether that world is presented as actual, fictional, dreamed, etc.), conveying (iii) what it's like to live through that disruption, that is, the 'qualia'[13] (or felt, subjective awareness) of real or imagined consciousness undergoing the disruptive experience.
>
> (Herman 279–280)

A precondition that follows for selecting YouTube narratives of undocumented youth for this study therefore is that there is 'a story to tell' (in the context of their undocumented status) and that undocumented youth are the narrators of these stories themselves. This becomes particularly important when interpreting the narratives as 'coming out' narratives, which, for this purpose, need to clearly identify the narrator as undocumented. The narrative situation, therefore, is first-person.[14] This combination of political context with narrative situation implies that within the stories that the undocumented youth narrators tell in their YouTube videos, the narrators are mostly also the protagonists in their 'story', forming an intradiegetic level of the story (cf. Kuhn 61). Here, the name, *You*Tube, actually reveals a lot about the media logic of YouTube as it was intended to be used.

The setting and other visual elements (such as props), as well as camera angle, movement, and montage, create further layers of meaning, which are not part of the 'story' the narrators tell. As such they could be termed the extradiegetic level (cf. Kuhn 60). On this level, we also find voice-overs, or the insertion of text in the visual, or music. As this level is peculiar to the narration in film, indeed, the use of editing programs and filmmaking techniques transforms many a video clip on YouTube into a short film, connecting all elements into one coherent production (cf. Mittell 160).

The fact that the narrators are recounting *their* stories, however, does not mean that their narratives were not also co-produced. Commonly, Kavoori maintains, "co-creators are engaged as collaborators as they upload, tag, organize, and categorize content on YouTube" (49). Consequently, in the narrative selection for analysis in this study, I choose narratives that seem co-produced and more 'professionally' edited as well as some which *seem* to have been produced exclusively by the narrators themselves. A comparison of sophisticated and amateur productions is likely to uncover alternative strategies for negotiating political and media logic in the narratives of undocumented youth as well as slight differences in agenda and/or ideology.

Through the individual assortment of (very broad) categories and (oftentimes misleading) tags that the producers may attach to the videos, researchers on YouTube immediately stumble upon problems of accountability. This renders choosing stories according to filters as ineffective, because of which the selection of narratives relies upon 'free search', sorted according to relevance by default (cf. Tao et al. 1).

As political logic (politics) denotes publicity- and attention-seeking strategies, heavy usage of relevance factors, as Tao et al., have shown, implies that the publishers (and narrators) of the videos perceived the successful publication as important. They wanted 'their video' to be viewed by many people, which is the key element of political logic (politics), and hence, important for the analysis in this study.

To make use of YouTube's keyword function, I developed a list of key terms that I searched for systematically on 10 pages in a row, each with 20 entries (limited to that due to practicability) (see Table 2.1).

The search terms are, at first glance, very similar, as I employed the approach recommended in "Search Strategy Effectiveness" and "Relevance" of the videos on YouTube that Tao et al., published recently, namely, the

Table 2.1 Keyword Search (Terms)

1	undocumented immigrant
2	undocumented immigrant youth
3	undocumented immigrant student
4	undocumented students
5	undocumented student
6	undocumented activist
7	undocumented name activist
8	undocumented student activist
9	undocumented youth
10	undocumented youth movement
11	undocumented family
12	undocumented life
13	undocumented immigration story
14	undocumented story
15	undocumented Dream Act
16	undocumented Dreamer
17	undocumented unafraid/undocumented not afraid/undocumented no longer afraid/undocumented student no longer afraid/undocumented, unafraid, unapologetic
18	undocumented not hiding/undocumented no longer hiding/undocumented student no longer hiding
19	undocumented coming out
20	undocumented queer

Source: Created by the Author.

authors explain that the visibility of videos was increased when multiple search terms were available and these thus became "more relevant" (3). Hence, "in a free text search, variations of search terms should be considered and used in order to retrieve as many results as possible [...] including different spellings, singular vs. plural, different names for the same concept" (ibid). As a result, all of the videos selected appeared more than once during the search with differing terms and spellings. What is more, these search terms change from a more general description of 'undocumented youth' to more specific terms or mottos that are used in the Movement and/or the news media and that also appear as a topic of the narratives.

I further reduced the scope of the narratives that appeared multiple times in this search according to my context: the politics of the Immigrant Rights Movement since 2006. The selection includes not only narratives that establish a concrete connection to the youth-led Movement and their political agenda (such as the DREAM Act) or the DACA[15] but also discursive strategies such as the use of 'unashamed' and 'unapologetic' for their Movement, which are explicit references to the gay rights movement and community and which also show in the search term 'undocu-queer', for instance.[16] Resisting strategies of anonymity, I chose only narratives in which the narrators 'came out' as undocumented. Finally, my selection of eight narratives reflects no preference regarding nationality; consistent with national statistics, it mostly features undocumented youth of Mexican origin. In order to reflect the intersectionality of the struggle of being undocumented in the narratives, I deliberately chose males and females in equal number. However, I took care to include at least one gay and one lesbian undocumented youth to reflect the connections of the youth-led Immigrant Rights Movement to the gay rights movement and community.

It is important to note at this point that any selection of YouTube videos remains in a sense arbitrary and is by no means representative of all undocumented youth and their stories, despite the *attempt* to create an objective and representative selection process, and should therefore rather be understood as case studies. However, this 'problem' is inherent in the media logic of YouTube, and therefore, a normative variable in interpreting the results of this study. As the results of this investigation will show, "YouTube presents not just a more efficient and creative means by which individuals can connect and create, but also a movement towards a change in the process of storytelling" (Kavoori 4–5). "Storytelling", after all, "is at the heart of all media" (2).

On the basis of this introduction to media logic on YouTube and its storytelling, I created the following list of criteria for the selection of narratives according to their format – the 'grammar' of YouTube video clips:

- They have 'radically reduced time frames' (between 2 and 8 minutes).
- Undocumented youth are the narrators of their 'stories'. For reasons of practicability, I selected only narratives that were technically produced

in such a quality that they were clearly intelligible and narrated in the English language.[17]

- The narratives incorporate multiple modes and media of communication in their video clips, yet mostly freely spoken (as opposed to read, for instance). Accordingly, a majority of the narratives are edited by video editing programs (five are edited; three are not).
- Some of the narratives are more 'professionally' created/co-produced than the others (three were created by professional producers; five were not).

Notes

1 Desai defines "collective identity" as "an individual's cognitive, moral, and emotional connection to a larger community (real or imagined), category, practice, or institution", essentially leading "to positive feelings for other members of the group" (421).

2 According to Edgar, Habermas frequently "revised his views of the public sphere, and suggested that he was less pessimistic about the erosion of the public debate", which he saw in "modern public relations and advertising" (127). Due to the lack of organizational interdependence of the individual narratives of undocumented youth on YouTube, Habermas' concerns and subsequent reformulations of the concept are not of essential relevance for this study.

3 "Die Öffentlichkeit selbst stellt sich als eine Sphäre dar – dem privaten steht der öffentliche Bereich gegenüber" (Habermas 12).

4 "Im Gespräch der Bürger miteinander kommen die Dinge zur Sprache und gewinnen Gestalt; im Streit der Gleichen miteinander tun sich die Besten hervor und gewinnen ihr Wesen – die Unsterblichkeit des Ruhms" (Habermas 13).

5 "Die Tugenden [...] bewähren sich einzig in der Öffentlichkeit, finden dort ihre Anerkennung" (Habermas 13).

6 The at-sign at the end of the word denotes the incorporation of the male and female – Chicano and Chicana – into one word.

7 The Civil Rights Act of 1964 prohibited "racial or sexual discrimination against individuals by employers and in restaurants, lodgings, and other public accommodations" (Levy 200).

8 Kymlicka adds that "minority rights cannot be subsumed under the category of human rights", either, because "traditional human rights standards are simply unable to resolve some of the most important and controversial questions relating to cultural minorities" (*Multicultural Citizenship*, 4). Different rights (and the lack thereof) therefore need to be negotiated for specific individuals and groups of a minority in the current cultural and political context. For further discussions of 'citizenship' (rights) see Chapter 4.

9 The legislation that many of these students and other immigrant activists press for is the DREAM Act (acronym for Development, Relief, and Education for Alien Minors); a path to citizenship for undocumented students if they succeed in graduating from college. It was first proposed in Congress in 2001 and has been furiously debated ever since (cf. Pérez 8). Further, the bill only benifited certain undocumented youth – those that entered the United States before age 16, had been present in the United States for at least five years prior to the bill's enactment, had obtained a high school diploma, and demonstrated "good moral character" (ibid).

10 Often, companies even pile into production processes on YouTube: Multichannel networks are established who aid YouTuber*s* to professionally create

their videos (and thus get more 'clicks'). It is through this process that YouTube has undergone a noticeable shift: From amateur television to professionalization. Along the same lines, YouTube's commercialization poses the "fundamental question [...] whether YouTube's domination of online video distribution, and the market logic behind it, represents a [...] threat to the viability of alternative or community media spaces" (Burgess and Green 75).

11 "Traditionally, literacy refers to the ability to read and write with printed and written materials associated with varying contexts", a notion which drastically changes in the twenty-first century, according to Tan and Tan (105).

12 The term "digital natives" denotes that "younger people do not regard digital technologies as new" and take "for granted the use of digital technology for communication in their personal, leisure, and commercial life" (White and Wyn 210).

13 Qualia is a strongly debated concept that broadly defines as the "intrinsic, ineffable properties of experience" (Caracciolo 105).

14 Because the aspect of 'coming out' is significant to the investigation of undocumented youth online, I also chose to exclude co-authored/multiple narrators in one narrative.

15 Deferred Action for Childhood Arrivals (DACA) is an executive order announced by President Obama on 15 June 2012 that created "a process by which undocumented youth can apply to get a work permit and avoid deportation for at least a two-year period" (Pallares, *Family Activism* 124).

16 See Chapter 6, for instance, for a detailed discussion of these latter aspects.

17 As the narratives that I was searching for were supposed to be narrated in the English language, during my search for digital narratives of undocumented youth, I chose "English (US)" as the language and "worldwide (all)" as the general settings on YouTube. Another language I frequently encountered was Spanish. One should bear in mind that choosing other languages in a selection of narratives might alter the results of analysis significantly, as language is a phenomenon that always carries great cultural meaning.

References

Abrego, Leisy J. "'I Can't Go to College Because I Don't Have Papers': Incorporation Patterns of Latino Undocumented Youth." *Latino Studies* 4 (2006): 212–231. Web. 15 Jan. 2013.

Altheide, David L., and Robert P. Snow. *Media Logic*. Sage Library of Social Research 89. Beverly Hills: SAGE, 1979.

Baca, Michael A. de. "History: 1965-Present." *Latino History and Culture: An Encyclopedia*. Ed. David L. Leonard and Carmen R. Lugo-Lugo. Vol. 1. Armonk, NY: Sharpe, 2010. 19–30.

Benítez, Gabriela. Personal interview. 13 March 2014.

Bennett, W. Lance, and Robert M. Entman, eds. Mediated Politics: An Intro-duction. *Mediated Politics: Communication in the Future of Democracy*. Cambridge: Cambridge University Press, 2001. 1–29.

Bigler, Ellen. "Chicano Movement." *Latino History and Culture: An Encyclopedia*. Ed. David L. Leonard and Carmen R. Lugo-Lugo. Vol. 1. Armonk, NY: Sharpe, 2010. 109–111.

Briggs, Vernon M. *Immigration Policy and the American Labor Force*. Baltimore, MD: John Hopkins University Press, 1984.

Burgess, Jean, and Joshua Green. *YouTube: Online Video and Participatory Culture*. Digital Media and Society Series. Cambridge: Polity Press, 2009.

Butler, Judith, and Athena Athanasiou. *Dispossession: The Performative in the Political.* Cambridge: Polity Press, 2013.

Caracciolo, Marco. *The Experientiality of Narrative: An Enactivist Approach.* Narratologia 43. Berlin: De Gruyter, 2014.

Curry, Agnes B. "Chicanisma." *Latino History and Culture: An Encyclopedia.* Ed. David L. Leonard and Carmen R. Lugo-Lugo. Vol. 1. Armonk, NY: Sharpe, 2010. 101–103.

Dencik, Lina, and Oliver Leistert, eds. Introduction. *Critical Perspectives on Social Media and Protests: Between Control and Emancipation.* London: Rowman & Littlefield International, 2015. 1–12.

Desai, Manisha. "From This Bridge Called My Back to This Bridge We Call Home: Collective Identities And Social Movements." *The SAGE Handbook of Identities.* Ed. Margareth Wetherell and Chandra T. Mohanty. Los Angeles, CA: SAGE, 2010. 421–436.

Edgar, Andrew. *Habermas: The Key Concepts.* Routledge Key Guides. London: Routledge, 2006.

Esser, Frank, and Jesper Strömbäck, eds. "Mediatization of Politics: Towards a Theoretical Framework." *Mediatization of Politics: Understanding the Transformation of Western Democracies.* New York: Palgrave Macmillan, 2014. 3–28.

Fenton, Natalie. "Multiplicity, Autonomy, New Media, and the Networked Politics of New Social Movements." *Discourse Theory and Critical Media Politics.* Ed. Lincoln Dahlberg and Sean Phelan. New York: Palgrave Macmillan, 2011. 178–200.

Flores-González, Nilda, and Elena R. Gutiérrez. "Taking the Public Square: The National Struggle for Immigrant Rights." *Marcha! Latino Chicago and the Immigrant Rights Movement.* Ed. Amalia Pallares and Nilda Flores-González. Urbana: University of Illinois Press, 2010. 3–36.

García, Justin D. "Illegal Immigration." *Latino History and Culture: An Encyclopedia.* Ed. David L. Leonard and Carmen R. Lugo-Lugo. Vol. 1. Armonk, NY: Sharpe, 2010. 249–252.

Gilroy, Paul. "Urban Social Movements, 'Race' and Community." *Colonial Discourse and Post-Colonial Theory: A Reader.* Ed. Patrick Williams and Laura Chrisman. New York: Columbia University Press, 1994. 404–420.

Ginsburg, Faye. "Rethinking Documentary in the Digital Age." *Cinema Journal* 46.1 (2006): 128–133.

Gladwell, Malcolm. "Small Change: Why the Revolution Will Not Be Tweeted." *The New Yorker.* 4 Oct. 2010. Web. 8 Oct. 2017.

Gómez-Quiñones, Juan. *Roots of Chicano Politics, 1600–1940.* Albuquerque: University of New Mexico Press, 1994.

Gutiérrez, Antonio. Personal interview. 25 March 2014.

Gutiérrez, José Á. "The Chicano Movement: Paths to Power." *The Social Studies* 102 (2011): 25–32. Web. 7 Oct. 2015.

Habermas, Jürgen. *Strukturwandel der Öffentlichkeit: Untersuchungen zu einer Kategorie der bürgerlichen Gesellschaft.* Neuwied: Luchterhand, 1969.

Hands, Joss. *@ for Activism: Dissent, Resistance and Rebellion in a Digital Culture.* London: Pluto Press, 2011.

Hartley, John. "Uses of YouTube: Digital Literacy and the Growth of Knowledge." *YouTube: Online Video and Participatory Culture.* By Jean Burgess and Joshua Green. Digital Media and Society Series. Cambridge: Polity Press, 2009. 126–143.

Herman, David. "Introduction." *The Cambridge Companion to Narrative*. Ed. David Herman. Cambridge: Cambridge University Press, 2007. 3–21.

Jenkins, Henry. *Convergence Culture: Where Old and New Media Collide*. New York: New York University Press, 2006.

Jenkins, Henry, Sam Ford, and Joshua Green. *Spreadable Media: Creating Value and Meaning in a Networked Culture*. New York: New York University Press, 2013.

Kavoori, Anandam. *Reading YouTube: The Critical Viewers Guide*. New York: Peter Lang, 2011.

Kress, Gunther. *Literacy in the New Media Age*. Literacies. London: Routledge, 2003.

Kuhn, Markus. "Narrative Instanzen im Medium Film: Das Spiel mit Ebenen und Erzählern in Pedro Almodóvas La Mala Educatión." *Mediale Ordnungen: Erzählen, Archivieren, Beschreiben*. Ed. Corinna Müller and Irina Scheidgen. Marburg: Schüren Verlag, 2007. 56–76.

Kymlicka, Will, ed. Introduction. *The Rights of Minority Cultures*. Oxford: Oxford University Press, 1995. 1–27.

———. *Multicultural Citizenship: A Liberal Theory of Minority Rights*. Oxford: Clarendon Press, 1995.

Lange, Patricia G. *Kids on YouTube: Technical Identities and Digital Literacies*. Walnut Creek, CA: Left Coast Press, 2014.

Levy, Peter B. *The Civil Rights Movement*. Westport, CT: Greenwood Press, 1998.

Lundby, Knut, ed. "Introduction: Mediatization as Key." *Mediatization: Concept, Changes, Consequences*. New York: Peter Lang, 2009. 1–20.

Mittell, Jason. "Film and Television Narrative." *The Cambridge Companion to Narrative*. Ed. David Herman. Cambridge: Cambridge University Press, 2007. 156–171.

Munck, Ronaldo. *Globalization and Contestation: The New Great Counter-Movement*. London: Routledge, 2007.

Orner, Peter, ed. "Introduction: Permanent Anxiety." *Underground America: Narratives of Undocumented Lives*. San Francisco, CA: McSweeney's Books, 2008. 5–13.

Pallares, Amalia. *Family Activism: Immigrant Struggles and the Politics of Noncitizenship*. New Brunswick, Canada: Rutgers University Press, 2015.

———. "Representing 'La Familia': Family Separation and Immigrant Activism." *Marcha! Latino Chicago and the Immigrant Rights Movement*. Ed. Amalia Pallares and Nilda Flores-González. Urbana: University of Illinois Press, 2010. 215–236.

———. "The Chicago Context." *Marcha! Latino Chicago and the Immigrant Rights Movement*. Ed. Amalia Pallares and Nilda Flores-González. Urbana, Chicago, and Springfield: University of Illinois Press, 2010. 37–61.

Pallares, Amalia, and Nilda Flores-González, eds. "Introduction." *Marcha! Latino Chicago and the Immigrant Rights Movement*. Urbana, IL: University of Illinois Press, 2010. xv–xxix.

Pérez, William. *Americans by Heart: Undocumented Latino Students and the Promise of Higher Education*. New York: Teachers College Press, 2012.

Preston, Julia. "Deportation Up in 2013; Border Sites Were Focus: Deportation Surged in 2013, Data Shows." *The New York Times* 1 Oct. 2014. *The New York Times*. Web. 14 Oct. 2014.

Ramírez, Leonard G. "Preface." *Chicanas of 18th Street: Narratives of a Movement from Latino Chicago*. Ed. Leonard G. Ramírez et al. Urbana, Chicago, Springfield, Illinois: University of Illinois Press, 2011. xi–xvi.

———. "Social Action." *Chicanas of 18th Street: Narratives of a Movement from Latino Chicago*. Ed. Leonard G. Ramírez et al. Chicago: University of Illinois Press, 2011. 166–200.

Reinfandt, Christoph. "'Texture' as a Key Term in Literary and Cultural Studies." *Text or Context: Reflections on Literary and Cultural Criticism*. Ed. Rüdiger Kunow and Stephan Mussil. ZAA Monograph Series 15. Würzburg: Königshausen & Neumann, 2013. 7–22.

Rivas, Jorge. "Associated Press Stylebook Drops 'Illegal Immigrant'." *Colorlines* 2 Apr. 2013. *Colorlines*. Web. 16 Aug. 2015.

Rolfe, Brett. "Building an Electronic Repertoire of Contention." *Social Movement Studies* 4.1 (2005): 65–74. Web. 28 Oct. 2017.

Rusin, Sylvia. "Addressing the Elephant in the Room: Understanding the Daily Life of Undocumented Latino High School Youth." *Honors Projects* 41. n.p.: Illinois Wesleyan University, 2013. Web. 8 July 2013.

Ryan, Marie-Laure. "Toward a Definition of Narrative." *The Cambridge Companion to Narrative*. Ed. David Herman. Cambridge: Cambridge University Press, 2007. 22–35.

Tan, Seng-Chee, and Aik-Ling Tan. "Developing Students' New Literacies with Computer Supported Collaborative Argumentation." *Transforming Literacies and Language: Multimodality and Literacy in the New Media Age*. Ed. Caroline M. L. Ho, Kate T. Anderson and Alvin P. Leong. London: Continuum, 2011. 105–121.

Tao, Donghua, et al. "Search Strategy Effectiveness and Relevance of YouTube Videos." *Proceedings of the American Society for Information Science and Technology* 49.1 (2012): 1–4. Web. 25 Oct. 2015.

Tarrow, Sidney. *Power in Movement: Social Movements, Collective Action and Politics*. Melbourne: Cambridge University Press, 1994.

———. *Power in Movement: Social Movements and Contentious Politics*. 2nd ed. Cambridge: Cambridge University Press, 1998.

Tilly, Charles, and Sidney Tarrow. *Contentious Politics*. Oxford: Oxford University Press, 2007.

White, Rob, and Johanna Wyn. *Youth & Society: Exploring the Social Dynamics of Youth Experience*. 2nd ed. Oxford: Oxford University Press, 2008.

Yoshikawa, Hirokazu. *Immigrants Raising Citizens: Undocumented Parents and Their Young Children*. New York: Russell Sage Foundation, 2011.

Zamarripa, Manuel X. "Chicanismo." *Latino History and Culture: An Encyclopedia*. Ed. David L. Leonard and Carmen R. Lugo-Lugo. Vol. 1. Armonk, NY: Sharpe, 2010. 103–106.

3 Reframing *testimonio*

Mediatizing political storytelling on YouTube

1. *Testimonio*: narrating resistance

Traditionally, testimonial narratives were produced in interview(-like) situations, in which the narrator addresses "a specific interlocutor" (Roth 194). As in oral history, this production process includes "the different phases of listening, recording, and transmitting others' voices" (Randall 64). The status that this narrator obtains, however, is a central distinction from other genres, as he/she rises in status over the interlocutor, who merely 'uses' the interlocutor to publish his/her story in a public sphere that he/she does not usually have access to due to "the very conditions of subalternity to which the *testimonio* bears witness" (Beverley, *Narrative Authority* 556). Thus, the testimonial narrator usually finds him/herself in some kind of oppressive situation that leaves him/her "politically and socially marginalized, voiceless and submissive" (Logan 200).

What is more, *testimonios* are "told in the first person by a narrator who is also the real protagonist or witness of the events she or he recounts" (Yúdice 42). Accordingly, the line between *testimonio* and autobiography is thin. While autobiography affirms a "self-identity that is separate from the group or class situation it narrates", *testimonio* seems to "erase" any "textual presence of the 'author'" (Beverley, *Narrative Authority* 556). Despite the fact that autobiography, too, "provides powerful means for marginalized or subjugated people to turn from 'subjects *of* discourse' to 'subjects *in* discourse'" (Swindells in: Döring 66–67), this position of the narrator differs noticeably in *testimonio*. The shift in status that the narrator undergoes also differs: The opportunity to write on one's life, in *testimonio*, "implies necessarily that the narrator is no longer in the situation of marginality and subalternity that his or her narrative describes, but has now attained the cultural status of an author" (Beverley, *Narrative Authority* 556). It follows that, in order for them to be called '*testimonios*' and not, simply, autobiographical 'stories', the undocumented narrators of narratives chosen for this study must form a collective identity that speaks for their Movement.

Testimonios originated in liberation movements and social struggles inspired by Marxism in the 1970s and 1980s (cf. Zimmermann 107). In Western academia, the *testimonio* itself became popular through indigenous activist Rigoberta Menchú, whose story was published in *I, Rigoberta Menchú* in order to call attention to organized crimes committed against the indigenous Guatemalan population that she experienced on a personal basis in 1984. Yet, her book was debated ferociously at the time of its publication on the basis of the question whether the testimonial narrative actually lost its "counter-hegemonic quality" due to its academic discussion and publicity (that amounted in the winning of the Nobel Peace Prize in 1992) (Do Mar Castro Varela and Dhawan 77). Secondly, the narrator's (alleged) 'subaltern' identity was questioned. In particular, Gayatri Spivak's logic of the 'subaltern' was used to deprive Menchú of her subaltern status. The argument was that the subaltern could not 'speak' "because if the subaltern could speak in a way that really mattered to us, that we could feel compelled to listen to and act upon, then it would not be subaltern" (Beverley, *Testimonio* xvi).

In order to comprehend the role of the narrators as the 'voice for the subaltern' in *testimonios*, Beverley underlines the importance of understanding that the testimonial narrator is not "the subaltern *as such*" (*Narrative Authority* 557, *emphasis added*). Rather, Beverley finds that the narrator in *testimonio* "functions as an organic intellectual (in Antonio Gramsci's sense of this term) of the subaltern, who speaks to the hegemony by means of a metonymy of self in the name and in the place of the subaltern" (ibid). Nevertheless, it is widely acknowledged that *testimonios* do, in fact, "represent [...] in particular those subjects – the child, the 'native', the woman, the insane, the criminal, the proletarian – excluded from authorized representation when it was a question of speaking or writing for themselves" (Ashcroft, Griffiths, and Tiffin 259). In line with Dube, this study therefore understands the concept of the 'subaltern' as a "metaphor for the general attribute of subordination [...] – whether such subordination was expressed in terms of class, caste, age, gender, race or office" (127).

The issues of 'truth' and 'authenticity' in *testimonio* appear equally unsolvable as those revolving around the subaltern because measuring the degree of authenticity and truth is equally problematic in the scholarship of new media. Burgess and Green report that experiences trigger "tensions between 'expression' and 'exhibitionism,' performance and surveillance" (27). Jenkins argues that "in a hybrid space like YouTube, it is often very difficult to determine what regimes of truth govern different genres of user-generated content", since "the goals of communicators can no longer be simply read off the channels of communication" (122). Connecting the indeterminability of the medium's content to its logic, he observes: "There seems to be a fascination with blurry categories at moments of media in transition – it is one of the ways we apply our evolving skills in a context where the ca-tegories that organize our culture are in flux" (123). Likewise, Hoffmann and Eisenlauer argue that "the degree of narrative authenticity of weblogs [...] is difficult to determine for bloggers can deliberately suspend the tension between biographic details of their life and episodic make-believe" (84). Therefore,

I suggest seeing all digital *testimonios* telling stories of varying degrees of truths instead of trying to establish categories that measure these degrees of truth.

Taking a step further, Benmayor simply *personalizes* those degrees of truth expressed in *testimonio*. She states that it is the specific place and moment when the narrators decide to "speak *their* truth" rather than *the* truth that makes up a central part of the creation of meaning itself (512, *emphasis added*). The political voices in *testimonios*, thus, do not portray reality *itself* but an impression of reality, which could be called a 'reality effect', proposing the existence of different "degrees of truth" (cf. Maier 7).

In the following sections, the major task will be to establish a framework that negotiates the political logic in the *testimonios* of undocumented youth with the media logic, that is, in particular, the devices of storytelling on YouTube.

2. Reframing *testimonio*: the mediatization of storytelling and the digital *testimonio* on YouTube

2.1. Digital testimonio *vs. storytelling*

In the article "Digital *Testimonio* as a Signature Pedagogy for Latin@ Studies", published in 2012, Rina Benmayor introduces the 'digital *testimonio*'. Understanding the '**digital *testimonio***' as an amalgamation of the traditional *testimonio* and digital stories, Benmayor stresses the tight integration of the logic of the *testimonio* into this new form. As with *testimonio*, digital stories also express the collective level of experiences that are coined by "marginalization, resistance, and strength" (508). Yet, in contrast to the form that became known as the 'digital story' or 'digital storytelling', the digital *testimonio* is a story that "gives urgent and powerful voice to individual and collective Latin@ experiences and allows for broader, more democratic authorship, dissemination, and reception" (ibid). All throughout the story, it is therefore not the individual voice that counts, rather, the voice always "signifies a collective referent" (511) and speaks with "urgency" for its cause (cf. 510). The digital *testimonio*, therefore, 'inherits' the social purpose of the tradition of the *testimonio* and points to "acts of oppression and injustice that subjugate, marginalize, and silence communities" (523), while digital storytelling clearly emphasizes the medium (cf. 510).

Her definition of the digital *testimonio* places Benmayor in a wide range of scholars who are attempting to delineate the meaning of digital storytelling practices. Couldry similarly defines digital storytelling as "the whole range of personal stories now being told in potentially public form using digital media resources" (42). 'Digital storytelling' refers to a variety of digital media products (Lundby 1). Typically, a 'digital story' has been defined as short movie (only a few minutes long) in which the narrator tells a story in the own voice and uses images and sound to underline the message (cf. 2).[1]

The difference between Lundby's and Benmayor's understanding of digital storytelling and *testimonio* lies in the production process and setting: Rather than at home, by oneself, in Benmayor's form of the digital *testimonio*, the institutional setting has an inevitable influence on the final products – the *testimonios* – that are produced and published there. In the university setting (Center for Digital Storytelling, California), Benmayor explains that her students produce, publish, and theorize their own *testimonios* within the group, yet with professorial instruction and university equipment (cf. 507; 510).

Problematic with Benmayor's definition of the digital *testimonio* as a *testimonio* "in a medium that is digital" (510) is the de-emphasis of mediatization processes: Benmayor depicts the digital medium as a mediator of content. She does not attend to the 'social factors' in the production process other than that she stresses the collaborative production process. Further, the choice of YouTube as the medium, containing its own socio-technological affordances that shape its content (cf. Schulz 62), dictates that digital *testimonios* are absorbed into the medium and can be regarded as *testimonios* with a critical eye only. As my definition for 'politics' includes ways of "power- and publicity-gaining presentational politics" (Esser and Strömbäck 16), social-shaping or 'self-mediatization' on YouTube needs to be redefined for the (digital) *testimonio*, before one can analyze the actual use of the semiotic resources that YouTube offers to undocumented youth as narrators.

2.2. Media logic and testimonio: *negotiating 'public spaces' on YouTube*

The oldest known function of social media such as YouTube is the formation of a public space for issues and opinions (Schmidt 10). Accordingly, YouTube integrates major social and interactive functions into the platform, located at the intersection of mass media and interpersonal communication (cf. 11). From its very beginning, it "offered basic community functions such as the opportunity to link to other users as friends" (Burgess and Green 1) and the opportunity to 'like' a video, share it with others or comment on it. However, these social functions transpire primarily *after* uploading of content, in contrast to network platforms such as Facebook, where the interpersonal networking is much more important, or blogs, where the diary-like recounting of individual experiences is predominant (cf. Kim 10, 12). However, this multipath communication is what makes digital (social) media *social* (cf. Esser and Strömbäck 18).

The question that emerges out of the *social* 'potential' of YouTube for this study is whether the platform also has the means to fulfill *political* functions. Advocates of 'technological determinism', on the one hand, clearly understand YouTube as "the apparent link between more accessible digital technologies, user-generated content, and some kind of shift in the power relations between media industries and their consumers" (Burgess and Green 10). Further, its great assemblage of tools used to produce narratives in Web 2.0 contexts is believed to enable "collaboration between multiple users" (208). The videos are therefore "shaped significantly by the participatory qualities of their surrounding discourse context" (ibid). As we have seen earlier, the data gathered for this study suggest that YouTube is an environment for participatory culture for the Immigrant Rights Movement, which this study shall therefore explore.

Conditioned by the space and (relative) freedom to negotiate the latter, Burgess and Green define YouTube as a "cultural public sphere" (77). This space represents, according to Kim, "an updated version of Habermas' public sphere on the Internet" (10), significantly moving "the dividing line between private and public behavior in a print-oriented society" (Meyrowitz 308). This blurring of boundaries between the private and the public sphere on YouTube has an important implication for the videos of an undocumented youth published on the platform: As the interviewees Marcela Hernandez and Antonio Gutiérrez have stressed, the publishing of personal information in a 'story' serves as a form of political activism for Movement, as the individual storyteller acquires a public face in name of the Movement's cause and agenda. Undocumented youth thereby transgress the dividing line between private and public behavior. Their private activism becomes public and vice versa.

Kavoori observes that stories on YouTube are "fundamentally informed" by the identities of the storytellers and "their attempts at self-definition through digital means" (4). Esser and Strömbäck describe this phenomenon as 'personalization', confirming that media "increasingly permeate *all* aspects of [...] life, from the micro (individual) to the meso (organizational) and the macro (societal) level" (10). YouTube, too, serves as a public sphere – a 'new space for the performance of the self, in which "self-representations" make up the most important part (Lundby 4). The performance of the self, however, does more than 'represent' the self – it allows the narrator "to pass through a variety of roles", "inhabiting new spaces" and 'trying on' "authority in a productive way" (Jones 82). Hübler, here, stresses the 'life as a show' metaphor, arguing that it is one of the most salient effects allowing "the 'theatricalization' of ordinary life" through "the possibility of participating in all sorts of video activities" (39).[2]

Nevertheless, this 'show' – the performance of personal narrative – remains political, according to Langellier and Peterson, "because it does something; and in doing something in and with discourse that is neither uniform nor stable, performing may reinscribe or resist the bodily practices and material conditions in which they are embedded" (164). Likewise, Baym finds that "the individual self is inseparable from the group in which it is situated" (157), as people in online communities "define themselves not just in relation to their offline selves or the medium but also in relation to one another and to the group as a whole" (158). This overlapping of self and community can be explained by the ways in which individual identity is shaped by interaction with others, namely, by how "speakers position themselves relative to other voices in their communities" by, for example, commenting directly on others' posts (ibid) but also how users manage to find "a voice" – the "process of making oneself distinct from the others through the creative use of existing discourse" (159). "When taking all of the communicative modes into consideration that people use in their everyday lives to *perform the actions* that they perform", Norris explains, "suddenly the connections between actions and belongings, between individual and society, and between the hidden and the overt begin to make sense" (xiii). Viewing the digital stories on YouTube as performances within the Immigrant Rights Movement, modes for communicating and performing, in particular, gain relevance.

2.3. Medium-conscious narratology: multi-, intermediality, and multimodality

With the arrival of new media in the field of narratology, "the question of how the intrinsic properties of the medium shape the form of narrative and affect the narrative experience can no longer be ignored" (Ryan, *Introduction* 1). Underlying this need for study is the fact that "media technology pressures" its producers "to adapt to and take advantage of" (Esser and Strömbäck 18).

When embarking on the search for a 'media language' on YouTube, in which the stories are told, we find that there is no single or homogenous media logic that is useful for the analysis of stories in new media (cf. Schulz 61). It follows that in measuring the narratological options that a single medium obtains, we need to figure out "what stories can be evoked or told, how they are presented, why they are communicated, and how they are experienced" (Ryan, *Introduction* 18). In contrast to early work on *the* media logic in new media, current research proposes that digital technologies such as those employed in digital storytelling "definitely do not obey just a single logic", but rather that "the multimodality of digital media operates according to mixed logics" (Lundby 11).

The combination of distinct media such as those on the platform YouTube, offers multiple levels in the creation of meaning(s) in narrative. The study of 'intermediality' – defined as "relations between (at least) two conventionally distinct media" (Schwanecke 18) – has partly answered the demand for investigating the results of media combination, media transfer, and intermedial references (cf. Rajewsky 12 and 18–21).

The process of combing media naturally includes two or more semiotic systems (category one) which "work together in the constitution of meaning", "contributing to this meaning with their inherent medial particularities and by the distinct way in which they are combined" (Schwanecke 21). Media combination, or *multimedia*, hence, denotes the combination of the two media systems into a whole, while multimodality can be found outside of media combination but in one of the semiotic systems already. On a more narrow level, multimodality refers to "the way that communicational structures can invoke different senses (hearing, sight, touch), using different semiotic channels (text, image, audio recording, video)" within one medium, while it, phrased more polemically, "generally strip[s] out cultural and material history to construct their models of the fundamental elements of human perception" (Punday 20). The merit of a multimodal approach in the analysis of the video clips of undocumented youth, in contrast to a multimedia one, is the need to decipher the use of very small signs of the sensory systems used for getting political messages across.

While Hoffmann notes that "multimodal narratives exist in both old and new media contexts", he stresses the fact that new media particularly "encourage (and enable on a technological plane) authors and users to co-deploy a complex web of semiotic moves in their online stories" (1). One important property of digital media, Ryan likewise emphasizes, is the "multiple sensory and semiotic channels" (*Will New Media Produce* 338). This leads to the necessity "for narrative scholars, in particular," to remodel "existing methods of analysis" of "the multimodal extension of texts" (Hoffmann 2). Consistent with mediatization theory, we should stress at this point that affordances that new media offer seem to have a vital influence on the form and content of online narratives and make the study of the resources used in the narratives even more important. In other words: storytelling in video format on YouTube naturally employs multimodality.

Kress and Van Leuuwen, who have investigated, in particular, the (socio) cultural aspects of meaning production through multimodality in narrative, emphasize that the study of multimodality is, most prominently, about "how [...] people use the variety of semiotic resources to make signs in concrete social contexts" (vii). Consequently, "the emphasis is on the sign-maker and their situated use of modal resources" (Jewitt, *Different Approaches* 30). Therefore, signs need to be understood in their particular situations and social contexts, as they are "governed by a common set of rules" to these communities (Stöckl 11). This further implies that there is much subjective interpretation of modes and their signs, which we need to keep in mind for the interpretation of the multimodal meaning-making in digital *testimonios* of undocumented youth.

Determining the functions of modes, so-called 'meta-functions', Stöckl proposes three categories: Any mode is, he argues, "able to depict states-of-affairs (ideational), design some social interaction between the communicators (inter-personal) and contribute to organizing and structuring the text (textual)" (25). Further, while the 'design' – the "(uses of) semiotic resources, in all semiotic modes and combinations of semiotic modes" – is means "to realise discourses in the context of a given communication situation" (Kress and Van Leeuwen 5), the production of multimodal output "refers to the organisation of expression, to the actual material articulation of the semiotic event or [...] artefact" (6), which is of particular relevance in this investigation. In videos on YouTube, performance is a major part of the social shaping, and hence, of the socio-technological affordances of the medium. It plays a central role in the analysis of the interplay among different modes and the "cultural work performed with the different materials" chosen by the undocumented narrators (cf. Kress, *What is mode?* 67).

2.4. Multimodal 'design' of digital testimonios *of undocumented youth*

Due to the close relationship of YouTube video clips to film, parallels in narrativity and narration of the different media highlight similar ways of producing meaning. As film is intermedial and multimodal by nature, it offers open-ended repertoires. According to Wildfeuer, film's "semiotic resources interact and operate according to various principles and in order to create the film's overall meaning potential" (2). Storytelling genres on YouTube, however, includes "the relation or interaction between media texts and their environment" such as "linking, instant distribution, indexing and searching, and above all, interactivity" (Kavoori 12). Burgess and Green further point to the "residual character of interpersonal face-to-face communication" (54). In contrast to television, for example, digital videos are "technically easy to produce, generally requiring little more than a webcam and basic editing skills" (ibid). Because a personal video seems more direct in its communication, it "inherently invites feedback" (ibid).

In a political context, the potential for attention and reaction on part of the audience is of immense importance. The YouTube video's capacity for eliciting attentive audience response will be evident in our analysis of the interpersonal function in the different modes employed in the samples used for this study. Which meaning does the incorporation of links into the video, for instance, create? For hypertext applications such as YouTube, how do narratives create (political) meaning through the use of semiotic codes/modes/sensory channels *other* than *exclusively* language? YouTube videos deliberately focus on the visual – moving images that form really short films, as the reference to television in the name of the website, You-*Tube*, already indicates.

While the digital *testimonios* chosen are unique short films which create new hybrids of pictures (static and moving), music, verbal and non-verbal, and background sounds, for the most part, the visual image (moving) and verbal sounds (spoken language) dominate. According to Doloughan, "the emphasis has been on a move away from the primacy of the verbal towards an interest in exploring the impact of other modalities on verbal or written communication, most notably, though not exclusively, the influence of the visual" (127). Likewise, Kress emphasizes the revolutionary character of this shift from "the now centuries-long dominance of writing to the new dominance of the image and, on the other hand, the move from the dominance of the medium of the book to the dominance of the medium of the screen" (*Literacy* 1). Thus, the analysis of the narrative's meaning production also begins with the moving image and face-to-face narrative effect created by the narrators in Chapter 5.

Realized through the combination of the logics of time and space, moving image, is "realized by a succession of frames of images, each of which is itself organized by the logic of space and simultaneity" (Kress, *What is mode?* 56).

Visual means of communication such as gestures or facial expressions play an important role for this analysis because the digital *testimonios* chosen mostly employ an eye-level medium shot or medium close-up, showing the narrator as if in an interview. In this performance, Hübler explains, the presence of a camera has an "impact on the narrative performance", as non-verbal modes of narration are visible, such as the "prosodic and kinesic/gestural" modes (40). Therefore, with regard to the visual, there is a stronger emphasis on the "narrator as actor (rather than on technical possibilities that the medium offers and the repercussions on the narrative format)" (ibid).

This observation resonates with current performance studies, which focus upon the speech act, addressing the question, in Butler's words, of "what [...] it mean[s] for a word not only to name, but also in some sense to perform and, in particular, to perform what it names?" (43). This view purports, in particular, the tremendous impact words have on our actions (cf. 44). Yet, the production of spoken language works according to a very different logic, compared to image: Speech is strongly dependent on time, as words and sentences appear in succeeding sequences (cf. Kress, *What is mode?* 55). Still image, in contrast to speech and moving image, is dependent on (framed) space and its "simultaneously present" or oddly arranged elements (55–56). Based on the logic of space more strictly than moving image (as the latter incorporates sound), still image also creates its meaning by the "relations between the depicted entities" (56). The question, at which point (logic of time) the moving picture combines the audiovisual narrative with the medium of the still image, such as pictures or photos, is particularly relevant for this study. Which 'story' does the still image add to the narration of the moving image?

There has been a noticeable move from the written language to the image in digital text. However, writing assumes a prominent role in the creation of meaning in digital text by the use of hyperlinks or captions.[3] The choice of written captions or filming written text illustrates an important semiotic source in the narratives chosen for this study. Potential for creating meaning through written language, however, is less easy to define according to the logics of time and space: Writing is "spatially displayed," yet visually 'mimics' speech "in its logic of sequence in time" (Kress, *What is mode?* 56). As the use of written language in the digital *testimonios* of undocumented youth is fairly restricted – sound, however, is used in *all* of the narratives – I chose to separate modes, both spoken and written language, into different chapters.

As the multimodal ensemble just introduced shows, "multimodal capacity is a key to understanding Digital Storytelling" (Lundby 8). Central in this understanding is the "semiotic power of multimodality" that lies "in the blending of new and old textual forms" (ibid), which, through digital media, has become more available to the average user to employ and reshape according to his/her communication needs (cf. Hedberg vii). However, we also need to emphasize that "multimodal composing depends on computer technologies" (ibid). While Burgess and Green have observed a "noticeable focus on video as a technology" and "fascination with the technological capabilities of digital video editing" in video stories on YouTube (52), this affordance also presupposes a necessary knowledge of how to use the different semiotic resources that produce a multimodal ensemble. The production process, as Beach observes, forces users to learn "how best to combine texts, images, audio, and/or video designed to craft a visual argument" (209). Participating on YouTube via consuming or producing multimodal videos, in sum, requires media literacy. Here, "technology plays an increasing role in changing media into modes, and hence in controlling how meanings can be made", Kress and Van Leeuwen observe (79).

"Being literate", in this context, "means more than just being able to read and write the printed word" (Ho et al. 2), if we wish to "participate in meaning-making communities as producers and not just consumers – to shape the landscapes in which we participate" (1). Producing digital *testimonios* becomes a "literacy practice" – "the knowledge, experience, feelings, values and capabilities that play a role in the reading and writing of [multimodal] texts" (Jewitt, *Glossary* 299). While "human cognition is multimodal" by nature (Grishakova 329; see also La Rose 301), clues on digital sites such as YouTube need to be learned, which transforms its use into a "cultural practice" (Street et al. 200). The turn to the use of the visual (moving) image, as in digital *testimonios* on YouTube, as a concluding thought, "will have profound effects on human, cognitive/affective, cultural and bodily engagement with the world, and on the forms and shapes of knowledge" (Kress, *Literacy* 1). This, predicts Ryan, creates "new forms of narrativity" and discourse but also "pragmatic factors: new modes of user involvement; new types of interface; and new relations between the author (or, rather, system designer), the plot (or plots), and users" (*Digital Media* 333).

The analyses will deduce the political meaning produced by the different modes and media and examine the specific resources of film montage with regard to the ideational, interpersonal, and textual meta-function of modes. They also assess the socio-technological affordances of YouTube's media logic and their socio-cultural context in terms of participation, personalization, and performance within the tradition of the *testimonio*.

The figure below provides a collection of (selective) designs provided in the digital *testimonios* chosen for analysis in this study. The categories for this chart are deduced from Hartmut Stöckl's collection of "network of modes, sub-modes and features in TV-and film media" (12–13).

The table presents, first of all, a focus on visual and verbal modes that produce essential political meaning. The specific modes, or 'sub modes' (cf. Stöckl 12) of communication and representation used in the narratives can be found in Category 2. They represent subcategories of more general modes and media listed in Category 1. The latter includes, first of all, the sensory channel (visual or auditory), the core mode (image, language, sound, or music), and, lastly, the medial variants (moving, speech, noise, performed, static). The number in brackets/italics indicates the number of narratives that utilize the particular mode/medium listed. The names of the undocumented youth narrators are indicated by their acronyms and chronological number of publication (see Table 3.1).

Table 3.1 Multimodal Design in Digital *Testimonios* of Undocumented Youth on YouTube

Category 1 *(Sensory Channel) Core Modes* *(Medial Variants)* (Total No. Used)	*Category 2* *Sub Modes*	*1.* *S.S.*	*2.* *M.A.*	*3.* *C.R.*	*4.* *D.R.*	*5.* *A.V.*	*6.* *M.C.*	*7.* *I.R.*	*8.* *L.M.*
(Visual) **Image** (Moving) *(8)*	A Non-verbal means: gestures (movement of arms, hands, head); posture; facial expressions (movement of facial features and gaze: 'eye contact')	+	+	+	+	+	+	+	+
(6)	B Montage: cuts, zoom, fading in & out	+	+	+	+	–	–	+	+
(5)	C More than one setting and/or distinct objects/'props' (mise-en-scène)	+	+	–	–	+	–	+	+
(Auditory) **Language** (Speech) *(8)*	D Voice quality: pitch, volume (dynamics), intonation, rhythm, speed, pausing	+	+	+	+	+	+	+	+
(3)	E Voice editing: voice-over/off-stage commentary	+	–	+	–	–	–	–	+
(Auditory) **Sound** (Noise) *(3)*	F Non-verbal sounds (background) in original soundtrack and their quality	+	–	–	+	–	–	+	–
(Auditory) **Music** (Performed) *(2)*	G Instrumental music in soundtrack: provenance, melody/theme, rhythm	–	–	+	–	–	–	–	+
(Visual) **Language** (Static Writing) *(5)*	H On props/in background (e.g. signs, posters, clothes)	+	+	–	+	–	–	+	+
(4)	I Captions	+	–	+	–	–	–	+	+
(3)	J (Hyper)links	+	–	+	–	–	–	+	–
(Visual) **Image** (Static) *(4)*	K Photographs	+	+	+	–	–	–	–	+

Source: Created by the Author.

Notes

1 It needs to be noted, at this point, that this "classic model" of digital storytelling incorporates still 'images' rather than moving pictures. Naturally, the technological affordances of YouTube allow short films, including moving images, however, and all digital *testimonios* selected for this study consist of filmic material to the most part. Which effect this transformation of the 'digital story' has for the *testimonio* will be addressed, in particular, in the analysis of the visual mode in Chapter 5.

2 The so-called 'affective turn' is proof for the advanced status that individuality has recently gained recent years. While the linguistic turn in the 1970s acknowledged that language helped "to constitute reality", likewise emotions are said to have a "fundamental role in human experience" (Lemmings and Brooks 3). The performance of the self and subjective experience therefore implies a sense of 'individual agency' which is strongly informed by "affect" (4). Emotions may build up a sense of urgency, making people 'ready to act' and engage in political criticism.

3 The hyperlinks are not links per se but written website addresses and references.

References

Ashcroft, Bill, Gareth Griffiths, and Helen Tiffin, eds. *Postcolonial Studies. The Key Concepts.* 3rd ed. Routledge Key Guides. New York: Routledge, 2013.

Baym, Nancy K. *Tune in, Log on: Soaps, Fandom, and Online Community.* Thousand Oaks, CA: Sage Publications, 2000.

Beach, Richard. "Digital Tools for Collecting, Connecting, Constructing Responding to, Creating, and Conducting Media Ethnographies of Audience Use of Media Texts." *Media/Cultural Studies: Critical Approaches.* Ed. Rhonda Hammer and Douglas Kellner. New York: Peter Lang, 2009. 206–228.

Benmayor, Rina. "Digital 'Testimonio' as a Signature Pedagogy for Latin@ Studies." *Equity & Excellence in Education: University of Massachusetts School of Education* 45.3 (2012): 507–524.

Beverley, John. "Testimonio, Subalternity, and Narrative Authority." *Handbook of Qualitative Research.* Ed. Norman K. Denzin and Yvonna S. Lincoln. 2nd ed. Thousand Oaks, CA: Sage Publications, 2000. 555–565.

———. *Testimonio: On the Politics of Truth.* Minneapolis: University of Minnesota Press, 2004.

Burgess, Jean, and Joshua Green. *YouTube: Online Video and Participatory Culture.* Digital Media and Society Series. Cambridge: Polity Press, 2009.

Butler, Judith. *Excitable Speech: A Politics of the Performative.* New York: Routledge, 1997.

Couldry, Nick. "Digital Storytelling, Media Research and Democracy: Conceptual Choices and Alternative Futures." *Digital Storytelling, Mediatized Stories: Self-Representations in New Media.* Ed. Knut Lundby. New York: Peter Lang, 2008. 41–60.

Do Mar Castro Varela, María, and Nikita Dhawan. *Postkoloniale Theorie: Eine Kritische Einführung.* Bielefeld: Transcript Verlag, 2005.

Doloughan, Fiona J. *Contemporary Narrative: Textual Production, Multimodality and Multiliteracies.* London: Continuum, 2011.

Döring, Tobias. *Postcolonial Literatures in English.* Uni-Wissen Anglistik-Amerikanistik 4. Stuttgart: Klett Lernen und Wissen GmbH, 2011.

Dube, Saurabh. "Critical Crossovers: Postcolonial Perspectives, Subaltern Studies and Cultural Identities." *The SAGE Handbook of Identities*. Ed. Margaret Wetherell and Chandra T. Mohanty. Los Angeles, CA: SAGE, 2010. 125–143.

Esser, Frank, and Jesper Strömbäck, eds. "Mediatization of Politics: Towards a Theoretical Framework." *Mediatization of Politics: Understanding the Transformation of Western Democracies*. New York: Palgrave Macmillan, 2014. 3–28.

Grishakova, Marina. "Intermedial Metarepresentations." *Intermediality and Storytelling*. Ed. Marina Grishakova and Marie-Laure Ryan. Berlin: De Gruyter, 2010. 312–331.

Hedberg, John G. "Foreword." *Transforming Literacies and Language: Multimodality and Literacy in the New Media Age*. Ed. Caroline M. L. Ho, Kate T. Anderson and Alvin P. Leong. London: Continuum, 2011. vii–x.

Ho, Caroline M. L., Anderson, Kate T., and Alvin P. Leong, eds. *Transforming Literacies and Language: Multimodality and Literacy in the New Media Age*. London: Continuum, 2011.

Hoffmann, Christian R. "Introduction: Narrative Revisited: Telling a Story in the Age of New Media." *Narrative Revisited: Telling a Story in the Age of New Media*. Ed. Christian R. Hoffmann. Amsterdam: John Benjamins B.V., 2010. 1–18.

Hoffmann, Christian R., and Volker Eisenlauer. "Once Upon a Blog…: Storytelling in Weblogs." *Narrative Revisited: Telling a Story in the Age of New Media*. Ed. Christian R. Hoffmann. Amsterdam: John Benjamins B.V., 2010. 79–108.

Hübler, Axel. "The Role of Electronics in the Perception of Everyday Narratives." *Narrative Revisited: Telling a Story in the Age of New Media*. Ed. Christian R. Hoffmann. Amsterdam: John Benjamins B.V., 2010. 39–55.

Jenkins, Henry. "What Happened Before YouTube." *YouTube: Online Video and Participatory Culture*. By Jean Burgess and Joshua Green. Digital Media and Society Ser. Cambridge: Polity Press, 2009. 109–125.

Jewitt, Carey, ed. "Different Approaches to Multimodality." *The Routledge Handbook of Multimodal Analysis*. London: Routledge, 2009. 28–39.

———. Glossary. *The Routledge Handbook of Multimodal Analysis*. London: Routledge, 2009. 293–308.

Jones, Leigh A. "Postcasting and Performativity: Multimodal Invention in an Advanced Writing Class." *Composition Studies* 38.2 (2010): 75–91. Web. 16 Apr. 2015.

Kavoori, Anandam. *Reading YouTube: The Critical Viewers Guide*. New York: Peter Lang, 2011.

Kim, Gooyong. "The Future of YouTube: Critical Reflections on YouTube Users' Discussion over Its Future." *InterActions: UCLA Journal of Education and Information Studies* 5.2 (2009): 1–30. Web. 21 Aug. 2014.

Kress, Gunther, and Theo van Leeuwen. *Multimodal Discourse: The Modes and Media of Contemporary Communication*. London: Hodder Education, 2001.

Kress, Gunther. *Literacy in the New Media Age*. Literacies. London: Routledge, 2003.

———. "What is Mode?" *The Routledge Handbook of Multimodal Analysis*. Ed. Carey Jewitt. London: Routledge, 2009. 54–67.

Langellier, Kristin M., and Eric E. Peterson. "Shifting Contexts in Personal Narrative Performance." *The SAGE Handbook of Performance Studies*. Ed. D. Soyini Madison and Judith Hamera. Thousand Oaks, CA: SAGE, 2006. 151–168.

La Rose, Tara. "Digital Media Stories through Multimodal Analysis: A Case Study of Erahoneybee's Song about a Child Welfare Agency." *Journal of Technology in Human Services* 30.3–30.4 (2012): 299–311. Web. 16 Apr. 2015.

Lemmings, David, and Ann Brooks, eds. "The Emotional Turn in the Humanities and Social Sciences." *Emotions and Social Change: Historical and Sociological Perspectives*. New York: Routledge, 2014. 3–18.

Logan, Kathleen. "Personal Testimony: Latin American Women Telling Their Lives." *Latin American Research Review* 32.1 (1997): 199–211.

Lundby, Knut, ed. "Introduction: Digital Storytelling, Mediatized Stories." *Digital Storytelling, Mediatized Stories: Self-Representations in New Media*. New York: Peter Lang, 2008. 1–17.

Maier, Linda S. "Introduction: The Case for and Case History of Women's Testimonial Literature in Latin America." *Woman as Witness: Essays on Testimonial Literature by Latin American Women*. Ed. Linda S. Maier and Isabel Dulfano. New York: Peter Lang, 2004. 1–17.

Meyrowitz, Joshua. *No Sense of Place: The Impact of Electronic Media on Social Behavior*. New York: Oxford University Press, 1985.

Norris, Sigrid. *Identity in (Inter)Action: Introducing Multimodal (Inter)Action Analysis*. Trends in Applied Linguistics 4. Berlin: De Gruyter Mouton, 2011.

Page, Ruth. "Interactivity and Interaction: Text and Talk in Online Communities." *Intermediality and Storytelling*. Ed. Marina Grishakova and Marie-Laure Ryan. Berlin: De Gruyter, 2010. 208–231.

Punday, Daniel. "From Synthesia to Multimedia: How to Talk about New Media Narrative." *New Narratives: Stories and Storytelling in the Digital Age*. Ed. Ruth Page and Bronwen Thomas. Lincoln: University of Nebraska Press, 2011. 19–34.

Rajewsky, Irina O. *Intermediales Erzählen in der Italienischen Literatur der Postmoderne: Von den Giovani Scrittori der 80er zum Pulp der 90er Jahre*. Tübingen: Gunther Narr Verlag, 2003.

Randall, Margaret. "Reclaiming Voices: Notes on a New Female Practice in Journalism." *The Real Thing: Testimonial Discourse and Latin America*. Ed. Georg M. Gugelberger. Durham, NC: Duke University Press, 1996. 58–69.

Roth, Julia. *Occidental Readings, Decolonial Practices: A Selection on Gender, Genre, and Coloniality in the Americas*. Inter-American Studies 10. Trier: Wissenschaftlicher Verlag Trier, 2014.

Ryan, Marie-Laure, ed. Introduction. *Narrative across Media: The Languages of Storytelling*. Lincoln: University of Nebraska Press, 2004. 1–40.

———. "Part 5: Digital Media." *Narrative across Media: The Languages of Storytelling*. Lincoln: University of Nebraska Press, 2004. 329–335.

———. "Will New Media Produce New Narratives?" *Narrative across Media*. Lincoln: University of Nebraska Press, 2004. 337–359.

Schmidt, Jan-Hinrik. *Social Media*. Wiesbaden: Springer, 2013.

Schulz, Winfried. "Mediatization and New Media." *Mediatization of Politics: Understanding the Transformation of Western Democracies*. Ed. Frank Esser and Jesper Strömbäck. New York: Palgrave Macmillan, 2014. 57–73.

Schwanecke, Christine. *Intermedial Storytelling: Thematisation, Imitation and Incorporation of Photography in English and American Fiction at the Turn of the 21st Century*. Studies in English Literary and Cultural History 52. Trier: Wissenschaftlicher Verlag Trier, 2012.

Stöckl, Hartmut. "In Between Modes: Language and Image in Printed Media." *Perspectives on Multimodality*. Ed. Eija Ventola, Cassily Charles, and Martin Kaltenbacher. Document Design Companion Series 6. Amsterdam: John Benjamins Publishing Company, 2004. 9–30.

Street, Brian, Kate Pahl, and Jennifer Rowsell. "Multimodality and New Literacy Studies." *The Routledge Handbook of Multimodal Analysis*. Ed. Carey Jewitt. London: Routledge, 2009. 191–200.

Wildfeuer, Janina. *Film Discourse Interpretation: Towards a New Paradigm for Multimodal Film Analysis*. New York: Routledge, 2014.

Yúdice, George. "*Testimonio* and Postmodernism." *The Real Thing: Testimonial Discourse and Latin America*. Ed. Georg M. Gugelberger. Durham, NC: Duke University Press, 1996. 42–57.

Zimmerman, Marc. "Testimonio in Guatemala: Payeras, Rigoberta, and Beyond." *The Real Thing: Testimonial Discourse and Latin America*. Ed. Georg M. Gugelberger. Durham, NC: Duke University Press, 1996. 101–129.

4 Stories of the dispossessed

1. Introduction

As we have seen in the preceding chapter, the powerful fusion of digital storytelling and *testimonio* affects the digital *testimonio*, as the latter employs – in their mediatization – multimodal affordances and the socio-technological format of YouTube. Despite this predominant connection to the mediatization of storytelling, Baym cautions us that "the topics and purposes around which online communities organize are at least as important as the medium in shaping a group's communication patterns" (200). Subjecting the political logic, the history of marginalization and exclusion, as well as current political goals of the Immigrant Rights Movement since 2006 to the mediatization of storytelling, and, in particular, the genre of the *testimonio*, calls for new terms to refer to the politics of digital *testimonios*. The personalization and performative aspects of stories on YouTube, and the melding of the *testimonio* with digital storytelling (affordances), in particular, employ a distinct understanding of a *testimonio* and its narrator for the political purposes of undocumented youth in the Movement. This chapter offers an approach to framing the political logic of testimonial narratives produced by marginalized and/or oppressed identities that are *not* excluded from participating in public discourse through websites such as YouTube, an approach that does not "abstract [...] *testimonio* from its real and painful", as Bartow cautions (47). The theoretical framework of Butler and Athanasiou's 'dispossession', in contrast, offers a new understanding of 'the human' in circumstances of oppression and/or marginalization and his/her agency and activism in the public sphere through understanding spaces of appearance as general constructs that enable 'the human' to *perform* his dispossession and, thereby, resist it. This agency need not be bound to a specific medium but materializes dispossession *through* the bodily performance. It is precisely this literal visibility, and a central socio-technological affordance on YouTube, that gives undocumented youth a 'face' in the public sphere.

The following section formulates a common structure in the YouTube narratives of undocumented youth – the *stories* of oppression that the narrators tell – and relates them to the genre of the *testimonio*. Section 3 links this structure to Butler and Athanasiou's dispossession. The greater part of this chapter introduces these core stories of dispossession for each of the eight digital *testimonios*, analyzing their political message and content in detail. The last section of this chapter formulates a scheme that will serve as the grounds for analyzing the performance in the context of the political.

2. Framing experience of dispossession: the core story in digital *testimonios*

Story-oriented narratology reminds us of the assumption that "narrative texts (in contrast to descriptive, discursive and other types of texts) are characterized by a chronologically organized sequence of events, in which an event brings about a change in the situation" (Nünning and Nünning 103). Although this investigation focuses on the mediality and performance of the stories and their use of multimodality to get their political message across, when viewing the digital *testimonios*, a pattern of chronological events embedded, integrated, yet separate and distinct in each of the narratives becomes visible. All digital narratives seem to be composed of a central story that the narrator introduces with variants of the claim that 'this is my story'. The core story, as I term this orderly structured unit, is a tight sequence of events and the most central element in the digital narrative. It seems that often, precisely *because* of the core story's centrality, the whole narrative is referred to as 'the story', 'my story', or 'a student's story' on the Web not only by the narrator him-/herself but also in the very title of the digital narrative. It tells a sequence of events that constitutes an important moment in the narrator's biography in the narrative and often even signals a turning point for the narrator. The *core* story is the densest unit of content in the form of events. Core story events are narrated in much length and detail, while the narrator rapidly and casually narrates introductory matters, 'additional information' such as the announcement and outing of the undocumented status of the narrator, potential political messages and conclusions, and a forecast of current and potential future activism. Further, it seems as if the events that make up the core story are more actively *performed*, as the narrator visibly and audibly re-lives the moments that seem to be so crucial. The rest of the narrative is, by contrast, dispassionately reportorial.

Pointing to these core stories in the digital narratives shows that digital *testimonios* are composed of 'life experiences', 'emergency situations', or 'significant episodes', just as traditional *testimonios*. What is more, the core stories in digital *testimonios* incorporate much more than a simple chain of autobiographical events. The content structure of the stories shows that they are summoned to recount in detail a situation of 'dispossession' and/or 'exclusion' in the narrators' lives that they regard as crucial, due to their lack of citizenship status and attached rights. In other words, the core stories are accounts of the core moments of powerful negative experiences that highlight this dispossession of citizenship and reinforced exclusion. Each narrator uses this core story as a basis or an apparent reason for producing his/her *testimonio*. However, the core story itself does not formulate any specific political actions to follow. It is rather the grounds for their digital *testimonios* to *perform* dispossession in Butler and Athansiou's sense, not 'on the streets' but in digital form with YouTube being the public space for this action.

The most salient aspect with regard to narrative structure and content of *testimonios*, one might argue, is their depiction of an important event or sequence of events in the life of the narrator. In the words of Ashcroft et al., the *testimonio* can thus be described as a "unit of narration [that] is usually a life or a significant life episode" (259). The genre imposes clear boundaries upon the nature of this experience, as it is "a story that *needs* to be told – involving a problem of repression, poverty, subalterneity, exploitation or simply struggle for survival, which is implicated in the act of narration itself" (Vidal and Jara in: Ashcroft et al. 260, *emphasis added*). Hence, without this bleak condition in which the narrator finds him-/herself, there would not be the *testimonio*. This leads Beverley to describe the *testimonio* as "an 'emergency' narrative" (556). The term – *testimonio* – further implies that the narrator "bear[s] witness in a legal or religious sense" to this significant life episode and problem, "distinguishing it from simple recorded participant narrative" (Ashcroft et al. 260).

3. A claim to Butler and Athanasiou's "dispossession"

3.1. "Dispossession"

In their most recent book, *Dispossession: The Performative in the Political*, Butler and Athanasiou[1] seek to gain a normative understanding of political or economic dispossession that marginalizes different people worldwide through, for instance, the loss of citizenship, property, or land. It especially exists in capitalist states, according to Athanasiou, that support strict migration policies and the "abjection of stateless people, *sans papiers*" (29). These bodies, which Athanasiou then understands as "human capital", are becoming "disposable, dispossessed by capital and its exploitative excess, uncountable and unaccounted for" (ibid). But why would Athanasiou and Butler's approach to this kind of marginalization be more useful for the analysis of digital *testimonios* by undocumented youth on YouTube than other theories similar to the subaltern/organic intellectual that the traditional *testimonio* proposes?

In their definition of dispossession, Athanasiou and Butler work out two senses of 'dispossession'. In the first sense, the two scholars define dispossession as a fundamental relationality to others. As Butler maintains, "dispossession can be a term that marks the limits of self-sufficiency and that establishes us as relational and interdependent beings" (*Dispossession* 3). Similarly, Athanasiou argues that dispossession leads to a "sense of agency" and a sense of conditions imposed by others that leads to this autonomy (2). According to the scholar, this sense of agency rises "as a limit to the autonomous and impermeable self-sufficiency of the liberal subject through its injurious yet enabling fundamental dependency and relationality" (ibid). Butler adds emphatically that without this peculiar dependency there would not be dispossession and vice versa, as the following quote shows: "We are dispossessed of ourselves", she claims, "by virtue of some kind of contact with another, by virtue of being moved and even surprised or disconcerted by that encounter with alterity" (*Dispossession* 3).

Applied to digital *testimonios*, we find that the core story events also recount precisely this dependency and 'being moved' by others: They depict what undocumented youth feel (which they, hence, *perform* for the viewer of their videos) when they learn they are undocumented in particular life situations that they recount, in which they are *dispossessed* by a higher normative and policing power. This dispossession transpires either formally, through institutions such as schools or universities or informally through, for instance, bullying in school upon their 'outing' or social exclusion and lack of empathy for their situation. These core stories are, really, *stories of dispossession* as recounted in this first, more internal sense of dispossession understood by Athanasiou and Butler and portrayed above.

The second, more direct sense of dispossession that the authors define points to the concrete violations inherent in the dispossession such as land loss, material expropriation, military violence, and the loss of citizenship (cf. Butler, *Dispossession* 3). Athanasiou adds that being dispossessed relates to "processes and ideologies by which persons are disowned and abjected by normative and normalizing powers" (2). While this study has no room to attempt an analysis of these ideologies per se, it certainly seeks to carve out the ideological traces that undocumented youth themselves ascribe to their dispossession in the succeeding analysis. Because Athanasiou points to the underlying ideologies, one could argue that any analysis of dispossession demands this postcolonial endeavor. Nevertheless, what unites both senses of dispossession is that it "involves the subject's relation to norms, its mode of becoming by means of assuming and resignifying injurious interpellations and impossible passions" (2) that eventually lead to the "performative in the political" (3).

Both senses of dispossession – that by normative forces as well as the dispossession that highlights our relationality to others and robs us of our autonomy – need to be understood in multiple complex sociopolitical and historical contexts. According to Athanasiou, we need to pose the question of how dispossession is "legitimized, normalized, and regulated through, and in the name of, discourse of reconciliation" (26). I understand 'reconciliation' in one particular way: While it often also takes material forms, for me, it especially highlights the negotiation of changing legal situations for those who are dispossessed. In this concrete legal context, we need to ask what kind of statement current and changing policies on undocumented immigrant make and how they influence processes of dispossession. As Athanasiou implied in her quote above, postcolonial subjection and dispossession are *ongoing*, which means that the policies that are changed never come from scratch – they are always based upon another, discriminating, subjectifying and dispossessing context. Therefore, policies that 'reconcile' undocumented students, for instance, with exceptional high school records by granting them a work permit after graduation (in order to finance their college or university education) – the DACA – may result in other processes of dispossession: Many legislative changes are still not all-embracing, and by making them available to only some, others are again dispossessed as legal changes neither reach nor actively exclude their relatives or friends, or even themselves. This leads to an ongoing dispossession within the context of prior dispossessions.[2] Likewise, Langellier and Peterson argue that "no one element" in the personal narratives " – a canonical story or a counter-narrative, a performer's intention or identity's body, a liberatory or ritualized setting – can anchor normativity or guarantee transgression outside the multiple and meshed workings of context" and therefore, the authors declare "performing personal narrative as a radically contextualized practice" (166).

One concrete dimension crucial to the effect of dispossession that can also be found in all of the digital *testimonios* of undocumented youth online is the "complicated affective, psychic, and political dynamic" of the act of dispossessing others or becoming dispossessed (Athanasiou 6). The effect that Butler ascribes to this sense is that "we sometimes no longer know precisely who we are, or by what we are driven" (*Dispossession* 3). It is "these forms of experience [that] call into question whether we are, as bounded and deliberate individuals, self-propelling and self-driven" (4). Butler reminds us what dispossession feels like due to its consequences. It is

> lived feeling of precariousness, which can be articulated with a damaged sense of future and a heightened sense of anxiety about issues like illness and mortality (especially when there is no health insurance or when conditions of labor and accelerated anxiety converge to debilitate the body). This is just one example of how a condition crosses the economic and cultural spheres, suggesting that what we need precisely are a new set of transversal categories and forms of thought that elude both dualism and determinism.
>
> (43)

The affective dimension of dispossession is an aspect that asks for a multimodal analysis, since emotions can be particularly well portrayed through a combination of different modes.

As ways of dispossessing people, Athanasiou understands the process of withholding them "from means of survival" (26). Not only does land deprivation become an issue but essentially "subjective and epistemic violence" as well as the inherent "discursive and affective appropriation with crucially gendered and sexualized implications" (ibid). In her point of view, potential to dispossess someone or even entire groups via the application and implications of sexual norms (e.g. displaying homosexuality as a taboo) is particularly strong. Even more so, when homosexual identities, to pick up the example from above, intersect with other minority group identities, such as immigrants, tension is enhanced through the multiple dispossessions the individual has to suffer (cf. Athanasiou 166). Tension might, on the other hand, inspire the countering of such constellations by the sometimes "allied constellation of anti-racist, immigrant, and queer communities against the violence of precarity and abjection in both national and transnational frames" (ibid). For our analysis, the workings of dispossession at different intersections and in critical conflict with each other therefore need to be considered.

3.2. Dispossession of citizenship rights: exclusion vs. belonging

Dispossession manifests itself in undocumented youth as the feeling of legally *not belonging* anywhere. The strong political goal of finally 'belonging' to a nation – the United States – is the central motive of the Movement, after all. More concretely, activists "work together to produce the situation in which the targeted population belongs, finally, to no land, a situation that embodies one clear impasse of dispossession" (*Dispossession* 24). While many more individuals and groups of people might be dispossessed in the same way, I argue that undocumented youth offer unique political resistance to dispossession via their narratives on YouTube by actively claiming a belonging (to the United States), undocumented youth counter precisely this type of dispossession.

Understanding 'dispossession' as outside the logic of actual, material 'possession', Butler claims that it also denotes other "forms of human deprivation and exploitation" prone to capitalism (*Dispossession* 7). In fact, undocumented youth have not been dispossessed of their U.S. American citizenship, because they have never actually *possessed* it. Further, they are not dispossessed of their citizenship of their country of origin. According to Butler's and Athanasiou's understanding of 'dispossession' outside the logic of 'possession', undocumented youth are dispossessed in *not having* citizenship *rights*. As the call for an actual claim to citizenship is not very loud in undocumented communities, it is, instead, the dispossession of the *rights* granted with citizenship that undocumented decry. The deprivation of rights distinguishes two groups of people, those who possess rights attached to citizenship and those who do not. This distinction, as we can see, brings the discussion to a more elementary, human level: Who is included, who is excluded? Who is 'of more worth'?

These speculations about the workings and effect of citizenship[3] and its rights need to be explained from a sociological standpoint to gain a full understanding of the workings of dispossession: As Isin and Turner explain, "'modern citizenship rights that draw from the nation-state typically include civil (free speech and movement, the rule of law), political (voting, seeking electoral office) and social (welfare, unemployment insurance and health care) rights'" (in: Albiez et al. 19). Citizenship, in this sense, "captures the formal status of an individual within a state" (20). This understanding points to a postmodern 'dilemma': Who defines citizenship and which rights are attached to it? (cf. ibid). The dispossession of immigrants of all citizenship rights once they are of 'undocumented status' is further problematic in the sense that many of these citizenship rights arguably overlap with civil and even human rights – a topic which undocumented youth also engage in with their core stories. Machado Pais, too, reminds us that "the concept of citizenship establishes boundaries and margins between societies and groups" and that "some fall within the framework (the 'included'), while others lie outside (the excluded, the marginal)" (231). The access to these definitions is limited to few people in that "the margins are defined from the centre, in other words, on the basis of values which belong to 'us' (the included), as opposed to 'them' (the excluded)" (ibid). The inner workings of inherent exclusion and active dispossession of those at the margin could not be clearer. To the sense of dependency on and relationality to the state that Butler and Athanasiou stress, Bendit adds the need for the state "to recognize young people as full citizens, who are entitled to individual and direct allowances from the state" (35–36). In other words, for youths to develop as adults, they need to be citizens.

When contemplating the idea of citizenship rights, one needs to bear in mind that these rights "also have responsibilities or obligations attached to them, as has been the case with military service" or the "citizen's obligation to pay taxes" (Albiez et al. 19). Although mandatory, obligation is also a 'right' of citizenship 'responsibilities' as it still provides the possibility of exclusion. The lack of both – the rights and privileges as well as the responsibilities – show that, as Albiez et al. have argued, citizenship is a social category that can be understood as a criterion for "expressions of collective belongings, [...] be they imagined or assigned, [they] undeniably con-vey processes of inclusion and exclusion in order to distinguish between in-groups and out-groups" (13).

Butler forcefully articulates how the lack of citizenship rights evokes a feeling of 'non-belonging' that establishes an immutable and conflicting condition in the dispossessed person:[4]

> The state signifies the legal and institutional structures that delimit a certain territory [...]. Hence, the state is supposed to service the matrix for the obligations and prerogatives of citizenship. It is that which forms the conditions under which we are juridically bound. We might expect that the state presupposes modes of juridical belonging, at least minimally, but since the state can be precisely what expels and suspends modes of legal protection and suspends modes of legal protection and obligation, the state can put us, some of us, in quite a state. It can signify the source of non-belonging, even produce that non-belonging as a quasi-permanent state [...]. This 'state' – that signifies both juridical and

> dispositional dimensions of life – is a certain tension produced between modes of being or mental states, temporary or provisional constellations of mind of one kind or another, and juridical and military complexes that govern how and where we may move, associate, work and speak.
>
> (*Who Sings* 4)

Altogether, this sense of 'exclusion' and consequential expression of 'non-belonging' is a severe consequence of the dispossession, as the introduction of the core stories will show in the following section: Undocumented youth enact this sense of non-belonging that Butler proposes, defining core moments in which this immediate consequence of dispossession comes to the fore.

As we have seen, Butler connects dispossession to internal processes and effects. The immediate issue raised by the core stories in the narratives of undocumented youth is 'belonging' as a structure of feeling[5] that is affected by dispossession of citizenship rights. 'Belonging' can be "prone to effecting social exclusion, but also the opposite – widening borders, incorporating, defining common grounds" (Pfaff-Czarnecka 203). Hannah Arendt, we recall, similarly described the right to have a home as the *ne plus ultra* human right (cf. Schlink 40). Author Bernhard Schlink argues along the lines of undocumented youth in their narratives – not for direct citizenship – but for the rights and privileges that come along with citizenship. He calls the right to be protected, live, and work in a country one can call home a fundamental human right.[6]

'Belonging to' the broader U.S. American people, to American societies/communities, and to 'humanity', are central issues involved in the core stories of the narratives. Adding to the sense of 'belonging to', translated in German as 'Zugehörigkeit', Pfaff-Czarnecka narrows down a broader sense of the 'belonging with', meaning 'Zusammengehörigkeit'. The former "denotes an individual's belonging to a collective" but also stresses "a tension inherent in belonging, namely a distance between the self and a we-collective" (201–202). 'Belonging *with*, on the other hand, "stands for togetherness" and "ideally combines commonality, mutuality and attachment" (202). The reason for bringing up this distinction is, when viewing the digital narratives, we find that while all of these digital *testimonios* express belonging with, to say, the 'whole undocumented community', we also acknowledge and at times express the different political interests that develop in the Immigrant Rights Movement since 2006.

The intersections at which dispossession is at work also find expression in the second sense of belonging, the concept of 'belonging to'. Pfaff-Czarnecka argues that

> this distinction becomes of interest when we shift our perspective from group dynamics geared at maintaining the collective status quo to a consideration of an individual's embeddedness in a collective, its seeking access to it ... or trying to abandon it.
>
> (202)

For three of the undocumented youth narrators in this study, for example, it is not enough to 'come out of the shadows' with regard to their undocumented status. They frequently also express the need to align themselves with other communities, such as the 'gay' one, and establishing a distinct connection between undocumented immigrants and homosexual identities and a very personalized logic within the general, greater logic of YouTube as a channel for communicating the political logic of the Movement. Within the frame of protest against dispossession, Manuel et al., publishers of a set of (written) stories by undocumented youth, "believe that if only they [the narrators of the stories published] were known and understood by their neighbors, their request for legal inclusion into American society could not be denied" (xi). A step in precisely this direction is what is taken by the undocumented youth narrators of digital *testimonios* selected for this investigation.

4. Core stories of dispossession in digital *testimonios* of undocumented youth

4.1. Core story: digital testimonio *of Stephanie Solis, "Lost & Found (Story of a DREAM Act Student)". Published: 12 May 2009*

The core story of Stephanie's digital *testimonio* is divided in two sequences (narrated in minute 00:00:11–00:01:10 and 00:01:47–00:02:57).[7] Both parts recount specific situations that are highly important to her. The situations she describes are experiences with dispossession that are already indicated by the title of the digital *testimonio*, "Lost & Found". First, she recounts how all her childhood pictures taken in her country of origin, the Philippines, got *lost* in a public storage place, where her mother deposited family belongings. Her family "moved around so frequently" that the place apparently lost track of them and got rid of all of her family's belongings (00:00:17–00:00:26). *Finding* a few baby photos again in a book she had loaned to a friend and just gotten back, she tells us that she finally could picture herself as a baby again and this way retrieve part of her memories. What follows this sequence is one that provides the viewer with information on Stephanie and her family's 'immigration story'.

The second moment of dispossession that she recounts in lively detail is the moment when she learns that she is undocumented. Stephanie tells the audience that, prior to the event, she found herself feeling at home in the United States just like any other American with an immigration background (as the sequences that recount her father's immigration story highlight). Finding out that she is undocumented and, hence, living in the United States illegally shortly before her 18th birthday, she not only feels robbed of her U.S. American identity but also realizes what her status does to her life – *dispossessing* her of vital elements of adulthood. She recounts that she now has no official national identity – neither a Philippine nor an American one, losing safe home at the same time. In more literal terms, Stephanie does not have access to in-state tuition, to a passport, or to activities for which a form of government identification is needed. It is this *loss* – a literal and symbolic dispossession – according to Stephanie, that 'delays' her transition to adulthood. In sum, her narrative recounts dispossession induced by the undocumented status, and the impacts on the inner workings, relationships, and national identity of the multigenerational, immigrant family.

The following aspects distinguish Stephanie's dispossession. "Literally, at the age of twenty," she says, "I did not remember what I looked like as a kid anymore" (00:01:06). In connection to her legal situation, I argue, it is apparent that in those early years of adulthood, Stephanie has not only lost the link to her Philippine cultural identity, but her identity development is further 'on hold'. This is primarily caused by the fact that she is denied all rights that are automatically granted to adult citizens once they turn 18.

The state's legal system becomes, in this story, the main normative policing power that causes Stephanie's suffering. Her dispossession highlights her dependency on the state to *grant* her these rights and de-emphasizes the undocumented immigrant family's responsibility for the situation. The end of their time in high school makes them realize their difference to other students of their school in terms of career options, in particular (cf. Pérez 24). The bitterness and, hence, affective dimensions of this situation, which Stephanie performs with the help of multiple modes, lie in the sudden exclusion experienced by undocumented children who grew up in the United States. Inclusion and exclusion, defining markers of the construct of 'belonging' to a culture or group, turn into momentous mechanisms in these youths' lives. As Machado Pais explains:

> Traditionally, the concept of citizenship establishes boundaries and margins between societies and groups. [...] But the margins are defined from the centre [...] on the basis of values which belong to 'us' (the included), as opposed to 'them' (the excluded).
>
> (231)

Determined to become an 'other' in U.S. society, Stephanie has, as we have seen, also been turned into a 'them' through the literal loss of her original cultural identity. Losing access to her Philippine culture and identity as well puts her in a double state of loss, as she is denied, literally, other memory repertoire.

The second sense of dispossession that connects to this dilemma is induced by the first part of the story. Stephanie describes how her family moved around so frequently that nobody was able to track them down. They were living a life in the shadows, of course. However, the effect of her life in the shadows influences Stephanie's relation to her mother, whom the narrator accuses of having put her childhood photos in the storage place in the first place, and hence, who is at least partly responsible for the subsequent loss as well. Further, she tells us that she only learned of her undocumented status after she directly and forcefully confronted her mother to tell her the truth. Stephanie's struggle shows how dispossession is further fortified in relations to 'others'. In this case, she is dispossessed in an interaction with her own mother, putting a strain on inner-family harmony. In this situation, Stephanie's multiple states of dependency become especially clear.

4.2. Core story: digital **testimonio** *of Mohammad Abdollahi, "My name is Mohammad and I am undocumented". Published: 19 March 2010*

'Mo', as the narrator of the succeeding digital narrative in our selection introduces himself, starts his personal story by introducing the fact that his parents migrated from Iran and stayed in the United States illegally, depicting his undocumented status as something that always was a known and 'given' to him, although he "never really understood what it meant until it was that time when everybody was applying for colleges" (00:00:37–00:00:42).

His core story then revolves around not being able to go to university because of his undocumented status, or, more precisely, because he was "not a citizen" and 'not born in the U.S.' Mohammad tells a detailed story of how he sat in the admission office at Eastern Michigan University in September 2007 and got handed his acceptance letter, yet how it was taken away from him after the registrar realized that he was undocumented. Consequently, he lost the right to a university education that, for a brief moment, had been his.

In contrast to many other undocumented students, Mohammad claims that he first was "personally fine" with community college (00:00:57–00:01:02). This is distinctive considering that his narrative was published in 2010, and when many other narratives at that time – just as Stephanie's – aimed at illustrating educational excellence and personal qualification for a legislative path to citizenship. Mohammad, too, emphasizes his parents' faith in the American Dream. He recounts that his mother, in particular, had high hopes for her son's education and future, identifying her dreams as one of the reasons why his family migrated (illegally). This depiction reminds us of the mythical American Dream that apparently many of the undocumented DREAM Act students had and still claim. Unlike many other students in the Movement, he was not worried about his future in early high school. Mo powerfully juxtaposes his high school tranquility regarding the future to the humiliation he experienced in the counselor's office at Eastern Michigan University, how he was devastated and, thus, dispossessed.

The dispossession of Mohammad, as he recounts it in his story, works in multiple ways. It is important to mention that the official profusely compliments him for his strong academic qualifications. It seems as if this raises not only Mohammad's hopes and pride, it also positions him slightly above or at least on the same level as the counselor, an 'elevation' presumably new for Mohammad, a recent high school graduate who had not assumed he would be attending university. He was aware that his undocumented status could limit his options. The circumstance that Mohammad's hopes for his future were *created* by the university counselor and *taken away* from him in the same moment, highlights the normative powers at work in that moment of dispossession, Mohammad's dependence on the institution's policing power, and his limit to function autonomously in the university system and the dependency thereon. The 'loss of citizenship' that Butler and Athanasiou describe as one condition of and for dispossession is not a 'given' to Mohammad prior to that experience. Rather, it is created in this moment, as the institution – the university – actively *dispossesses* Mohammad, albeit the citizenship never really existed in the first place. This situation, depicted in slowed discourse time, results in Mohammad's thinking that, in his words: "because of I wasn't born here, I wasn't good enough for the university" (00:02:58–00:03:01). Mohammad's status and his place of birth become the all-decisive reason(s) to *exclude* him.

Distinct, again, from many other undocumented students is Mohammad's deliberations over what to do after being denied access to American universities. He argues that, because there was no legal option at that time – the DREAM Act failed in Congress a month later – he considered "going back to Iran" first neutrally, then thought, that this was not "a reality" for him because he "was also gay…and so going back to Iran was just not a reality for me" (00:03:25–00:03:45). In contrast to many other producers of 'coming out' narratives, who use their sexual identity at the *beginning* of their digital narrative as a major identity marker in the introduction of themselves, Mohammad 'drops the bomb' about such a crucial point in his identity fairly late in his narrative, subordinating his sexual identity to his U.S. American identity and future plans.

At the same time, Mo uses the United States' obsession with stereotyping Muslim, Middle Eastern countries in order to argue for his stay in the United States because, surely, every scared U.S. American had the worst pictures in his head about how Iran treated gay people. This makes Mo, automatically, almost a case for political asylum and makes the rejection he received at university seem even more cruel. Further, due to these circumstances, Mohammad highlights that an access to higher education *rightfully* belongs to him, as there is 'no option' for him to obtain education in his 'home country' Iran, where the state's powers would, as he argues, dispossess him of even more basic human rights due to his homosexuality. Mohammad draws a concrete link to the political exclusion at work in both countries that can be understood through the "prisms of colonially embedded notions of belonging and unbelonging" (Athanasiou 24–25). By actively claiming this belonging (to the United States) through highlighting basic human rights violations (his homosexuality and his right to education), Mohammad makes us alert to this type of dispossession by means of the core story.

4.3. Core story: digital **testimonio** *of Carlos Roa, "The story of an undocumented student". Published: 21 July 2010*

Carlos' core story connects his undocumented status and immigration background to the topic of the American Dream, Manifest Destiny, and patriotism to the United States. Through this manifold connection, Carlos reinstates the myth of the 'autonomous' self with inherent dreams to strive for a better life through immigration to the United States. In sum, he tells us of the situation he found himself in after his high school graduation in 2005. Namely, Carlos "*wanted* to get into college", "*wanted* to join the military" but due to his undocumented status, he had to realize that "those options … like … weren't … couldn't do any of that" (00:00:58–00:01:09).

Carlos recounts in detail how this denial and lack of 'options' makes him feel. His state of mind illustrates well Butler's claim that the dispossessed person feels a heightened sense of a "damaged sense of future" (*Dispossession* 43). He further emphasizes this feeling as follows: "And so, it's frustrating, you know, the fact that I wanna give back, you know, I'm willing to serve this country … ehm … in the military service … and I don't even have the option to do so" (00:01:10–00:01:20). On a symbolic level, Carlos' sense of frustration causes self-dispossession: he lacks any understanding of why he is being denied the chance to live up to his dreams. Dramatically, Carlos expresses a deep sense of patriotism and loyalty to the United States that he cannot live up to because he is not 'allowed' to 'give back', as he is not accepted as a citizen in the country. His exasperation with the policing forces dispossessing him of his sense of belonging to the United States builds in intensity during this sequence. His future plans in the military, to him, earn him a *rightful* belonging to the United States, as he is not only wishing to belong and obtain the rights that a U.S. citizen 'enjoys' but also to perform obligations and duties, such as military service. Carlos feels he is a victim of injustice, carried out by a personified 'state', which he in the same moment turns into something in-between "modes of being or mental states […] and juridical and military complexes that govern how and where you move" (cf. Butler, *Who Sings* 4). What Carlos' story shows, ultimately, is that people dispossessed of themselves through the interdependency that immigrants (and others) simply do not have the power to eradicate in a country like the United States.

Carlos particularly emphasizes his dispossession when he connects his situation to similar struggles that immigrants experienced in the history of the country. He incorporates the immigration background of his parents, reciting how his parents were denied citizenship, although his grandfather was a "U.S. citizen for over forty years" and it was the sole purpose of, especially, his mother to 'give back' to the country in the form of her three children as 'professionals'. It is this aspect that Carlos highlights in particular. Within the anger that Carlos apparently feels with regard to his family not being granted legalization, he concludes that this denial is "bad for *everyone*, not just immigrants" (00:01:27). This is the first time that Carlos explicitly mentions 'immigrants', arguing for equal status of both citizens and non-citizens by claiming that denying immigrants citizenship has negative effects for "everyone", which includes and, in fact, defines 'everyone' as *Americans* without the distinction between citizens and non-citizens.

Likewise, Carlos determines that 'everyone', including undocumented immigrants, are *all humans* and at this point connects the myth of the American Dream as an all-incorporating potential inhabited by immigrants without exception. Carlos argues that "this country has prided itself on" the possibility to "change this country for the better", that "we've seen that at the turn of this century we saw how immigrants ... em ... you know, changed this nation for the better of Irish, of Polish, of Italian descent". Then providing the connecting link to himself and his family, he argues that "we are no different than the immigrants from the past" (00:02:35–00:03:01). It is the human 'merit' which immigrants have 'contributed' to the nation that Carlos emphasizes with this statement. On the next level, when denying current undocumented immigrants, the opportunity to work or join the military – as rights and obligations included in the construct of 'citizenship' – Carlos talks about the fact that he feels that this is, in fact, "shooting down people's dreams" (00:01:21), dehumanizing them – the most gruesome agenda of dispossession. However, Carlos does not specifically say *who* is doing that, using the pronoun "you" as a generalization of the 'other'. It is apparent, nevertheless, that Carlos is actually accusing the United States for excluding him and his family – a country he would, technically, 'kill for'.

4.4. Core story: digital **testimonio** *of David Ramirez, "David Ramirez, Immigrant Youth Justice League". Published: 5 April 2011*

David's core story of dispossession is less easy to distinguish from the rest of the narrative than the core stories of the other seven digital narratives, perhaps because his narrative is comparatively short, slow speech tempo, and full of pauses. Further, instead of performing the affective dimension of his dispossession, he presents to the viewer the current situation he finds himself in, arguing that he has "spent the last decade realizing, struggling through and really recently coming to terms with being undocumented" (00:00:12–00:00:22). In his story, David reports that his undocumented status transformed into a psychological burden, which accompanied him throughout most of his teenage years. We see that David's state of dispossession is an affective one that influenced him on a long-term basis rather than in one concrete situation or event that he experienced.

David expresses the precariousness of his status in more explicit terms than the previous three narrators. He explains that in his teenage years, being undocumented made him feel "absolutely alone" (00:01:07–00:01:08) and that he was constantly confronted with "all this hate that's been shot at [him]" (00:00:39–00:00:41). The *precarious* life he led up to this point forms a particularly literal mental image through this choice of his words. David further reports that whenever he tried to "reconcile" hateful confrontations with his undocumented identity, he felt even more lost. The fact that David felt the need to 'reconcile' his identity with the reactions of others implies that he is dispossessed of the 'belonging to' a group in society. However, the attempts to reconcile the 'hate' he perceives from others with his undocumented 'identity' failed. "Every time that I compromised with the hate; every time that I tried to reconcile with it, ehm, I felt that I was digging myself further into a hole", he claims (00:00:45–00:00:57).

David's claim stands for the impossibility of fighting the hate on his own, suggesting the need for a plural resistance against dispossession and a united protest against the forces of dispossession that agonize him. As the first of these four narratives, David explicitly mentions the *need* for activism through his personal story, which bears immediate consequences for the performance of personalized activism that David displays in form of his YouTube *testimonio.*

4.5. Core story: digital testimonio *of Angelica Velazquillo, "An undocumented immigrant, Angelica, tells her story". Published: 2 March 2012*

After introducing herself and her undocumented status, as well as several consequential impediments in her everyday life that are due to her undocumented status, Angelica begins to tell the core story: She recounts the night of her brother's arrest and subsequent detainment, as well as the emotional consequences this incident has for her and her mother. Angelica narrates this event in a more structured way than the previous core stories we have discussed.

Angelica's core story begins with a precise date (October 2010), thus marking her dispossession as a clear and separable event in her life to which she is witness as in the tradition of the *testimonio.* The core story is further marked by the fact that that digital *testimonios* apparently have a solid integral part; a personal story within the greater narrative account of the dispossession that is felt by each of the narrators and can be referred back to the life they are leading as undocumented immigrants in the United States. This 'core story' includes a series of events that are emotionally laden, major happenings in the lives of undocumented youths.

Angelica recites the events that happened in the night that distinctly marked her dispossession in clear and logical order. As hinted in several of the other stories, the topics of 'family' and 'community' become a central one in this digital *testimonio*: Angelica's core story revolves around her (also undocumented) brother's arrest "for driving with his high beams on" (00:00:33–00:00:36). She also tells us that because the officers learned that her brother was undocumented, "ICE took a hold of him" (00:00:41–00:00:42), and after that spending three days in jail, his family could save him from being brought to a detention center in a different state only by paying "a

5,000 immigration bond" (00:00:46–00:00:48).[8] While it is inherently her brother's dispossession, Angelica becomes dispossessed as she is affected emotionally. Here, family unity and community becomes an important aspect. As Athanasiou stresses, dispossession "rises from [...] a limit to the autonomous and impermeable self-sufficiency" (2). Angelica's brother's arrest becomes the event in the story that builds the structural basis for the whole narrative. In this particular instance, dispossession becomes a community issue, in which all the other (remaining) family members become dispossessed at the same time. The police officers who arrest the brother symbolize the institutional, regulating and *policing* forces of the state, which seemingly work randomly to dispossess whole communities. Thereby, it is seemingly not even important who her brother really is – the viewer is not even told a name, which altogether highlights the arbitrariness of the event. The arrest, we conclude, could have happened to any other member of Angelica's family or even community. For the digital *testimonio*, much more crucial for the narrative outcome and means of protest is the actual effect his arrest – and the family's consequential dispossession – has on Angelica herself, as the following quote shows:

> This was a turning point for me, ehm, up to now I had faced challenges because of being undocumented but nothing compares to ... to that night. Ehm ... coming to my brother's empty room and realizing that he was spending the night in jail. And to see my mom falling apart because we didn't know when we were gonna see him again or if we were gonna see my brother again.
>
> (00:00:53–00:01:18)

4.6. Core story: digital testimonio *of Mitzy Calderón, "I am no longer hiding! I am no longer afraid!". Published: 13 November 2012*

The digital *testimonio* of Mitzy, a college student in Georgia, utilizes a moment in her senior year at high school as the major situation of dispossession for the core of her story. For this, an additional character appears in Mitzy's core story: The nice but 'not helpful' high school counselor whom Mitzy meets to inquire about college options at some point in her last high school year. Mitzy finds the latter, however, inexperienced with undocumented students, which raises her level of frustration and, simultaneously, builds a stronger awareness of her undocumented status, which, she finds, stands in her way to obtain a proper secondary education.

Before Mitzy retells the moment of dispossession (unconsciously) triggered by the institutional representative, she explains how she feels toward her undocumented status throughout her high school years. In detail, Mitzy argues that she kept her status a secret, not comfortable with "sharing" it, because she was afraid of deliberately getting turned in by her 'peers' and then detained (and eventually deported) by *la migra*

(00:00:50–00:00:59). While these circumstances show how Mitzy already feels and *is* dispossessed – restricted in living out her life freely and utterly afraid of policing consequences – in 00:01:28, she explicitly begins narrating a strictly secluded sequence that describes the core of this dispossession: Her experience in the counselor's office.

Mitzy recounts this changing sequence of events, the core story of her digital *testimonio*, in much detail. This leads to a slowing down in narrative time, allowing much room to all emotions and thoughts that Mitzy connects with that situation. However, this makes Mitzy's digital narrative the longest in this selection. Dispossession, here, again, is depicted as a process, unfolding in the order that Mitzy tells us 'her story': First, Mitzy highlights her hopes and dreams for the future, in her talk with the counselor as well in her retelling of the story to 'us'. Then, however, she narrates the experience of indirect rejection by her favorite educational institution, Young Harris College, which, at that time, only accepted undocumented students who would pay out-of-state tuition. In consequence, Mitzy is dispossessed of her dreams much more than of a real, tangible, and graspable college education. Implying that "the American experience", as she calls it (00:01:36–00:01:42), is not meant for her, Mitzy feels that she is being excluded from the experience that seemingly all other students at that school, and perhaps even all other immigrants, in her mind, are granted. On a deeper level, the right to that dream and to even have the option to have that dream, excludes Mitzy from a sense of 'belonging with' American culture. Being identified as an international student (at least in a financial sense), to Mitzy feels like an immense insult and "definitely not an option" to her, since she identifies as an American (00:02:45–00:03:18).

The fact that this rejection is mediated and indirectly carried out by the high school counselor points to the policing instances that the state employs in order to regulate and punish those that it dispossesses. However, the dependency of the counselor on the institution also shows that dispossession works with multiple dependencies: Mitzy interprets the counselor's lack of knowledge of "how to help" undocumented students like her as an institutional ill that is based on racism. Although allegedly 95 percent of the school's students are white, Mitzy feels that the other five percent should also be shown options by the counselor. The lack of educational options, such as attending her college of choice, and the fact that she does not have "legal status" or "a social", to Mitzy, is "a modern way of segregation" (00:04:20–00:04:21).

In sum, the moment that Mitzy is denied the "American experience" that she claims to appreciate so much (00:01:40–00:1:41), not only dispossesses her of belonging with and to American society but also dispossesses her altogether of being American at all. The racism she connects with this experience could be explained in terms of dispossession, which Athanasiou explicitly reconnects to colonial and imperial histories of racism (cf. 26). While one can clearly see the connections to this form of dispossession with regard to the immigrant worker, Mitzy herself does not epitomize the latter per se. However, she aligns herself with the American Dream, which commends hard work in order to achieve the best and, thus, identifies with the immigrant worker in the United States at least in a symbolic way. The result, after all, remains the same: Mitzy feels 'useless', robbed of all ideas for her future, and discriminated against.

4.7. Core story: digital **testimonio** *of Ivette Roman, "Maryland's undocumented immigrant students". Published: 5 January 2013*

The core story of this digital *testimonio* relies on the intersection of homosexual identity and dispossession as determined earlier. It is important to note that in contrast to Mohammad's core story, undocumented narrator Ivette directly centers her story of dispossession on the intersections of her undocumented status, her homosexual identity, and the period of transnational motherhood that she experienced when her mother went to the United States to find work, as well as struggles of cultural adjustment in the United States. This difference is noticeable when Ivette introduces herself as undocumented and gay in two consecutive sentences, "I'm an undocumented immigrant. And I'm a lesbian" (00:00:10–00:00:14). This is even before she begins to talk about her family's immigration story and the hardships that she encountered in the first years of living in the United States, including bullying in school, initial language problems as well as being forced to reject a scholarship and placement in a college she would have liked to attend because her family was too poor to pay the rest of the tuition. The strongest hardship and core story, however, depicts her 'coming out' as a lesbian to her mother.

Ivette tells her 'coming out' story in more detail than the rest of her biographical events depicted in the narrative. She recounts sitting on the couch next to her mother one evening, when she comes out to her mother. More precisely, Ivette takes a news report on television about somebody being beaten for 'coming out' as the impetus to come out to her mother as well, in that very moment of watching. Upon this, her mother rejects her for several months, not speaking to her and treating her very coldly, "she wouldn't even look [Ivette] in the eye" (00:03:05–00:03:08). Her mother's rejection dispossesses her of her will to life, inducing inherent suicidal thoughts, as she reports: "I didn't even wanna live anymore", because she "thought [she] had lost her [mother]" (00:03:09–00:03:15). In multiple ways, Ivette's sense of herself is precarious, as she identifies most strongly with 'non-being' (cf. Athanasiou 19).

Athanasiou's comments on sexual dispossession help us understand Ivette's dispossession. First of all, one has to determine the "multilayered traumas of subjection" (6). We learn of Ivette's trauma(s) prior to this incident in the core story as well – informal ways to dispossess her by discriminating her for her 'insufficient' language skills as well as the abandonment of her mother in early childhood.[9] Deciding to be homosexual, in Ivette's case, hence puts a complicated burden on the relationship to her mother due to the latter's particular conservatism that needs to be understood in the general framework of dispossession, as Athanasiou has stressed above. Telling the viewer immediately after narrating this traumatizing incident about the impediments of undocumented status on her future plans – inherently dispossessed of the rights to go to college or university – Ivette connects the mechanism of being an (undocumented) immigrant to her personal crisis. Both have put a tremendous strain on the relationship to her mother, which follows her throughout her whole life – from the beginning of her first high school years to the (current) wish to enter university as an undocumented student. In the face of all of her intersecting and similarly traumatizing events in life, Ivette exclaims toward the end of her story: "I want the same ... I want the same rights as they do. I'm still just like them" (00:04:12–00:04:21). However, she does not specify to whom "they" refers, experiencing the workings of dispossession at the multiple intersections of her selves.

4.8. Core story: digital **testimonio** *of Luis Maldonado, "A brief look into the life of an undocumented American". Published: 20 September 2013*

Luis' core story of dispossession differs slightly from the core stories in the previous digital *testimonios*. Similar to Ivette's story, the first hint of dispossession is Luis' statement that he is "queer" (00:00:04). While Luis does recount his experiences within the undocumented immigrant community and identifies, in particular, the widespread discrimination of homosexuals to be his motivation to 'fight' for legal changes for undocumented (and undocumented homosexuals), his core story does not refer to himself. Like Angelica's core story, Luis' story relates to the topic of family and an experience with family separation. And again, it is the separation from a sibling. However, while Angelica is dispossessed in the moment of learning of her brother's detention, the situation for Luis' family has already escalated: His sister got deported a few years prior to the recording of his *testimonio* and while this seems indeed painful, it is not the major dispossession that Luis' family experiences. Rather, as he tells us from minute 01:34 on, it is the story of his nephew, the son of his sister, which occupies him: While the mother got deported back to Mexico, Luis' nephew is a U.S.-born child and, therefore, a U.S. citizen who is now separated from his mother.

In detail, Luis explains that he feels emotional distress and responsibility to fight for his nephew. This complicated situation characterizes Luis' own situation of dispossession and emphasizes the responsibility and connectedness within his undocumented community that transforms his family's problem into his own: "The separation of families that are constantly happening...on a day-to-day basis...is affecting me", he claims, explaining the cause in more detail: "It affects me because my nephew, his parent is not with him, and I see the pain that he has, and how much that hurts him, and not only him, but also his mother" (00:01:48–00:02:08). Directly confronted with his family's constant pain, Luis' *testimonio* emphasizes the fact that immigrant stories, and especially those by undocumented immigrants, are stories that *need* to be told, because they involve the dispossession of children's rights. As the quote further implies, not only does his sister's deportation affect Luis in his role as her brother but their dispossession also makes Luis' nephew completely dependent on him. Luis has been thrust into the life of an adult caring for a child because the state deported the child's mother. Any type of self-sufficient and autonomous family life is put to an end. In addition, the state took a policing role, 'punishing' not 'only' Luis' sister and nephew but the whole family. Luis' core story thus highlights that 'the state' does not even 'spare' its own *citizen* children, therefore dispossessing them of their (human) right to protection (cf. Schlink 47).

Since Luis describes himself as an undocumented "American" in the very title of his narrative, he implies that this experience might be real for potentially many more (undocumented) Americans, while he personifies the state, the United States as the predominant perpetrator of their dispossessed state. Simultaneously, Luis explains that this situation is the major trigger for his activism in the revived Immigrant Rights Movement. At this point, Luis explicitly connects his activism against deportation to his identity, claiming that these causes inspire him to fight against them. Particularly striking in Luis' core story is the fact that he highlights the intersections of his multiple identities at which dispossession takes place. However, dispossession, to him, is a unifying cause to spur activism. He emphasizes these intersections, first of all, by introducing himself as follows: "I'm undocumented and unafraid, queer and unashamed. My name is Luis Maldonado" (00:00:00–00:00:07). The order in which Luis makes claims about his identity suggests that his undocumented identity comes first, and the queer second (even before his first name). With regard to the debate on immigration in the United States, and his "immigration story" (as the narrative is named), both identities, however, are the ones that dispossess him (and his family) of the right to 'live a normal life'. Luis' activism thus stresses that he is convinced that the undocumented status is accentuated as it intersects with the queer one. He expresses this relation by arguing, for instance, that "what some people might take for granted [...] ... are actually the dreams of other people, especially the dreams of people in *my* community" (00:02:20–00:02:30, *emphasis added*). Through this, Luis actively claims a belonging *with* the undocumented immigrant community but, at the same time, also resists the exclusion from *American* society, despite his status.

On the other hand, Luis also shows how this queer identity, in contrast to his undocumented identity, is a very solid part of his complete. To illustrate this, he gives the term 'unashamed' an additional meaning: In the current Movement, 'unashamed' is used by undocumented youth (now most likely to have DACA) for referring to their parents – taking away the blame and guilt that was thrust upon them in an early phase of the Movement that focused on a national 'DREAM Act'. However, Luis now actively uses shamelessness to refer to his homosexual identity. Still, he does explicitly detail the emotional impacts of coming out as gay. Instead of telling us how coming out as homosexual was a major event in his life, he tells us that "it was a very nerve-wracking moment prior and during me coming out as an *undocumented person*" (00:00:47–00:00:57, *emphasis added*). Here, too, Luis ascribes his immigration status a greater power of his well-being than his sexual identity. LGBT community rights, however, in part depend on the undocumented status and vice versa. One important interface between the two is that before its repeal in July 2013, it was not possible for a U.S. citizen to get immigration benefits for his undocumented partner due to the Defense of Marriage Act (Pallares 141). While Luis' personal family struggle (that of his nephew and sister, in particular), becomes the trigger for his *testimonio*, Luis underscores the ongoing nature of this struggle that he is engaged in, which includes the rights of undocumented gay people: "I still feel that that's another battle of my identity, of my immigrant story" (00:01:28–00:01:33), he exclaims.

5. The performative in dispossession: dispossessed bodies in the digital sphere

Dispossession in digital *testimonios* is openly performative, meaning that it connects the performative of the political to those groups who are dispossessed as a possible strategy for counter-movement. By framing dispossession as they do, Butler and Athanasiou seek a sense of agency, a "performative occasion in an ongoing process of socially regulatory self-formation, whereby under different circumstances the self struggles within and against the norms through which it is constituted" (68).

The logic of YouTube narratives is strongly connected to the performative. As a part of its political logics, this Movement poses interesting dynamics of the logic of media – YouTube – and the intertwinement of both as an expression of the mediatization of politics. How the performative becomes a logic of the Movement, Butler and Athanasiou explain through performativity and dispossession: Judith Butler connects performativity to movements and their claim to exercise the right to public protest. According to Butler, performativity in movements implies a sense of "appearing" and "exercising" the individual rights (*Dispossession* 101). This situation is then "precarious", yet bound to produce a "political subject" that "seeks to overcome its own precarity" (ibid). Applied to the context of undocumented narrators, this means that by the exercise of their right through the narratives, undocumented youth narrators seek to overcome their fear. Inherent in the concept of dispossession lies the performative that constitutes the individual experience as the author/narrator relives, retells it in his/her digital *testimonio*.

The performance studies perspective that the authors stress, according to Madison and Hamera, can "interrogate and enrich our basic understanding of history, identity, community, nation, and politics" (xii) and is "radically interdisciplinary" (xiii). It is further "employed across disciplines to decipher the multiple operations of performance (performativity and the performative) within a written text, a life world, and in domains of cognitive and imaginary expressions", of which "the *performance turn*" is a major part "in western academic theory" (xxiv). Performativity refers to identity construction through repetitions in utterances and behavior. Judith Butler's work has been considered as ground-breaking in the field in the sense that she shifted the "focus from identity and history to performativity", which had major effects on research in feminist and queer studies, in particular (cf. Chinn 105).[10]

According to Butler's basic argument, all identities are constructed in discourse (cf. Chinn 106), "while making room for repetition, reiteration, durability and stability, and the psychoanalytic", as Wetherell claims (17). Essentially, performativity "is the argument that an identity based on gender, for instance, is nothing other than persistent regulatory performances materialized over time" and "not biologically given" (ibid). More importantly, performativity materializes as performances in stories, according to Madison and Hamera, like those selected for this study (cf. Madison and Hamera xix). Inherent in this definition is the difference between performance and performativity – while the latter focuses on speech acts, which contributed actively in negotiating meaning, the former denotes bodily actions and inherent perceptions (cf. Velten 549).

Studying 'performative language', it was J.L.Austin who first used the term 'performativity' (cf. Chinn 106). He distinguished between, primarily, "constative language", which is descriptive of our environment and "performative language", which actually "makes something happen [...] by saying something" (ibid). Goffman adds the integration of performance into everyday life. One of his central theoretical assumptions refers to performances as "all the activity of an individual which occurs during a period marked by his continuous presence before a particular set of observers and which has some influence on the observers" (22) – basically declaring most behavior and thought a performance. In a theoretical approach to performativity and performance nowadays, according to Hamera, "we move beyond Ervin Goffman's [...] notion of the presentation of self in everyday life to examine how performance illuminates the deep structures of community in/and [...] practice" (47). Butler, most famously, revises both theoretical trains of thought thoroughly, applying them to, most famously, gender as an "embodied act in the same way that performative language is a speech act", according to Chinn (110). Thus, it is mainly the cultural context – the Movement – and forms of resistance and potential role-playing that is of importance in the analysis. The central question becomes how performativity is materialized as performance in concrete terms. Does multimodality have an effect on the production of meaning through differently materialized, multimodal performances?

Inherent in the performative of dispossession is the allocation of humanness and the resignification – the reclaiming – of humanness on part of the dispossessed. Because "colonially inscribed forms of power involved in the property-propriety economies of the modern subject", humanness and the definition of who is considered 'more human' than others is a central issue in even more recent processes of dispossessions (Athanasiou 31). For the purposes of this investigation, we need to pose the question of how undocumented youth address and express the allocation of humanness in their stories of dispossession. Do they choose multimodal forms to express humanness?

In sum, narrating dispossession provides new forms of resistance, enabled by the performative in dispossession itself. Although Butler and Athanasiou refer to public protest 'on the streets' more than to other forms of resistance, "sometimes a performative politics seeks to bring a new situation into being, or to mobilize a certain set of effects", Butler ascertains, "through language or through other forms of media" (*Dispossession* 102). The main question to be addressed in the chapters to follow is:

- How do the narrators perform their dispossession in *testimonio* via the means of other multimodal affordances of the YouTube video to give political meaning and give shape to resistance to their narrative?

Notes

1 Since the book consists of a dialogic correspondence between the two authors, I quote the individual authors' statements with the respective name of the author of the statement rather than with both names. Since this study quotes several works of Judith Butler, I additionally mark the Butler's quotes with "*Dispossession*" (I do not for Athanasiou). The Works Cited List refers the book with both authors' names, beginning with Butler.

2 As of November 2014, dispossession is further reformulated by newer legislations on deportation relief. Thus, current campaigns of the Movement also focus on those *who are excluded* after Obama's announcement of a second executive order on undocumented immigration. While Obama granted "deportation reprieves" to those undocumented parents whose children are American citizens or legal permanent residents "if they have lived in the country for five years and have not committed serious crimes", the "claim for relief" is denied to those parents whose children are included in the DACA, as the latter have deportation deferrals and work permits (Preston n.pag.). Interviewee Uriel Sánchez from Chicago, who was also granted the DACA, once jokingly called himself 'un-DACA-mented' with regard to his '*non*-status' (personal interview).

3 According to Albiez et al., the current debate about the concept of citizenship, as we can also see in the current immigration debate in Congress, questions "the restructuring of socio-political spaces; globalisation and the increased bypassing of the state, and the extension of rights of non-citizens, in particular those of migrants", as well as a "reassignment" in "an age of growing globalisation, deterritorialisation and post-nationalisation" (21). In addition, scholars such as Saskia Sassen "acknowledge that citizenship is a process that can be enacted through people" (ibid). The latter is aware of the concept as being impacted by globalized and transnational trends (such as the "human rights regime") and the increase in impact on states all over the world and approaches the discussion in

a theoretical manner not of immediate 'use' to undocumented youth, calling for postnational concept of citizenship as alternative to the traditional, nationally defined one (cf. 288), even if undocumented youth certainly call for a redefinition of the concept in terms of inclusion and exclusion.

4 *Who Sings the Nation-State* is co-authored by postcolonial and feminist scholar Gayatri Spivak, highlighting the postcolonial context of the concept of dispossession and marginalization through normative powers such as the state. As I only quote Butler's words here, I do not mention Spivak in the in-text quotations.

5 Pfaff-Czarnecka defines 'belonging' as "an emotionally-charged social location" which combines "perceptions and performance of *commonality*", "a sense of mutuality and more or less formalised modalities of collective *allegiance*" and "material and immaterial *attachments* that often result in a sense of *entitlement*" (201). The scholar further explicitly argues that "both, social inclusion and social exclusion underlie regimes of belonging [...] buttressing commonality, mutuality, and attachments, while simultaneously excluding outsiders" (205–206). For more detail, see the three definition of 'belonging' that Albiez et al. establish in their book.

6 "Das Recht auf Heimat als elementares Menschenrecht ist das Recht darauf, an einem Ort rechtlich anerkannt und rechtlich geschützt zu leben und nicht nur zu leben, sondern zu wohnen und zu arbeiten" (Schlink 47).

7 As of now, I quote the spoken word or visual passages of the eight YouTube videos by providing the exact minutes and seconds as the duration of the passages in combination with the narrator's names. All detailed information of the videos is listed in the References.

8 ICE is the acronym for "Immigration and Customs Enforcement", which was "created in March 2003" and "is the largest investigative branch of the Department of Homeland Security" (Orner 376). It "is charged with enforcing deportation orders, investigating employers of illegal workers, targeting smugglers of counterfeit products, and various counterterrorism responsibilities" (376–377).

9 It is important to point to research carried out on transnational motherhood: As Gjokaj et al. stress, for instance, "like other social practices and relations, families are always in motion, continuously transforming and being transformed by transnational spaces" (283). Transnational motherhood is one example of these transnational transformations that change the relationship between individual family members eternally. In their study, Bacallao and Smokowski, for instance, found problems appear especially at reunification and the following "adjustment period in which structural changes created new configurations of roles, boundaries, and communication processes, as well as a stormy period after reuniting" (57).

10 It is important to "point out the intimate links between gender, race and class", according to Chinn, "and that certain gendered performatives require specific racial or class identities to go along with them" (113) as well as that "what those genders mean, particularly in the context of histories of white supremacy and European and US colonization and imperialism, varies significantly depending upon the context" (113–114). Likewise, Butler and Athanasiou stress the intersectionality at work in the re-inforcement of norms that dispossess persons (cf. 45–46).

References

Abdollahi, Mohammad. DreamActivist. "My Name is Mohammad and I am Undocumented." Online video clip. *YouTube*. YouTube, 19 Mar. 2010. Web. 22 Dec. 2014.

Albiez, Sarah, et al., eds. *Ethnicity, Citizenship and Belonging: Practices, Theory and Spatial Dimensions*. Madrid: Iberoamericana, 2011.

Ashcroft, Bill, Gareth Griffiths, and Helen Tiffin, eds. *Postcolonial Studies. The Key Concepts*. 3rd ed. Routledge Key Guides. New York: Routledge, 2013.

Bacallao, Martica L., and Paul R. Smokowski. "The Cost of Getting Ahead: Mexican Family System Changes after Immigration." *Family Relations* 56 (2007): 52–66. Web. 8 July 2013.

Bartow, Joanna R. "Essential Subversions: Reading Theory with Latin American Women's Testimonial Discourse." *Woman as Witness: Essays on Testimonial Literature by Latin American Women.* Ed. Linda S. Maier and Isabel Dulfano. New York: Peter Lang, 2004. 47–61.

Baym, Nancy K. *Tune in, Log on: Soaps, Fandom, and Online Community.* Thousand Oaks, CA: Sage Publications, 2000.

Bendit, René. "Growing Up in the Context of Globalization and Social Change: Present and Future of Youth and Challenges for Youth Research and Youth Policies." *Youth Transitions: Processes of Social Inclusion and Patterns of Vulnerability in a Globalised World.* Ed. René Bendit and Marina Hahn-Bleibtreu. Leverkusen, Germany: Barbara Budrich Publishers, 2008. 27–40.

Beverley, John. "Testimonio, Subalternity, and Narrative Authority." *Handbook of Qualitative Research.* Ed. Norman K. Denzin and Yvonna S. Lincoln. 2nd ed. Thousand Oaks, CA: Sage Publications, 2000. 555–565.

Butler, Judith, and Athena Athanasiou. *Dispossession: The Performative in the Political.* Cambridge: Polity Press, 2013.

Butler, Judith, and Gayatri C. Spivak, *Who Sings the Nation-State? Language, Politics, Belonging.* London: Seagull Books, 2010.

Calderón, Mitzy. SUDDENmovementDotOrg. "I am No Longer Hiding! I am No Longer Afraid!" Online video clip. *YouTube.* YouTube, 13 Nov. 2010. Web. 22 Dec. 2014.

Chinn, Sarah E. "Performative Identities: From Identity Politics to Queer Theory." *The SAGE Handbook of Identities.* Ed. Margareth Wetherell and Chandra T. Mohanty. Los Angeles, CA: SAGE, 2010. 104–124.

Gjokaj, Linda, Baca Zinn Maxine, and Stephanie J. Nawyn. "Connecting Family and Migration." *Routledge International Handbook of Migration Studies.* Ed. Steven J. Gold and Stephanie J. Nawyn. New York: Routledge, 2013. 283–294.

Goffman, Erving. *The Presentation of Self in Everyday Life.* Garden City, NY: Doubleday, 1959.

Hamera, Judith. "Performance, Performativity, and Cultural Poiesis in Practices of Everyday Life." *The SAGE Handbook of Performance Studies.* Ed. D. Soyini Madison and Judith Hamera. Thousand Oaks, CA: SAGE, 2006. 46–64.

Langellier, Kristin M., and Eric E. Peterson. "Shifting Contexts in Personal Narrative Performance." *The SAGE Handbook of Performance Studies.* Ed. D. Soyini Madison and Judith Hamera. Thousand Oaks, CA: SAGE, 2006. 151–168.

Machado Pais, José. "Young People, Citizenship and Leisure." *Youth Transitions: Processes of Social Inclusion and Patterns of Vulnerability in a Globalised World.* Ed. René Bendit and Marina Hahn-Bleibtreu. Leverkusen, Germany: Barbara Budrich Publishers, 2008. 227–243.

Madison, D. Soyini, and Judith Hamera. "Introduction: Performance Studies at the Intersections." *The SAGE Handbook of Performance Studies.* Ed. D. Soyini Madison and Judith Hamera. Thousand Oaks, CA: SAGE, 2006. xi–xxv.

Maldonado, Luis, and Sheridan Lagunas-Aguirre. "Luis Maldonado: A Brief Look into the Life of an Undocumented Immigrant." Online video clip. *YouTube.* YouTube, 20 Sept. 2013. Web. 9 Sept. 2014.

Manuel, José, et al., eds. Foreword. *PAPERS: Stories by Undocumented Youth.* Portland, OR: Graham Street Productions, 2012. iv–vii.

Nünning, Vera, and Ansgar Nünning. *Methoden Der Literatur- Und Kulturwissenschaftlichen Textanalyse.* Stuttgart: Metzler, 2010.

Orner, Peter, ed. Glossary. *Underground America: Narratives of Undocumented Lives.* San Francisco, CA: McSweeney's Books, 2008. 375–379.

Pallares, Amalia. *Family Activism: Immigrant Struggles and the Politics of Noncitizenship.* New Brunswick, Canada: Rutgers University Press, 2015.

Pérez, William. *Americans by Heart: Undocumented Latino Students and the Promise of Higher Education.* New York: Teachers College Press, 2012.

Pfaff-Czarnecka, Joanna. "From 'Identity' to 'Belonging' in Social Research: Plurality, Social Boundaries, and the Politics of the Self." *Ethnicity, Citizenship and Belonging: Practices, Theory and Spatial Dimensions.* Ed. Sarah Albiez et al. Madrid: Iberoamericana, 2011. 199–219.

Preston, Julia. "Deportation Reprieve May Exclude Parents of Young Immigrants." *The New York Times* 19 Nov. 2014. The New York Times. Web. 23 Dec. 2014.

Ramirez, David. Thedreamiscoming2011. "David Ramirez, Immigrant Youth Justice League." Online video clip. *YouTube.* YouTube, 5 Apr. 2011. Web. 22 Dec. 2014.

Roa, Carlos. Cccvideovault. "Carlos: The Story of an Undocumented Student." Online video clip. *YouTube.* YouTube, 21 July 2010. Web. 22 Dec. 2014.

Roman, Ivette. MsKYYoung. "Maryland's Undocumented Immigrant Students – Ivette." Online video clip. *YouTube.* YouTube, 5 Jan. 2013. Web. 22 Dec. 2014.

Sánchez, Uriel. Personal interview. 24 March 2014.

Sassen, Saskia. "Toward Post-National and Denationalized Citizenship." *Handbook of Citizenship Studies.* Ed. Engin F. Isin and Bryan S. Turner. London: SAGE, 2002. 277–291.

Schlink, Bernhard. *Heimat als Utopie.* Frankfurt am Main: Suhrkamp, 2000.

Solis, Stephanie. UndergroundAtBrown. "Lost & Found (Story of a DREAM Act Student)." Online video clip. *YouTube.* YouTube, 12 May 2009. Web. 5 Nov. 2013.

Velazquillo, Angelica. Mercy Sister. "An Undocumented Immigrant, Angelica, Tells Her Story." Online video clip. *YouTube.* YouTube, 2 Mar. 2012. Web. 22 Dec. 2014.

Velten, Hans R. "Performativitätsforschung." *De Gruyter Lexikon: Methodenge-schichte der Germanistik.* Ed. Jost Schneider. Berlin: De Gruyter, 2009. 549–571.

Wetherell, Margaret. "The Field of Identity Studies." *The SAGE Handbook of Identities.* Ed. Margaret Wetherell and Chandra T. Mohanty. Los Angeles, CA: SAGE, 2010. 3–26.

5 Visual dispossession(s) and the dynamics of the performative

Moving image

1. Introduction: face-to-face *testimonio* – on screen!

I would like to begin this chapter with the most literal type of performance – the corporeal performance – a performance which, in digital *testimonios*, is mediatized as a motion image, filmed by a camera and 'starring' the narrator of each of the eight *testimonios*. Quite literally, as Benmayor claims for the digital *testimonio*, in motion image, "the invisible becomes visible" (523). The sheer visibility and presence of the undocumented 'body' enabled and mediated through film gives a literal sense to the act of 'coming out of the shadows' that the undocumented narrators undertake. The undocumented body – narrator and 'actor' in one – *performs* his/her dispossession on the screen.

As the major focus of socio-technological affordances on YouTube lies on the moving image of the video clip, this aspect also represents the first body of analysis.[1] At the same time, this part of the analysis is also the primary one, as moving images are used most of the time in all digital *testimonios*, in combination with their original soundtrack (actual voice and also voice-over). The subsequent two chapters narrow down the film analysis to the elements that further constitute the individual narrators' performances. While in all narratives, the creation of meaning in speech is prominent, Chapter 7 also addresses static pictures and written language in their multimodal and intermedial combination. With reference to this, Wildfeuer defines any film's textuality as the "textual logic operating within the film", made visible through "structural composition and the resulting coherence" (6). The moving image, though, is the tissue that connects all other modes. For this, "the pattern of *time* plays a central role in film, since the filmic content unfolds in temporal succession and, at the same time, the film as a medium is played linearly in *narrative time*", according to Wildfeuer (12), and "spatial information" is rather "often additionally provided, for example visually described in the depiction of the setting or as inserts giving concrete locations" (ibid).

In the narratives chosen for this study, the focus of the visual (moving image) lies on the body of the narrator, which is mostly filmed in an eye-level medium shot or a (medium) close-up. It is the *movement* and positioning of the narrator's body in the video's framed space which creates much of the meaning. This movement needs to be evaluated with regard to the sound to which the body moves – or does *not* move. Thus, meaning is created in accordance with the logic of time and its verbal sound: the original soundtrack or a 'voice from the off' and nonverbal expressions of sound (noise and music). In very few instances does orality stand by itself, in combination with a simple black screen. There is an urgent need for the visual image to literally *fill* every second of the video clip, a condition crucial to the textual logic of film that seems to be transferrable to video clips on YouTube as well.

There are great differences with regard to form and content of meaning making in the different genres in which moving images are used. The "visual dimension of moving images", to name a commonality, adds "layers of expression and evidence as it captures human interaction and settings" (Sipe 379). If we consider this a valid argument, how is truth created through the visual? Do the moving pictures capture events "that take place independently of the camera", implying a sense of truth, or fictional in the sense that they are "staged to be filmed" (ibid)?

Considering these questions, Hübler reminds us that "the presence of a TV camera will have an impact on the narrative performance", as "the narrative will show particular features of entertainment and specific rhetorical elements as regards not only the verbal, but also the nonverbal, i.e. the prosodic and kinesic/gestural, modes" (40). Since the distinction between 'staged' and 'not staged' moving image material is not assessable, the performative lens views all performances of the self as either 'learned' (performativity) or explicitly staged (performance), uniting the unconscious with the conscious performances. Personal narrative, as Langellier and Peterson confirm, has become the site for performance (cf. 152). Likewise, due to the focus upon the narrator's body and speech in the videos, digital *testimonios* create their meaning in corporeal and vocal performance. Benmayor, too, stresses that the production of a digital *testimonio* incorporates a revised and performed process of creation (cf. 507). Thus, the performances of dispossession connected to undocumented status gain their major focus in the creation of meaning in these narratives that can constitute acts of resistance. Ginsburg sees great potential in the development of "indigenous" film productions,[2] as she points out that "the camera might be put in the hands of those who had historically been objects of the anthropological gaze" (566).

Gestures, for instance, play an important part in this performance through the movement of the narrator's body in the moving image of the video. Like the moving image, gestures generally combine the logics of time and space. As Kress explains, a gesture is "realized as a sequence in time of the movement of arms, hands, head, and facial features", yet these movements also relate to the body and surroundings in space (56). According to Mittell, "watching a narrative is an active ongoing process of comprehension, as views make and revise cognitive hypotheses and assumptions to create their own version of the storyworld" (170). Quite in contrast to speech, "the identification of kinesic gestures does not usually cause serious problems", Hübler points out. Vocal features are less easy to interpret, he further argues, "because man's auditory capacities lag behind the visual, at least in our Western culture" (47).

Herman identifies different "functions of speech-accompanying gestures used in narrative discourse", differentiating between "*gesticulations*" and "*emblems*", for instance (87–88, *emphasis given*). While all modes, as we have seen, essentially bear three key meta-functions – the ideational, the interpersonal, and the textual – Hübler adds that gestures, in particular, either add a "supportive" function to the "corresponding verbal expression" or a "complementary" one (46). Gestures have been classified into two types. First, there are those gestures that imitate verbal speech items or rhythm, such as emblems, which "have fixed meanings, similar to words" (45) or beats, which are "gestures that index discourse structures" (Ryan, *Face-to-Face Narration* 45).[3] The second type of gestures derives its meaning from its interaction with verbal means – the "interactional gesture space", as Herman names it (89). Among this category we find iconics, metaphors, and abstract pointing.

Iconics are "gestures that depict narrative action" (Ryan, *Face-to-Face Narration* 45) or highlight "pictorially some selected aspect of a concrete content item (verbally expressed)" (Hübler 45). Interestingly, **iconics** not only narrate the events, but also the speaker's point of view. Iconics, therefore, address the issue of who is speaking or who is being mimicked. **Metaphorics**, in contrast, are "gestures that display the vehicle of a metaphor inherent to language, such as mimicking the transfer of a solid object to announce the transmission of a story" (Ryan, *Face-to-Face Narration* 45). Moreover, space, shape, and movement all can pictorially highlight abstract concepts, "metaphorizing some aspect of such a concept in concrete terms" (Hübler 45). Finally, 'abstract pointing' or '**deictics**' is a type of gesture referring to the narrator's pointing to an object that is part of the story in the room. By means of abstract pointing, narrative "crucially mediate[s] between spaces and places", "saturating with lived experience what would otherwise remain an abstract spatial network of objects, sites, zones, and regions" (*Word-Image/Utterance-Gesture* 88). As indicated by this definition, abstract pointing can also locate entities in an "imaginary space" (Hübler 46).

However, Sipe stresses that verbally narrated content gains a primary status in the construction of the meaning of the visual image. The moving image that uses spoken language therefore sets the stage for orality: If used, "the spoken word will inevitably have primacy" (385). In contrast to Sipe, Kim argues that "compared to other communication modes, the visual is highly powerful in its communicative competence. As the cliché goes, seeing is believing" (9). In a combination of the two channels, the visual and the auditory, we thus need to note that "orality, at its core, is not purely a concept grounded in sound" but rather that "spoken word is embedded in a setting, a situation, a context", as they "respond to and refer to their setting and to objects" and "people speak with body language, expression, and tone" (379).

Specific about this type of narration in YouTube videos is, in particular, the fact that the audience, upon whomthe narrators center his/her gaze – materialized by the camera – becomes the interlocutor, since there is no other partner in this simulated oral storytelling setting. This plays an important aspect for oral storytelling. Thus, in simulated interaction with a simulated interlocutor that is represented by the camera, the 'performative dimension' plays a major role (cf. Ryan, *Digital Media* 42). In this dimension, a sense of simulated interaction with the imagined audience comes to the fore in digital media, in particular (330). "Speech", according to Stöckl, accompanies and shapes "non-verbal mode[s], i.e. gesture, posture and body language" (11). This distinctive property is reinforced by the corporeal performance visualized through gestures and facial expressions, and intonation, in particular (cf. Ryan, *Face-to-Face Narration* 41).

An idiosyncrasy of the medium of film, as a last aspect in this introduction, is montage – the film's editing devices. According to Wildfeuer, for instance, "filmic specificities such as montage, or continuity editing", in addition to the multimodal ensemble, "play a role and affect meaning-making constructions" (3). "These principles", according to Wildfeuer, "operate not only on the level of one single mode, but in particular across different modes", which the author calls "*intersemiosis*" (ibid). Due to this, montage will play a role in the analysis of meaning production throughout Chapters 5–7, but not be analyzed holistically in either of the three chapters. With the advance of the digital video, editing software is easily available (and often free) for users of a computer. Digital video editing devices produce yet another instance of narration in the videos. As they can reduce or stress the film's message by reducing/cutting (hence, de-emphasizing) or stressing (through visual effects, montage, or slow-motion) the originally taped material. As the focus of this study lies on the actual performances of the narrators – undocumented youth – the elaboration on film montage is kept to a minimum. However, prominent 'intrusions' into the production of meaning by the narrative are further highlighted throughout all chapters of analysis.

In the subsequent chapter, the body and its visualization become central devices for the creation of political meaning. I examine how the face-to-face oral storytelling might be imitated, action and resistance are implied, and dispossession is performed through the bodily and vocal enactment of the core story. The general question posed in all of the chapters of analysis, thus is:

- When do multiple levels of meaning-making occur and what is their semiotic outcome/the resulting political message communicated in context of the Immigrant Rights Movement since 2006? Which (multi)modal affordances do the narrators use and how do they contribute to the performance of the digital *testimonio*?

2. Visualizing dispossession

2.1. Gestures for resistance

This section contributes a major element to visual culture that is part of the media logic on YouTube. Gestures provide an immense "repertory" to "perform [...] narrative functions" (Ryan, *Face-to-Face Narration* 45). In the digital *testimonios* selected for this investigation, the narrators do this by explicitly using their hands or arms to illustrate (iconics) or represent (metaphorics) a certain action and object or "mimicking action" and "remediating" an abstract action or visual aspect (ibid), or they rely on mimicking speech (emblems).

Stephanie Solis (1): path to legalization via iconics[4]

Like Angelica Velazquillo (5), Ivette Roman (7), and Luis Maldonado's (8), Stephanie Solis uses only a small number of gestures in her digital *testimonio.* This is mostly due to the choice of a (medium) close-up, which shows her upper body facing us, to shoot the moving images, rather than representing Stephanie's personal preferences regarding the use of gestures to support or complement her speech. However, the use of those few gestures in the narrative is highly meaningful. In total, there are three instances in which Stephanie uses gestures. One of them, in particular, highlights the performance of dispossession and frames its rejection through a shift in roles. This happens in a very literal understanding of dispossession: Telling the viewer that she cannot participate in activities for which one needs a form of government identification (which she, of course, does not possess), she uses iconics to represent the imaginary 'post-it' she understands to be in all such places that, in some activity or another, require a form of identification to participate, such as banks or travel posters. As the function of a post-it is to remind oneself of something, Stephanie tells us that she is reminded of her undocumented status whenever she passes such as place or signs. Imitating the action of putting a post-it onto the wall, pretending the space between the viewer and herself was a wall, Stephanie performs the dispossession herself.

The act of performance carried out by herself redefines Stephanie's agency in the matter, as she assumes the role of the one who dispossesses (the role of the post-it in a literal sense, and that of the state who would not hand her government identification). At the same time, from the perspective in which the viewer finds him-/herself, Stephanie expresses a sense of forcefulness as she directs the post-it to 'us', facing the camera and her imagined audience directly. By this act, Stephanie passes on the dispossession to somebody else – her audience – inherently becoming the dispossessor herself and, hence, rejecting the role of the dispossessed that she finds herself in through verbal descriptions.

The second instance in which Stephanie uses iconic gestures in her digital *testimonio* expresses a similar rejection of dispossession. Recounting the paths she went to get legalized and describing how she imagined steps to legalization look like, Stephanie performs the pledge of allegiance (only the gesture, not the text) and the waving of a tiny American flag, which she imagines to be those symbolic acts that she would also have to perform in a formal legalization process. Recalling that Butler understands "the construal of the visual image as illocutionary speech" (*Excitable Speech* 65), *performing* legalization this way highlights not only Stephanie's rightful claim to legalization in the *moment* of the narration but also provides the viewer with an image that reduces the power of this formal process by 'suggesting' to the viewer what Stephanie's legalization might look like.

Presumably having internalized how to wave a flag and do the pledge of allegiance from an early age on, Stephanie's American identity constitutes the production of this identity that seems "'natural' through reiterative individual and cultural performances" (Jewitt 302). Performativity, then, is materialized in this performance. In the massive public protests of undocumented immigrants in 2006–2007, in expression of their alignment with the United States and their sense of national solidarity despite their lack of citizenship, "marchers wore white shirts as a symbol for peace, [...] and carried U.S. flags as a symbol of patriotism and loyalty to this country" (Flores-González and Gutiérrez 4) to express their American identity and the home they found in the country. Legalization, early in the year of 2009, also still assumes a greater part of the agenda. Activists, too, were optimistic that a path to legalization would pass (cf. Pallares, *The Chicago Context* 51). Consequently, Stephanie's use of these iconic gestures marks the persistence of a path to legalization predominant in the Movement at that time.

Mohammad Abdollahi (2): coming out of the shadows

Similar to the setting in which Stephanie Solis' (1) digital *testimonio* is recorded, Mohammad Abdollahi's video is also taped in a medium shot that, during one episode of his story of dispossession, most notably changes to a medium close-up. The angle of the camera is a little below eye level, as if the person taping the video was sitting. The setting and lighting of the video visualizes Mohammad's life 'in the shadows' in very literal terms: The room is dark and contains only few recognizable objects. There is only weak lighting compared to that in Stephanie Solis' video, which makes it impossible to discern Mohammad's gaze and the more refined facial features or expressions.

The dim lighting and the drawn blanks in the window further denote the time of the day that Mohammad has his digital *testimonio* taped: nighttime. He verbally confirms this fact when he explains that "it's about Thursday night or Friday morning" (00:00:11–00:00:13). The fact that there is darkness, combined with the awareness that it is 'nighttime' when the video was shot, creates a sense of urgency and emphasizes timing. Indeed, time and day play an important role for Mohammad's digital *testimonio*. In words, Mohammad confirms this impression, introducing his video with the words that "for the past week-and-a-half or so" the *DreamActivist* had been asking other undocumented youth "to share [their] stories and share [their] videos about 'coming out'". As the organization had been doing that, Mohammad reasons, he "thought it was about time to step up and actually do one" himself (00:00:04–00:00:11). The act of posting his video around this time becomes highly meaningful to the general message of the digital *testimonio*, making use of YouTube's direct distribution affordances. The publishing date on March 19, 2010, together with the timeline for posting coming-out stories 'within the past week-and-a-half' hint at an important day in the Movement's history: March 10, 2010; the first National Coming Out of the Shadows Event that took place in Chicago, Illinois.

The eventful spring of 2010 was the immediate result of the immigrant spring that had formed in the recent years prior to 2010. Rhetorically and culturally connected to gay rights movements, eight undocumented students held public 'coming out-speeches' at the Federal Plaza in Chicago in March 2010, despite the fact that this meant risking deportation and potential family separation. In a personal interview, Uriel Sánchez, an undocumented student activist who frequently attended the famous Coming out of the Shadows events in Chicago that would continue during the years after 2010, explains:

> 2010 certainly had a sense of urgency. 2011 didn't have…or 2012…no! 2013 and in late 2012 didn't have that large sense of urgency. I think, fundamentally, that's what it is. That urgency; or that sense of urgency or pressure on ourselves. You know, like, almost being, I think, pushed to the wall to decide and choose. Like, you're being pushed to a wall and somebody is making you decide.
>
> (personal interview)

Uriel describes the move out of the shadows as a counter reaction to internal and external pressure that undocumented status causes in immigrants. In a different interview, Marcela Hernandez, who came to Chicago from California, adds that she observed many youths taking center stage in the coming out events, but not that many older undocumented immigrants:

> We see that in the 'Coming Out of the Shadows' in Chicago, right? The first one that they had was in 2010 – most of us youth, you know, they were all youth. Most of them had or were in college, were educated, or had their degrees.

Pérez confirms in his book that the nation observed a special role that youth assumed in these events, arguing that "increasingly, undocumented student activists have moved to the forefront of these efforts" (85). He further summarizes the overall political goal of these events: "In an unprecedented demonstration of their leadership, political savvy, and organizational skills," he finds, "undocumented student activists and their allies responded with a well-coordinated youth-led national movement to pressure Congress and the president to pass the DREAM Act" (ibid).

By requesting his audience to post coming-out videos – implying that they are undocumented immigrant youths as well – Mohammad emphasizes the importance of activism in the offline Movement and explicitly connects his digital *testimonio* to other acts of coming out of the shadows, such as those in March of 2010.

A central feature that distinguishes Mohammad's narrative from Stephanie's, however, is the use of gestures. While Stephanie's video displays a few selective iconics, Mohammad frequently uses very large beats that also produce a clapping sound. We see almost his entire upper body, yet the span of his arms is so large that the cameraman[5] needs to zoom out in order to capture the whole movement of Mohammad's body, instead of simply cutting the hands off from the picture. Because of a rapid zooming *out*, the viewer is actually signalized to 'keep a distance', in striking contrast to the other video narratives, which primarily zoom in on people's faces, mostly at times when they would get very emotional and wrought up in their personal conflict. This move attributes a sense of power to Mohammad, reinforced further by his slightly higher angle over the camera. Also, the frequently moving beats give Mohammad's rather rapid and de-emphasized words more emphasis, connoting a sense of urgency and forcefulness. The beats dominate the whole video more than the setting or words he pronounces, establishing a hierarchy between the two modes that emphasize visual movement.

The power inscribed in Mohammad's visual performance enhances the leading role he seems to enjoy in his offline organization, *DreamActivist*. After introducing himself, Mohammad 'cheers' another member of the organization, for posting a video online that deals with explicit details discussed in the organization.[6] In this moment, his gesture performs the 'act of cheering' (he raises his right arm) in combination with an additional verbal exclamation ("wohoo!"). The iconic gesture fully exploits its potential to express the speaker's point of view, as well as his power.

Cheering another member's efforts in the name of the whole organization puts Mohammad in an executive position. Likewise, toward the end of the narrative he thanks people, especially those in the organization, for helping him and supporting him, claiming that this was what helped him "get through it the whole time", speaking *for* the other organizational members as well (00:04:42). The consequential effect of this performance of leadership in his offline organization leads to an empowerment over his imagined audience.

At the beginning of Mohammad Abdollahi's performance of his story of dispossession, the camera zooms in on him for the first time, emphasizing that the story of dispossession needs to be told in 'another frame' than the details that embed this narrative episode. Further, one could argue that the zoom is a meaningful instance indicating that affective dimensions need to be shown and telling the viewer that the cameraman is aware of the effects that dispossession has on an undocumented youth. It is very likely, thus, that Mohammad had his video recorded by another undocumented youth and/or youth activist.

Mohammad's (2) story of dispossession takes place in the registrar's office at Eastern Michigan University. He performs this story in the most literal sense possible: He uses his left hand to illustrate the acceptance letter of the university, keeping this hand up most of the time during this performance. With his other hand and his glances, he performs the actions happening to that letter. This way, he shows to us how he got rejected at the university because they had not noticed he was undocumented at first, and literally took his acceptance letter away from him. Mohammad enacts his thoughts verbally and the situation literally, with the help of his hands.

This performative act symbolizes the happenings in the office, giving the viewer a visual of Mohammad holding an acceptance letter from a university in his hands. As Mohammad is undocumented, the situation he performs is unreal, yet, becomes a reality through his performance. Moreover, the viewer becomes witness to the injustice that Mohammad experienced, which closely speaks to the tradition of the *testimonio*, which we recall is "told in the first person by a narrator who is also the real protagonist or witness of the events she or he recounts" (Beverley 555). Through the vivid reenactment of the moment his acceptance letter was taken away from him, Mohammad stresses the injustice with which he was treated as an undocumented student, appealing to the viewer's moral understanding, who is, through the performance, turned into a witness of the crime. Becoming a witness, the viewer, stirred by Mohammed's storytelling technique, feels the imperative to act in defense of the victim. The inherent message, thus, is to help Mohammad get into university.

A gesture that bears important meaning with regard to Mohammad's identity is metaphoric arm movement toward the beginning of his digital *testimonio*. The introduction of Mohammad's immigration background seems to be of less importance in the beginning of Mohammad's story of dispossession. "My parents emigrated here from Iran…which is on the other side of the world" (00:00:29–00:00:34), he claims, visually describing the location of his country of origin through a metaphoric gesture: He elevates his right arm and quickly moves it far to his right – out of the camera frame and thus the viewer's vision, as if portraying an airplane or other really fast object just to cross the ocean. This move implies that it does not really matter where Iran lies on the world's map, as Mohammad neither takes the time to explain it nor show it to the audience in any way.

The insignificance that Mohammad ascribes to his origins is reflected throughout the narrative. Toward the end of the narrative, Mohammad explains that he has no idea where to get the education that was denied to him in the United States through the failing of the DREAM Act. Without changing his vocal or nonverbal features of narration, he claims that he realized:

> The 'DREAM Act' wasn't a reality and so 'What do I do? Do I leave?'. Ehm, and so I realized that, you know, I couldn't…I couldn't go back to Iran because I'm also gay. And so going back to Iran was just not a reality for me.
>
> (00:03:25–00:03:44)

Mohammad subordinates his homosexuality to a sub-clause, spoken off-handedly. Given the fact that homosexuality is treated differently in Iran, and that he is finding himself in multiple discriminatory statuses, this monotonous style of narration is remarkable.

The most likely reason for this performance lies in the format of YouTube videos: According to Kavoori, YouTube only provides a "limited frame for issues of context, intent and, more critically, identity and culture" (12), as YouTube viewers, for instance, are 'used' to watching only short videos. "Watching YouTube", he explains, "is akin to scanning and sorting through a magazine catalog: […] the stories […] are skimmed through, with attention resting briefly on one or more items" (8). According to the logic of YouTube, therefore, it might be difficult for Mohammad to elaborate on his double state of oppression – being gay and undocumented – due to the strict time frame that he must stick to in order to keep the viewer's attention. A second reason lies in the organizational background itself. According to Wetherell, what it means to be, for instance, homosexual and Latin@ (or Arab) strongly "depends on how these social categorizations are worked through some of the other dichotomous identities dominating local situations and institutions" (18–19). It is possible, then, that being homosexual is an identity category that is widely accepted and positively attributed within the Immigrant Rights youth Movement. Being dispossessed by others due to one's homosexuality would then seem to be less pressing than the dispossession that undocumented status causes.

I personally posed the question of how undocumented status and homosexual identity are connected for an undocumented and homosexual youth activist from Chicago, Antonio Gutiérrez. The fact that he found that both identities are a "double the oppression in individuals" verbalizes "intersectional thinking", which offers "a critique of monolithic analyses in terms of social categories" (Wetherell 18). Intersectionality is "grounded", primarily in the understanding that "experiences and political struggles" are "not neatly contained or defined by […] singular identities" (ibid). However, Antonio also remarks that coming out as undocumented is "even more nerve-wracking than coming out as being gay", which indicates that although both identities are potentially triggers to dispossession by others, undocumented status weighs more in the process of coming out within a digital *testimonio*. In Mohammad's case, the situation is even more complicated, as he reasons his stay in the United States with the identity that he ascribes less room to in his digital *testimonio*: his gay identity. "Although the exclusion of gay foreigners was officially dropped in 1990", Patton argues, "subsequent legal activism was required to include homosexual persecution as a rationale for asylum" (364). Having this possibility, hence, of requesting asylum due to his homosexuality, Mohammad's *testimonio* instead focuses on fighting for the DREAM Act, emphasizing his identity as an undocumented student in the Movement. Although obtaining less weight in this *testimonio*, nevertheless, we can see the performative intertwinement of different identities, homosexuality as well as the immigrant identity, which are both essentially at stake for the dispossessed Mohammad.

Carlos Roa (3): 'shooting down' dreams

After introducing himself and recounting his family's immigration history (see Chapter 7 for detail), Carlos Roa (3) narrates his story of dispossession (00:00:56–00:01:27). Due to his undocumented status, Carlos Roa is dispossessed of the right to get a higher education or start a military career.[7] The fact that Carlos is not admitted to the military due to his undocumented status shows how undocumented youth are dispossessed of not only citizenship benefits and rights but also excluded from the whole concept of citizenship including the citizen's duties. Since joining the military is optional in the United States, Carlos offers a deep sense of patriotism which underlines his sense of belonging to the United States as a home. Carlos talks about the fact that he feels there is a "shooting down people's dreams", not specifically saying *who* is doing that, using the pronoun "you" as a generalization of the 'other' (00:01:21). It is apparent, however, that Carlos is actually accusing the U.S. legislation of excluding him – those, he would, technically, 'kill for'.

The first half of this roughly 30-second long episode is filmed in a medium close-up. Then, the episode is cut and what follows is a sequence filmed in the close-up. More drastic is the change from the close-up to the medium shot, which enables the viewer to see Carlos' gestures. The hand gesture he makes translates how his dreams are 'shot down' – destroyed – into a metaphoric gesture: Carlos lifts his right arm, forms a fist and lets his fist dash into his left hand, causing a loud clapping noise. This gesture (combined with the sound it creates) becomes very meaningful, as its performance expresses the violence of the dispossession which Carlos (and other undocumented youth in his situation) experience by this exclusion from the military and, ultimately, from the nation. Thus, Carlos metaphorically assumes the 'forcefulness' with which he is dispossessed and transforms it into his own means of power.

What follows is a moral judgment by means of which Carlos actively fights against his dispossession. Again, Carlos uses his bodily presence and the explicitness of gesture to support his spoken utterance. Through the following emblem, however, Carlos produces an additional meaning that conveys very clear cultural meaning: Lifting the index finger and moving his hand while keeping his finger lifted connotes a sense of rejection and denial, as well as powerful resentment. This meaning supports his verbal exclamation that the destruction of people's dreams is "bad" (00:01:24). The media logic of YouTube is not of little importance in this act, as 'vlogging' (video blogging) on YouTube is also part of the production of moral judgment and values in our culture. "The media hold the key to the public sphere and can have a major influence on public opinion formation", Esser and Strömbäck argue (4). Since Carlos does not name his offenders, the scolding symbolized by the finger assumes a function similar to the interpersonal in personal interaction – particularly because Carlos directly looks into the camera when he performs this gesture. Using emblems that convey value judgment, in this case, directly addresses viewers and urges them to respond to Carlos' testimony.

The connection of dispossession to Carlos' personal 'dreams' and to the American Dream is particularly apparent in the last of the episodes, which is introduced with a gray title screen, posing the written question: "What about the American Dream?" (00:02:20). "For all its faults as a concept", Campbell and Kean argue, the American Dream "does, however, express a dominant American national myth, a fundamental and long-held belief" which confirms "certain qualities and attributes that function to define an 'American spirit'" (11). The myths that inform the American Dream are highly ideological and subject to change. One constant, however, is "the purpose of the myth [...] to make the world explicable, to magically resolve its problems and contradictions" (ibid). Being posed the question of how he relates to the American Dream, Carlos defines the latter not only in verbal but also in visual terms. His undocumented status – and the undocumented status of his family and 'all immigrants' – dispossesses him especially because it prevents him from being a "contributing member to society" (00:02:29–00:02:31). Carlos chooses to express this definition by means of a metaphoric gesture, which creates powerful meaning for his digital *testimonio*. He moves his right arm up to his chest and grabs an imaginary object with his hand to then carry this content in his hand away from his body.

Metaphoric gestures highlight abstract concepts, in which all relations of the body to the space takes on metaphoric value. Through these gestures the viewer understands that Carlos does not specify any concrete contribution but shows that he wants to *personally* contribute to the society, offering 'content' that is very 'close to his heart'. Carlos' body, thus, becomes a highly performative occasion. Since the logic of dispossession is "interminably mapped onto our bodies", as Athanasiou has shown (18), Carlos performs how an undocumented immigrant like himself can easily 'give back' to society.

Mitzy Calderón (6): insiders and others

Mitzy Calderón's digital *testimonio* is the first (in this selection) that is published after the announcement of the DACA – the Deferred Act for Childhood Arrivals – which grants work permits and deportation reprieves to certain undocumented youth for at least two years (cf. Pallares, *Family Activism* 124). Through massive youth activism and campaigns around 'papers' (see, for instance, Manuel et al.), by that time, not having 'papers' and becoming aware of that fact through the last high school years – as Mitzy did – is a situation well-known to insiders and followers of the Movement. Manuel et al. even postulate that this was what affected a change in legislation: "The social activism and political organizing led by youth activists", the authors argue, "added to the pressure that brought the DREAM Act to a vote in 2010 and to President Obama's June 15, 2012 announcement of Deferred Action for Childhood Arrivals (DACA)" (xi).

Although Mitzy's video is shot in a close-up and the viewer generally cannot see her hands (if not lifted), when Mitzy describes her life with undocumented status, she forms virtual quotation marks with her hands to frame the word 'papers' when articulating that she "kinda always knew she didn't have [her] papers" (00:00:27–00:00:30).

This emblem imitates written language as it frames the word in space. Through the use of these imaginary quotation marks Mitzy visualizes that the term is politically laden and does not simply mean a couple of sheets of papers but official pieces of identification which become very significant to a person who does not possess them. However, this emblem also marks perspective: Mitzy specifically addresses those who do not know what 'papers' mean for an undocumented person and this way saves time to explain the meaning of the term in words. One could argue that this way, she attempts to reach out to a wide range of possible viewers. One could also argue, however, that the imaginary quotation marks add a sense of sarcasm to her statement, ridiculing how a 'piece of paper' can become so important in one's life. This reinforces Mitzy's story of dispossession, which revolves around the aporia she feels due to her status in the last year of high school.

While the announcement of the DACA certainly is a success for undocumented youth, having a work permit does not help much to finance out-of-state tuition all by oneself. Further, in states such as Georgia, as Mitzy shows, the top five universities of the country even refuse to accept undocumented students altogether (cf. Lozano n.pag.). Given the nationwide differences, undocumented students from Georgia like Mitzy are enraged at this exclusion, dispossessing them of options to build a future after high school.

After the introduction to her narrative, Mitzy noticeably leans back, signaling that a new episode in her narrative is about to follow. She then performs her process of self-dispossession – understanding "what it meant to be undocumented" (00:00:37), which led to her feeling that she needed to make her undocumented status as invisible as possible. Therefore, one could argue that by disguising her status and practically lying about it, Mitzy enforces a mutual distrust in people and, thus, cannot sustain close friendships. She recounts that her peers did ask about her personal life, such as, for instance, when she was getting her driver's license, and that then, she would have to make up excuses, and give them "whatever reason" for fending off the question (00:01:14). In these situations, she was dispossessed by others, stressing the relationality of the dispossessed subject and the 'other'. The 'other', here, "is important in defining the identity of the subject", as Ashcroft et al. argue (155): In Mitzy's view, 'others' are those who have 'papers' and are not like her, undocumented. The moment of telling this experience causes visible annoyance to Mitzy, since in her narrative, she needs to define herself as an 'other', differing from the (documented) center and, hence, reliving her own 'marginalization' (cf. ibid). Her hand gestures grow wilder, by primarily, on a visible level, fending off the questions of her peers, literally, with her left hand. At the same time, the viewer is put into the position in which those peers were earlier, when asking these questions that disturbed her. This means, clearly, that Mitzy is choosing her audience, be it consciously or subconsciously, namely, an audience which raises questions about her identity and against whom Mitzy has to defend herself.

We further see a gesture of 'protection': Mitzy explains that she "always had to cover up her life with lies" (00:01:19–00:01:22). The movement of this metaphoric gesture is the most important contributor to the production of meaning in this sentence: Not only does Mitzy cover up her chest with her hands, she also interchangeably places one hand in front of the other, causing quick up-and-down movements of her hands in front of her chest. Through this, the viewer understands that Mitzy had to 'cover up' her undocumented identity frequently in her past. At the same time as performing the past, Mitzy also covers up her identity once more – this time, in the eye of the viewer, shielding herself from and simultaneously othering him/her as 'documented'. Therefore, not only does the visual enactment of this part of the 'core story' emphasize *what* she is saying but also *to whom* she is saying it. As we have seen, Mitzy transforms the viewer of the online video into the people with whom she has had these uncomfortable experiences in the past and, hence, is given the chance, through the new medium, to vent her emotions and explain herself in retrospect, without running the risk of actually confronting them (her former peers could just as well be among the viewers).

Thirdly, through the use of gestures, Mitzy performs her anger about how she had to hide her undocumented status and cover up her identity with lies. The moving image of her digital *testimonio* allows the narrator, even if in retrospect, to perform her feelings through the use of beats that give her words emphasis, exclaiming repeatedly that she "hated it" (00:01:22–00:01:24).

The use of beats and a change in facial expressions express vividly the resentment she feels toward covering up her identity. Notably the paraverbal features of the words she articulates do not change significantly, reinforcing the impression that her voice mismatches the visuals she performs in this scene and, thus, signal that these feelings are not affecting her *just now*.

2.2. Marking the dispossessed: abstract pointing

Abstract pointing "crucially mediate[s] between spaces and places", "saturating with lived experience what would otherwise remain an abstract spatial network of objects, sites, zones, and regions", according to Herman (88). Abstract pointing, I argue, metaphorically translates into performative naming that constitutes Butler's performative dimension of the speech act. For the speaker, this creates a way to perform nonverbal naming while being able express additional information in the act of storytelling.

Mohammad Abdollahi (2)

Through abstract pointing, Mohammad translates the virtual space of the YouTube video – the "imaginary space" (Hübler 46) – into an abstract space in which he interacts with his audience. Through his slightly elevated position, he establishes a clear hierarchy between himself and his 'wider' audience.

Introducing the DREAM Act that again was up for a vote shortly after his experience of dispossession in 2007 (having been around for at least six years at that time), Mohammad directly addresses his imagined audience by gesturing toward the camera and saying: "And I'm sure that all of you guys are familiar with the 'DREAM Act' or else you wouldn't be looking at this video right now" (00:03:11–00:03:15). This statement not only saves him time to explain the meaning of the DREAM Act once more, the viewer also feels directly 'pointed at' and, literally, 'put on the spot', if he/she does not know about the political implications of the DREAM Act.

By pointing at himself, Mohammad victimizes his body, a process for which those politicians rejecting the DREAM Act could be accountable. By pointing at himself, he connects his personal story of dispossession to the DREAM Act, personalizing this political decision by accusing the "44 senators [who] decided that [he] didn't deserve a chance to go to college" of personally rejecting him (00:03:17–00:03:22). While saying this, his fingers *repeatedly* point to himself. Through this motion, Mohammed stresses the active and repeated denial of his apparently only chance to receive college education (the DREAM Act), which had been debated since 2001 and repeatedly failed.

Carlos Roa (3): speaking for the all

Returning to the myth of the American Dream that Carlos refers to in the last episode, he argues that the United States "has prided itself on" the possibility to "change this country for the better" and that "at the turn of this century we saw how immigrants…em…you know, changed this nation for the better of Irish, of Polish, of Italian descent", then providing the connecting link to himself and his family, arguing that "we are no different than the immigrants from the past" (00:02:35–00:03:01). It is the human 'merit' which immigrants have 'contributed' to the nation that Carlos underlines heavily with this statement. While the verbal content of this episode is dominant, Carlos actively *names* 'undocumented immigrants' as 'those like him' with abstract pointing to himself.

Since the viewer has been introduced to Carlos' ideals and dreams, he/she associates his story with that of 'all other immigrants'. Through Carlos' performance of 'the' undocumented immigrant identity which, as he stresses, has been the same for centuries, he proposes a homogenized idea of immigrants – undocumented and legal alike. This way, Carlos' *testimonio* assumes a 'voice for all', one could argue. However, the audiovisual format complicates the understanding of the 'voice for all' dramatically: Carlos' digital *testimonio* on YouTube personalizes his 'voice for all' by not only 'speaking' for other immigrants but also by performing visual associations with identity categories. Most prominent is Carlos' performance of gender in the combination of the verbal and the visual. While Judith Butler strictly disconnects corporeality and cultural frameworks (cf. Jagger 78; Butler, *Gender Trouble* 140), "denaturalizing gender" and avoiding "biological determinism" (Jagger 2), Carlos' verbal performances of masculinity appear quite gendered: As explained earlier, Carlos performs a version of masculinity that is based on the understanding of the desire of the patriotic male American to go to the army and serve his country; contributing to society. His verbal performance of strength and devotion is confirmed by his outer looks. Further, the shortly trimmed hair in particular visualizes this image of masculinity. Abstract pointing, thus, not only speaks for all other immigrants but also visualizes them, laying the grounds for stereotypes and generalizations.

Mitzy Calderón (6): racial exclusion and abstract pointing

Mitzy Calderón performs her story of dispossession by performing to us, the viewer, what the counselor said to her. She raises her left hand and displays her whole palm to illustrate that the latter could offer only 'limited help' with applying to colleges which do not require for students to provide social security numbers in order to be accepted.[8] Through this performance, the viewer experiences Mitzy's dispossession through her eyes, enabling viewers to understand her political statements. Realizing that she would have to pay out-of-state-tuition in order to attend college at all, Mitzy shakes her head, folds her arms in protest, and explains that it "was definitely not an option for [her]". Without explaining to whom she actually exactly refers, she then gives the following reason for her rejection of paying that tuition: "We are treated as international students" (00:02:46–00:02:49). Mitzy frames the words 'international students' with two slow, strong beats. Like typographical tools for written language, these beats underline the verbal utterance and give it emphasis; even while transmitting her disapproval. Secondly, Mitzy marks herself with abstract pointing as she talks about herself and undocumented students as 'we'. This gesture illustrates to the viewer that the ways she looks, acts, behaves, thinks, and talks resemble ways of all other undocumented students. The visuals therefore draw a representative picture for the viewer of what an undocumented student really is, instead of leaving it up to the viewer's imagination. This performance is automatically transferred to that of all other immigrants in her situation. This might eliminate, on the one hand, prejudices and stereotypes that unaffiliated viewers could have, but it also might create new ones. At the same time, her performance establishes a binary between herself (as representative of undocumented students) and 'internationals'. As Mitzy rebuffs the 'option' of attending university as an 'international', she distances herself from her immigrant background and does this not only for herself, but for all other undocumented students.

In a second step, Mitzy connects this visual performance of 'the undocumented immigrant', signified through abstract pointing, to racial discrimination. She exclaims angrily that she should be allowed to attend an American university, as she considers herself no different from any other American, except for the fact that she is "not white", does not have "blue eyes" and does not have "a damn social" (00:03:19–00:03:23). Here, as Gilroy stresses, race is "an analytical category" that "refers investigation to the power that collective identities acquire by means of their roots in tradition" (418). Accordingly, Mitzy connects racial discrimination (as a woman of Mexican origin) with her dispossession (in Butler and Athanasiou's second, literal sense) as an undocumented immigrant who does not possess a social security number and is hence excluded from citizenship rights, highlighting the intersectional character inherent in her performance – and, hence, protest – of dispossession.

As Elam and Elam point out, race "must always be considered as a shifting variable among many" (191), highlighting its intersectional character. Therefore, "race is salient at different moments in relation to class privilege, social position, gender, sexual orientation, nation, and so on" (ibid). Considering structures of dispossession that rise from racial or gender violence, to Mitzy, the exclusion from Georgia universities connects to racial discrimination. Mitzy's equation makes sense because quite literally, the logic of dispossession as 'mapped onto the body'.

Within this understanding of the performance of racial dispossession through the use of verbal utterances and gestures such as abstract pointing in Mitzy's digital *testimonio*, we should also turn to another instance in which she explicitly performs racial exclusion for the audience. She establishes this connection verbally through reasoning that she could expect only little help from her supervisor due to the fact that "most of them [the other students] were white" (00:02:22). Here, she not only reduces undocumented students to a 'non-white' race but depicts United States citizens as whites exclusively. Thus, she excludes white undocumented immigrants from continents such as Europe or Oceana. This equation, therefore, produces a racial binary which she visually performs to the viewer, narrowing down the representative character of her digital *testimonio* significantly as she defines herself as belonging to the racially dispossessed and dominated group. According to Gianettoni and Roux, Mitzy thus performs "the hierarchy" between the "dominant individuals" ("men, Whites, nationals") who control the process of inventing 'Others' and "the dominated groups generated by this process" ("women, Blacks, non-nationals") (375). Seeing herself belonging to that latter group, she – in the words of Ashcroft et al. – "gains a sense of [...] her identity as somehow 'other', dependent" (156) but at the same time refutes this being by claiming that she is "not less of an American than anybody else" (00:03:23–00:03:26). At this thought, she smiles and glances up to the ceiling, which creates the impression of her being at a remote place, which calls upon the viewer to reconsider his mindset on Mitzy's identity.

Indeed, the moving image portrays Mitzy as liberated when making her claim. Through this, Mitzy *addresses* and *responds* (cf. Athanasiou 133) to the violence of dispossession in her performance. However, when criticizing the need for a social security number as the prerequisite for attending university, it is not merely language that constitutes the performance of her resistance. The 'social', as she terms it, becomes a human characteristic, far from its material essence, but rather something that you either possess or not, just as 'blue eyes' determined by a human body's genetic code. Forming a small object in her left hand, Mitzy belittles the social security number visually, reminding us of a 'gene' or function that a human being either possesses or does not, but at the same time carries it in her hand metaphorically, thus, *possesses* it. Her eyes are squeezed together, her mouth slightly opened, and her head moved in the direction of the camera as she exclaims that "we might have everything that they're asking for, but, you know, we don't have that magic number" (00:04:59–00:05:05). The 'automatic denial' on the basis of this number, to Mitzy, is "a modern way of segregation" (00:05:11). Here, she enters a civil rights discourse that highlighted discrimination as materialized and 'mapped' onto the body of the discriminated (cf. Athanasiou 18). The preceding abstract pointing, in this context, fortifies her concluding statement that not having a social security number "does not make [her] less of an American as anybody else" (00:03:22–00:03:26), speaking for all undocumented immigrants at the same time. In combination with the visualization of the number through her metaphoric gesture, Mitzy exposes the arbitrary nature of the number and projects racist dispossession on those universities in Georgia that ban undocumented students from attending altogether *merely* due to their status. Mitzy repeats the gesture whenever she speaks about 'legal status' or the 'social security number', which serves a textual function that reinforces her logic.

3. Facial expressions: personal affect and resistance to dispossession

This section explores what happens when the body, which becomes 'a turbulent performative occasion' and, at the same time, the visual frame of the narrative, is reduced to no more than the narrator's face. In the following sequences, the narrators are shown in an eye-level medium-close-up shot, focusing on the narrators' faces, not even showing any other expressive body parts such as the hands. Dispossession, here, can be performed particularly well as a structure of feeling, expressed through the change in facial features. This feature reinforces the personalization that YouTube video clips integrate into their logic. As seen earlier, in Western culture, we tend to interpret nonverbal expressions and the emotions behind them more easily than those same expressions produced by voice; facial expressions are simple devices for making meaning. Therefore, emotions and the expression thereof are used to mark the affect of dispossession moments on undocumented youth. This is not to say, however, that all facial expressions are deliberately performed. Natural facial expressions occur with the words we say, and, hence, create a trigger for interaction, as we are usually prone to react to changes in emotions.

3.1. Narrative time and personal affect

Stephanie Solis (1): blame and shame

Stephanie's *testimonio*, narrated in her quiet voice, illustrates particularly well the emotional affect that dispossession causes and makes visible in moving images. In her digital *testimonio*, emotions are expressed through facial structures at particular points in the narrative: The second part of her story of dispossession, like the first, is told in an interview-like (staged) setting with a simple dark background. The color of the background sets the mood for both of these narrative episodes: The darkness underscores the seriousness and tragedy of the situation in which Stephanie finds herself. Her facial expressions, however, mark her emotions in only a few of the scenes, and become visible through the passing of narrative time.

The viewer can see clearly that the verbal narrative changed its topic and the emotions attached. After Stephanie narrates her father's immigration story (elements which are full of mythical images such as the American Dream and, hence, optimism),[9] via sad facial expressions she visually expresses that she was dispossessed of her assumed, American citizenship by her very own mother, and, on a macro level, by the state, realizing that she is denied all the plans she had for her then soon approaching adulthood. The inability to transition into adulthood seems to have been denied solely by the mother, which causes a mother-daughter struggle. Stephanie indicates that her father offered her 18 years of education and relative well-being, while her mother, symbolically, takes all this away in one single moment. Her wording, "cannot do that" reduces Stephanie back to a 'petulant' child, rather than the grown adult she would like to be. The two narrative events are only separated by a cut, accentuating this transition. "For most students", Pérez confirms in his study, "learning about their undocumented status and the limitations they would face [i]s devastating" (24). This indeed proves to be so, as we can see in Stephanie's body language when recounting this experience. Accordingly, her body is less rested, moving constantly. She shakes her head frequently, rolls and blinks her eyes hectically, as if searching for words.

This shift in visuals shows the contrast between Stephanie's immigrant experiences associated with her mother and her father. It is particularly noticeable in the way she talks about this experience in relation to her mother and the way she talks about her father's decision to come to the United States illegally, which is, after all, one of the main causes of her struggle. The mother turns out to be the decision-making unit in the household after immigration, while it is the father who decides to move his family away from their homeland in the first place. Yet, the mother seems to feel responsible for the decision and also for revealing this decision to her child. The irony that Stephanie seems to perceive in this situation could also lie in the fact that it is the mother who does the "hemming and hauling…and dodging the question", not Stephanie herself.

In the very beginning and end of the narrative, we learn that 'shame' triggers the behavioral patterns of Stephanie's mother. In those passages, Stephanie recounts that her family was too ashamed to tell her about her status earlier. This feeling is visualized by Stephanie's gaze in this scene, which is directed toward the floor rather than toward the audience. Hence, without verbally emphasizing the shame that some undocumented families feel, Stephanie conveys the emotion by adapting her facial expressions (consciously or unconsciously) to an expression of shame. The visual image in this scene further contributes to Athanasiou's idea of the dispossession as mapped onto our bodies (cf. 18). Shame, as the visuals show, is one of the most painful emotions that undocumented youth have to experience in 2009. Only after the repeated denial of a legislation such as the DREAM Act undocumented youth would appropriate the motto of 'undocumented, unashamed' into their political rhetoric. "Although the label 'undocumented' or 'illegal' continues to be a source of shame for most students", more recent legislation has "provided new, more neutral, and non-stigmatized social labels" such as "DREAMers", Pérez argues (82). It is "these new labels [that] help students not only conceal their stigmatized status but also reinforce their merits as students" (ibid), as some of the narratives published later than Stephanie's show.[10]

David Ramirez (4): performing precariousness

David Ramirez, who identifies as an undocumented immigrant from Chicago, Illinois, posts his digital *testimonio* only roughly four months before the

Illinois DREAM Act passed in August of 2011(cf. Rusin 6).[11] Clearly identifying with the struggle for the DREAM Act, as it says on his t-shirt (see Chapter 7 for a detailed discussion), David's digital *testimonio* highlights the precarity and urgency that his undocumented status imposes on him. Highlighting this urgency has an important political background, too. Toward the end of 2010, the federal DREAM Act is put up for a vote but fails (Sánchez). In a personal interview, Marcela Hernandez recounts the events of 2010:

> And also, you know, a lot of them fought to pass a national 'DREAM Act', which would actually allow a pathway to legalization, residency and citizenship. That didn't pass in 2010, so a lot of states just decided to work on their own 'DREAM Acts', which wouldn't give a pathway to legalization but would allow, you know, to have funding for students that the state would manage. And you know students could apply for that financial aid and actually be able to go to college.
>
> (personal interview)

Most important is the general frustration with the failure of the DREAM Act, which dashed the hopes of many people that a federal DREAM Act would ever be passed (cf. Pérez 85). David expresses the difficulty of his situation that becomes the central element of his digital *testimonio* visually in different ways. Constantly shifting and moving, David rarely gazes directly into the camera, as if the camera was merely observing him. Further, he is sitting on the ground, with his knees up high and his arms resting on them, yet moving as he speaks. David's eyes are constantly downcast or wandering through the room or staring at the floor.

David's absent gaze makes the viewer feel that the camera is observing David rather than interacting with him. He performs a distant and uneasy self, clearly troubled by some issue and not quite present in the virtual space that the video creates. His stance contrasts starkly with those of the other seven narrators, who seem very alert and eager to give their *testimonio*, wanting "to effect change" quickly and directly in their addressing of their interlocutor (Gugelberger 4). David's wandering gaze signals a disrupted interpersonal communication, which further breaks with the media logic of YouTube that stresses the direct attention-seeking interaction – enabled through the moving image and sound – with the audience, in order to increase the likeability of the video clip.

Equally noticeable is that David is constantly repressing his smiling. This is particularly visible in the first episode of the digital narrative until the first cut (00:00:23), in which David introduces biographical data and his undocumented status. The introduction of himself is kept short, however. David is cut off, right after saying that he had just recently come to terms with being "undocumented" – a word after which follows a short pause – and David looks up and smiles at the camera. The video is blended out and captions appear.

The smiling conveys a postmodern, playful awareness on David's part that his digital *testimonio* is published and viewed by many people on YouTube. The smiling, here, through the stark contrast, performs the uncertainty of what to say exactly about his status. Given the dramatic failing of the federal DREAM Act half a year prior to the production of his video, David might question the effectiveness of fighting for it and coming out of the shadows. David's smile and distracted gaze appear to be his way of alleviating his anxiety over the precariousness of his status and his unsettling doubts about the value of posting a digital *testimonio* in the cause of the DREAM Act. The second episode (00:00:24–00:01:03), which begins with David brushing over his head as if in thought or worry, confirms this interpretation. Running his hand through his hair while glancing down to the floor, David expresses his discomfort in telling his personal story for the sake of the campaign he is involved in (see Chapter 7 for details).

Angelica Velazquillo (5)

Angelica Velazquillo's digital *testimonio* is one of those narratives that were published shortly *before* President Obama's announcement of an executive action on immigration in June 2012: the Deferred Action for Childhood Arrivals; a success for those students that many trace back to their relentless fight for undocumented students' rights. Published on 2 March 2012, around major actions of activism such as nationwide Coming out of the Shadows events around March 10, Angelica's narrative needs to be contextualized in a heated debate and fierce fight among undocumented students. In a personal interview, Antonio Gutiérrez summarizes how he perceived the time before the announcement of DACA:

> At that point, the 'DREAM Act' failed, and I was still going through school. [...] Again, it was upsetting. [...] We had been fighting for this for *years* and for them to just not pass it, it was kinda insulting. It was: 'It doesn't matter what all you all do, we're still not gonna do this. You still don't deserve this.' So, I mean, I was very upset, but then the DACA – deferred action – policy passed.
>
> (personal interview)

Angelica's digital *testimonio* highlights the intersections of the student-led Movement with a focus on the "own exceptionalism as DREAMers" and a renewed focus on the "potential deportability of all the undocumented" which Pallares calls the beginning of "a new relational strategy" (*Family Activism* 123). Angelica does this by using no other core modes than spoken language and the moving image, which are produced together without any further montage devices. This strategy impacts the use of voice, posture, and facial expressions depicted in the moving image, especially since the camera frames the image through close-up shot that excludes the use of Angelica's hands from the sight of the viewer.

In the introduction to her digital *testimonio*, one can perceive subtle differences in attitude through altering facial expressions that mark the sentence about Angelica's received college degree on the one hand and the sentence in which she outs herself as undocumented on the other: Angelica first smiles and emphatically closes her eyes at the announcement of her degree. The closing of the eyes illustrates as the imaginary 'closing of the chapter of education', implying that she has managed to get her degree without the federal DREAM Act ever having been passed. Her facial expressions convey the impression that she is very satisfied with what she has achieved. There is no such affirmation in her gaze or a smile when she talks about her undocumented status.

This strong contrast between her facial expressions highlights Angelica's self-determination as a professional and sets this identity off against the undocumented status. In the first case, then, Angelica enacts performatively constituted 'self-determination' (cf. Athanasiou 65). By claiming that she obtained her degree with a "magna cum laude" in the early introduction to herself, she marks herself as a highly educated and ambitious person. It is clear that the money she must have invested and the trouble she went through to obtain that education actually paid off. Through the emphasis on education, Angelica transmits a sense of *legitimization* of the self and justification for why she is in the country illegally. Generally, her emphasis on immigrating in order to strive and obtain an education speaks to the commonly held emphasis of American exceptionalism, which could be defined as the belief in the United States' "unique mission in the world, idealism, high aspirations and sense of destiny" (Mauk and Oakland 2). Emphasizing the 'worthiness' of undocumented immigrant students in their campaigns and basing them on exceptionalism is something that is unique to the Movement's pro-DREAM Act students, in particular. Within the context of the Immigrant Rights Movement since 2006, thus, Angelica's self-determinism creates a sense of exceptionalism that had already circulated around undocumented youth for a while by the time of the publication of her *testimonio*. Pro-DREAM Act students around the year of 2012 call themselves DREAMers, in particular, and express that they qualify for higher education in every sense. By highlighting that she had already been through that educative toward which so many yet aspire, Angelica now stresses that she "cannot work in [her] field" (00:00:22) – a problem that the DACA would solve a few months later (see the analysis of Mitzy Calderón (6), for instance, for further details).

Ivette Roman (7)

The introduction to Ivette Roman's digital *testimonio* provides the most self-confident image of the whole narrative. Pronouncing that she is undocumented and homosexual, Ivette smiles and nods into the camera, expressing a confidence that these are precisely the categories by which she *wishes* to introduce herself.

Her smile after expressing that she is a lesbian is an act of gender performance confirming an 'other' type of identity (outside the norm) – an act that Judith Butler describes as "suggest[ing] that certain cultural configurations of gender take the place of 'the real' and consolidate and augment their hegemony through that felicitous self-naturalization" (*Gender Trouble* 33). We need to consider, however, as Chinn argues with reference to Foucauldian thought, that "sexual identities as we inhabit them today [...] are a product of the interlocking systems of power that form subjectivity" (109). Since performance is crucial to the establishment of gender identity, as we have seen, digital *testimonios* such as Ivette's provide the grounds for performing the intersectional workings of identity in the youths' dispossession, which is materialized in the act of narration itself. With reference to Athanasiou, thus, digital *testimonios* counter as they perform 'dispossession'. Ivette's facial expressions change drastically throughout the video, emphasizing the impact of these gendered and sexualized implications inherent in her dispossession.

First, her facial expression changes from confident to sad, as she starts talking about her immigration story and the hardship(s) that she encountered before and upon arrival in the United States. Her countenance is sad, her mouth downcast and her eyes are diverted away from the camera as she explains that her mother left her and her three brothers in Peru in order to work in the United States.

Framing the beginning of the narrative like this sets the tone for the upcoming story elements and moves the topic of family struggle into the foreground. The viewer immediately apprehends that the relation to her mother is one of the most important topics in Ivette's life and her narrative. Her physical ability to verbally tell the narrative is, as an effect that fortifies this impression, impeded by emotions – noticeable in hard swallowing, pausing, and an audible clearing of her voice. Since the captions explain indirectly that Ivette had not seen her mother for at least three years – until Ivette's arrival in the United Stated – the latter's childhood must have been powerfully affected by the consequences of transnational motherhood. The latter is a pattern that has occurred more frequently in recent years. Transnational motherhood entails, among many other things, leaving the family on its own in the home country, sending money back, and sending for the whole family to migrate to, in this case, the United States at a later point (Segal 333). This typical procedure exposes the family to precarious states of separation.

In the United States, mothers from Mexico, as Bacallao and Smokowski demonstrate in their study, enter the labor force, oftentimes, for the first time in their lives, reconfiguring their families into dual-earner households (cf. 62). Most families in their study report that this change challenged the marriage as well as the relationship between children and parents (cf. 59). Further, "family stress seemed to be worsened by the nature of the parents' work, which was physically exhausting and emotionally stressful" (Bacallao and Smokowski 59). Emotional stress, in Ivette's narrative, can be related to her experience of transnational motherhood in her family that directly affected her and might have permanently altered the relationship to her mother. Her sadness, which the facial expressions communicate in this part of the narrative, likely is connected to Ivette's conflict with her mother with regard to 'other' and 'new' forms of identity (such as Ivette's sexual identity), which Ivette performs in the second half of the narrative.

Secondly, her facial expressions change from sad to irritated as she recounts the problems that she faced due to her immigration background as a child in school. She explains that she had language problems and faced cultural differences in the American school system, making her feel "like an outsider" (00:00:42). Shrugging her shoulders and frowning, Ivette claims that she does not exactly know *why* she did not feel like she belonged. This topic then leads her into discussing her bullying experiences at school. The emphasis on this part of her personal story signals to the viewer that they are indeed a problem from the past that still affects her, although it is not directly connected to her *undocumented* immigration background.

These experiences were the first experiences of struggle in the new 'home' country that she encountered and had to fight off – just as she is *in this moment* of her digital *testimonio* – fighting for the education of undocumented youths like herself and against discrimination on the basis of her sexuality. This fight forms into an intersectional struggle that combines immigration background and lesbian identity, as Ivette has to claim her multiple ways to 'belong' not only in the new country but also in the inner circles of her family. The financial hardship that additionally lies on her shoulders, in this struggle, occupies a comparatively small part of the narrative. However, it again connects to Ivette's mother's wishes for "a better future" (00:00:25) for her children as a major reason for emigrating and Ivette's current struggle performed in the *testimonio*.

As her narrative was published in January 2013, the undocumented youth Movement had already experienced a relief from deportation for many undocumented youths who graduated from high school or obtained a GED, like Ivette, through the announcement of the DACA seven months before. Secondly, the Maryland DREAM Act, which "allows Maryland high school graduates who are undocumented immigrants the opportunity to qualify for the lowest tuition rates at their public colleges and universities upon meeting certain eligibility requirements and submitting required documentation", "became law on December 6, 2012" ("Maryland Dream Act" n.pag.). While we cannot, of course, fully determine whether Ivette really qualifies for the DREAM Act in Maryland or the DACA, the captions and her verbal reference to currently attending Montgomery College in Maryland, suggest that Ivette is also a resident in the state. Nevertheless, these two legislative changes indicate a de-emphasis of the urgency for political activism by undocumented students and a re-emphasis on the effects of immigration on the family, as well as the oftentimes unspoken issues of dispossession that penetrate the family unit. In digital *testimonios* like Ivette's, published shortly before or after major changes in U.S. immigration laws, narrative time becomes an indicator for the 'urgency' with which political campaigns have to be led. As YouTube videos generally are very short, the structure and narrative time in which issues are addressed expands and contracts in relation to their political context. Since Ivette's discussion of her struggle to pay tuition fees is brief compared to the discussion of her coming-out as homosexual, which assumes the whole second part of her narrative, she stresses the intersectionality in her dispossession, as discussed earlier, but clearly de-emphasizes the role of political urgency as an undocumented *student*.

What is more, the performance of emotions displayed by the change in facial expressions serves as an indicator of the current status with which the narrator negotiates his/her dispossession. In the end of the video clip, Ivette resolves the conflict with her mother for her audience by means of hand movement and a smile (thus, the covering of her initial, emotional composition). The slow and careful removing of tears in her face toward the end of her narrative is the first time that the viewer gets to see Ivette's hands (between minute 00:03:33–00:03:45). This movement – in which most of her speech comes to a halt, in connection to the strong zoom on the face – implies a sense of an *active* ending. Just as the hands suggest, within these seconds, the story comes to a resolution: Ivette has reconciled with her mother. Yet, without any further introduction, Ivette also announces that her mother and she are "now working together" (00:03:39–00:03:41) and that her mother is "proud of her for doing all of it" (00:03:46–00:03:48). The close connection between 'work' – by which she presumably means immigrant rights activism, and the reconciliation with her mother, visually produces an important statement in the context of her dispossession and the Movement: Dispossession is an inherently intersectional phenomenon, as Ivette recovers from her sadness, melding a smile into her sad face. The viewer receives the political message that for dispossession to be countered, it takes an *active* resolution, requiring hard work and a sense of family unity – no matter how diverse other aspects of identities are between family members.

3.2. Irony and resistance

Pérez found in his study that undocumented youth also used humor "as a way to cope with illegality collectively with others" (33). Baym shows that users on YouTube, too, can distinguish themselves from the other posts by embedding humor, irony, or cynicism as specific aspects of communication into their narratives. By this strategy, she argues, users might assume "more power to shape the perceived group consensus than do the other participants" (162). La Rose adds that acts of resistance "may be demonstrated through performances of tensions and contradictions, as well as through the use of irony, parody, wit, and humor, methods recognized as particularly effective in challenging taboos and abject subjectivities" (301).

For this reason, we need to address humor, irony, and cynicism in the digital *testimonios* chosen for this study as a communication and empowerment strategy that addresses the viewer more directly than other communication strategies (humor works, here, in 'collectivity', as Pérez has shown). For digital narratives, however, this also means that we need to view humor from the perspective of multimodality, as Kaindl does in his study. He shows, most importantly, that

> non-verbal elements in multimodal texts not only perform the function of illustrating the linguistic part of the text, but also play an integral role in the constitution of the meaning, whether through interaction with the linguistic elements or as an independent semiotic system.
>
> (176)

Three of the eight narratives in this selection express irony through a combination of the verbal dimension with nonverbal signs, depending "on a semiotic combination for their effect" (178).

Carlos Roa (3)

Carlos uses irony to express his disbelief that his grandfather was a citizen for over 40 years but his own father could not get legalized, even after spending high sums of money on legal assistance. Irony, in his digital narrative, works through contradictions. The visual channel shows a smiling Carlos, however, with arched eyebrows which symbolize alertness. Further, the bizarreness of this look reinforces resistance. Given the dramatic content of his words, smiling is, in Chinn's words, an "inappropriate performative act[...]" (115), which shows that Carlos is struggling with the current legal situation which requires children of immigrants to have been born in the United States in order to get U.S. citizenship as well. In contrast, the reverse case is a common subject in many campaigns in the recent Immigrant Rights Movement: Children have frequently been made the organizations' "local, national, and international spokespersons for the cause", Pallares argues (*Representing 'La Familia'* 222–223). Likewise, the Movement criticizes, as Yoshikawa finds, that "the undocumented are viewed in current policy debates as lawbreakers, laborers, or victims – seldom as parents raising citizen children" (Yoshikawa 2). The other side of this discourse, however, subsumes the strategy that emphasizes that these children are citizens, "future potential voters", and, therefore, need their parents to stay legally with them in the United States under the term "*anchor baby*", as Pallares reports (*Representing 'La Familia'* 224). The latter quote, in particular, illustrates well the complicated status of a mixed-status immigrant family living in the United States.[12]

In view of this context, Carlos performs mockery of a situation which he frames verbally to fit the discourse of the Movement just presented, even though his personal claim to legalization envisions a reverse situation: It is not his father who is a citizen and wishes his parents to become citizens as well, but vice versa. The use of irony – depicted in his digital *testimonio* by the connotative contradiction between the verbal and the visual channel of communication – distracts from his unique claim, through which Carlos further assumes potential power, effectively challenging the legal situation with the performance of the what he perceives as an ironic situation.

Angelica Velazquillo (5)

In one instance, Angelica uses multimodal irony to express her dispossession connected to the detention and deportation proceedings of her brother. Recounting that immigration officials 'offered' a 'voluntary departure'[13] to Mexico to her brother instead of direct deportation, Angelica smiles as she refers to Mexico as "a place we don't remember and where he hasn't been to in 21 years" (00:01:41–00:01:42).

Further, the timing of this utterance (a longer pause precedes it) and a change in breathing, tone, and facial expressions indicates that she had to search for a way to express her criticism at this 'proposal', which points to the absurdity that Angelica feels with regard to voluntarily returning to Mexico. What seems striking, though, is the fact that Angelica grew up at least bilingually, which she revealed when she code-switched to a Spanish pronunciation of 'Mexico' in the beginning of the narrative. There she implied that her resistance to the idea of moving back to Mexico is absurd despite the fact that she and her brother might have grown up biculturally. As this example shows, irony can be employed in digital narratives to express personal criticism, disbelief, and resistance via adding a facial expression contrary to the internal attitude to the verbal statement. Further, the interactive aspect of this strategy is greater than a direct, linguistic expression of a critical attitude, as the viewer needs to interpret the combination of those multiple signs, leading to the effect that the focus on Angelica's political statement is sharpened.

4. Occupying space

Through the performative in dispossession, Butler and Athanasiou single out a sense of solidarity and collectivity that open new possibilities for politics. Athanasiou sees current protest movements of dispossessed people as 'forms of plural performativity', in which stories of individuals in that group are linked to the collective (cf. 157). This role of the individual and his/her story is just as important in the *testimonio*. Further, the form of social agency described here assumes, at other times, a very literal form, in which the body of the dispossessed becomes a performative act of agency itself. Plural performativity, therefore, takes place, most commonly, in groups and in physical gatherings and protest. It then functions in a twofold way, "as performativity *of* plurality and performativity *in* plurality" (Athanasiou 176).

The emphasis on the dispossessed status, inscribed on the body, poses the question whether social media itself can be a 'space for appearance', as Butler and Athanasiou call this space in which the bodies appear. As argued in Chapters 2 and 3, YouTube becomes a 'site' for many possibilities for public/political protest. Does a video on the Internet also serve as a public space, in which dispossession can be countered by means of virtual plural performativity? To answer this question, it is helpful to point out that in addition to 'public space', Athanasiou and Butler add Arendt's theory of 'space as appearance' and mold the latter into "*spacing appearance*" to describe spaces for plural performativity (194, *emphasis given*). This space opens up plural performativity to other forms and spaces for appearance and 'actions taking place' (cf. Athanasiou 194). Further, protesters need not actually perform a certain protest activity. Rather, entering a space, being in a space, actively pronouncing this presence in a space in forms of 'we are here', she continues, effectively conveys the political message that the protesters are not absent from public life (cf. Butler and Athanasiou, *Dispossession* 196–197). In new media, Butler assures us that if there is a "media event that forms across time and space", then there is also a "crowd" (197).

4.1. Bodily movement and posture

'Coming out of the shadows' is an activity which is tightly connected to the multimodal event of a combined public 'showing of the body' and declaration of status. This act, itself, is highly performative. It implies that the 'body' is understood as the foundation, as well as a site and inherently connected and subjected to the power of regimes. Since the term 'undocumented' bears a sense of immateriality, or even a lack of corporeality and personality, opposition to such derogative and even stigmatized understanding of an 'undocumented' person can only be guaranteed by showing and, thus, reframing this understanding of the 'undocumented'. Performativity challenges this perception through the act of performing 'undocumented' identities and reiterating this aspect in plurality.

Displaying their face and undocumented identity online is a form of challenging their dispossession by means of their own bodies in a multifaceted and multimodal fashion. Not only do gestures become 'turbulent performative acts' but also the body itself becomes a 'performative occasion' (cf. Athanasiou 179). Further, the setting of the videos is the most obvious means for expressing and reframing space. This section thus focuses on the making of a 'public space' for the undocumented body – and materializing it in its most literal sense. We will identify the setting (and changes thereof) as well as the concrete bodily movement and posture as an occupation of this public space inhabited by digital *testimonios* of undocumented youth.

David Ramirez (4): 'pushed to the wall'

In a quote from a personal interview with undocumented university student Uriel Sánchez, the latter pointed to the "sense of urgency or pressure on ourselves" that activism in the Movement in the year of 2010 meant to undocumented youth. He further stressed the impression that he and other youth "still were, like, kind of being pushed to the wall" after the failing of the federal DREAM Act in the end of 2010.

The setting and David's movement in his digital *testimonio* performs exactly this metaphor. As the video is shot in front of a room's wall and David sits on the floor (at times, his knees are visible), David indeed is physically 'trapped' in a corner-like space (a right angle formed by the floor and the wall), from which he cannot escape quickly without moving past the camera. The frequent movement of his head, upper body, and arms, and hands in this space,[14] however, signal an *attempt* to escape the situation.

On a verbal level, David struggles to express the affective experience of dispossession that, for all of his teenage years, influenced him greatly, as he claims: "I spent the last 10 years ... ehm ... trying to reconcile...like...all this hate that has been shot at me ... with my identity" (00:00:31–00:00:43). Movement, in accordance with his interrupted verbal performances, expresses the discomfort that he felt with his status and the resulting dispossessing reactions of others during most of his teenage years.

In a literal sense, here, David performs the relationality to others that Judith Butler and Athena Athanasiou have called a fundamental aspect to dispossession. Athanasiou points out that the "narration of the self" has an inherent merit: It "assumes the norm and at the same time potentially deconstructs it" (93). In this self-narration, however, the self does not stand by itself (cf. 71). David is dependent upon others because it does not suffice, for him, to accept his (undocumented) identity without negotiating it with the perception of others. The result of this negotiation process is visible in the performance of this process: David moves in a rectangular-shaped space within the camera's frame but cannot escape this frame in the end; having to 'face' the camera once more. One could argue, then, that the visual space that a video on YouTube provides is actively used by undocumented youth to symbolically portray relationality between individuals in the offline political sphere. The movement becomes particularly visible to the viewer's eye when it is presented in contrast to a prior stillness of the body in the moving image, as in the case in David's narrative: Shortly before discussing the identity struggle of the 'past ten years', David sits very still and glances directly in the camera as he recounts that he does not have any memories of his home country, Mexico.

Separated by another cut, in the third episode (00:01:04–end), David describes his negative feelings during his teenage years when he realized that being undocumented was (and is) preconditioned by everlasting stigma in the anti-immigrant parts of society. During this episode, he lifts his head and tilts it up and down, as he counts each single year all the way from the age of 13 to the age of 20 to emphasize how *many* years he was struggling. Again, David's smiling increases in this performance, which one could, as before, associate with the awareness of and insecurity of being watched by potentially thousands of people as he recounts such intimate details as an identity crisis. The movement of the head further indicates a passing of story time and, thus, prolongs the dramatic effect that he creates to express the affective dimension of his dispossession.

Toward the end of this episode, David more explicitly connects his personal story to the campaign in which he places his narrative,[15] explaining that he can imagine many other '13-year-olds' (denoting the age in which his struggle with dispossession began) who might be in the same situation. Here, David assumes a 'voice' for other undocumented youth without explicitly saying so. Explaining that he is "doing this in hopes that he [the imaginary other undocumented boy] will hear about me doing it" (00:01:54), David settles his hands on his knees, and directs his gaze upward, which makes him look much younger, helpless, and innocent than before.

Given the fact that a civil disobedience action followed the publication of this video (the title of this shirt links his 'body' to a 'The Dream is Coming'-campaign), David decriminalizes himself through this posture. His resistance in this performance lies in the renegotiation of the common visual image of a 'criminal'. Through the visual image, there is no need to specifically *say* that he is 'not a criminal', as a traditional *testimonio* would have needed to do. Consequently, David's narrative serves as an example of the implicit workings of the visual logic in moving image that YouTube automatically imposes upon its viewers.

Angelica Velazquillo (5): self-determination through posture

In the seconds following the basic introduction of herself, Angelica tells us that there "is no way for [her] to change her immigration status" (00:00:25–00:00:28). This statement might, at first glance, end with an address to or a call on the viewer to help or even change her situation if possible. At a closer look, there is a noticeable change in posture between the previous introduction of herself and her claim that she cannot change her immigration status. Here, we see Angelica's head angle changes as she postulates the 'immutability' of her status as an irreversible circumstance with severe consequences for her life.

Further, the camera is located at a much lower point than Angelica's face. This causes the effect that Angelica *looks down* at the camera. She seems empowered through that angle – not necessarily 'bigger than she naturally is'. Rather, her eyes are always focused on the camera, which causes the effect that we can never clearly look into her eyes. Angelica thus empowers herself over the device that is filming her, as if retaining complete control over the intimate detail she publishes on YouTube.

The viewer then sees a change in posture. Instead of lifting her head slightly, *looking down* at the camera, Angelica now bows her head slightly, giving 'us' – the viewer – an eye-level 'glance' into the camera – the eye of the intended viewer. I propose that by this move, Angelica expresses a sense of personal agency. While lifting the head visually expresses a sense of keeping 'one's head above the water' by one's own power, the act of leveling the head down toward the addressee, reducing the virtual space between them, in a face-to-face digital *testimonio* like this translates into the performance of a call for mutual agency and a statement of dependency. Angelica thus includes the viewer in her activism, appealing directly to him/her through the reduction of distance between them. She, as Beverley stresses for the traditional *testimonio*, "uses (in a pragmatic sense) the possibility the ethnographic interlocutor offers to bring his or her situation to the attention of the audience" (556). Going a step farther, Angelica's digital *testimonio* appeals to the viewer as if in an actual conversation, "demand[ing] on our attention and capacity for judgment" and imposing on the viewer "an obligation to respond in some way or another" (558). In the end, as Beverley summarizes, "we can act or not on that obligation, but we cannot ignore it" (ibid).

Angelica again uses posture and movement to produce meaning in her *testimonio* when she connects her own activism to that of the Movement's organizations and activists. Posture, in this case, articulates, in Athanasiou's terms, "aspirations to self-determination" (99): On a verbal level, she exclaims: "When I was invited to participate in the civil disobedience, I accepted" (00:02:05–00:02:09), while at the same time her body leans toward the camera and she lowers the head, as if she wanted to be on the same level as the viewer, and smiles at the camera.

Here, Angelica determines her move to participate in a civil disobedience to protest against her brother's detention as a natural and self-evident act. The positive affirmation that this posture transmits, further, performs her 'agreement' (to the civil disobedience action) once more to her viewer, establishing a public space online for a revival of past offline activism. "Because of the public pressure", she then argues, "they dropped the case against us" (00:02:48–00:02:52). The reasoning and her asserting smile performs an awareness of what the pressure is causing and how effective this public strategy, publishing protest and resistance in multiple forms online like she does, really can be.[16] Confirming the pressure by her own video, Angelica opens up a new public sphere for the negotiation of political pressure.

In a second, yet similar example, Angelica stresses that when she "realized" that 'unjust' arrests like that of her brothers were "gonna continue to happen" (00:02:11–00:02:13), she shrugs her shoulders as if she actually had no choice but to act and protest against "the injustices [her] community is ... ehm ... is facing" (00:02:29–00:02:34). Most notably, through this claim and bodily enactment, Angelica, in the moment of her narration, builds "new knowledge from personal and collective experience" that is distinct to the *testimonio* (Benmayor 507). Specifically, Angelica makes her individual dispossession a collective one and, thus, transforms her narrative into a collective one too. The shrug of the shoulders, in particular, denotes the arbitrariness of who exactly is being dispossessed in her community. Having generalized the experience, what follows is an interpersonal call to her undocumented audience: In the fashion of a guardian, activist, and speaker for her community, Angelica pronounces that it is now "time to speak out and drop our fear" (00:02:18–00:02:22).

4.2. The everyday struggle: from the private to the public setting

Stephanie Solis (1): being a tourist

The first part of Stephanie's digital *testimonio* (00:00:00–00:02:58), as we have seen, mainly consists of moving images that convey a sense of a face-to-face conversation or interview – effects which are mostly realized through the editing of film sequences and which we discuss in a later section. Those sequences show her in, mostly, a frontal medium close-up. The second part of the digital *testimonio*, however, works with less-frequently edited instances of intermediality and consists of moving images that 'show' Stephanie *in action*. Due to the moving camera and the physical closeness to the narrator Stephanie, these images closely resemble those of a documentary film, taking the audience on a (virtual) bus and tram ride to her university campus. The destination of this ride is connected to offline activism on the university's campus, as the viewer learns, where a "mock graduation event" is held in which Stephanie, herself, participates as a speaker (00:04:05–00:04:09).

The change in setting produces significant meaning for Stephanie's digital *testimonio*. First, the 'virtual ride' to Stephanie's college campus inscribes a sense of normality and daily routine to the narrator's life, offering the viewer a feeling of what she endures on a daily basis due to her undocumented status: As she explains earlier in the video, she cannot get a driver's license and has to take bus and train, which "takes between an hour-an-a-half to, usually, more like two hours" (00:03:02–00:03:09). What we *see* in this half of the digital narrative, thus, enacts Stephanie's dispossession in very literal terms. Stephanie wanders through difference urban spaces, which are yet real, recognizable spaces. We see, for instance, a sign in the Los Angeles Union Station or the entrance to the LA Chinatown.

These spaces become 'real' to us as we can 'see' them, and as a consequence, the construction of Stephanie's world as 'true' follows immediately. Knowing which places she has to *pass* – as she does in the video – her complaint about the long time it takes her to get to university with public transportation becomes more real in the same step. The significant political context of this situation is that as of 2009, when undocumented immigrants did not have access to applying for a driver's license in California.[17]

With the core story in mind, the moving in literal (and even widely-known) public spaces, shown in the moving image, Stephanie's body is marked by dispossession, because the way she moves (via public transport) is determined by her lack of a driver's license. She, literally, performs her lack of options. Further, in this sequence, Stephanie performs what she expresses verbally in the face-to-face narration of her core story. While she verbally narrates that she feels like a child that never gets the chance to grow up (00:03:38–00:03:41), the visuals perform this image of a child very literally: Stephanie directly performs and, thus, emphasizes that her development in every sense of the word, is 'on hold': Wearing a bag shaped like a stuffed animal and riding the bus, ducked, worried and looking like a little child who has been *displaced* and *forgotten*, Stephanie performs the child that she claims to feel like. This effect is further reinforced by the use of camera angles that deviate from the eye-level. Stephanie is filmed from a slightly lower angle, which emphasizes the largeness of the room and de-emphasizes Stephanie's. In the tram scene, the angle causes a focus on Stephanie's head, which is bent upward. Her gaze is directed away from us and seems alert, as if wondering at her immediate surroundings. As Stephanie does not focus on the camera or interact with it at all, the viewer gets the impression that she is all by herself and, hence, assumes the position of observer. This builds a strong contrast to the face-to-face *testimonio*, in which the viewer is seemingly addressed directly and, at times, even challenged and called upon to 'get active' (see, for instance Mohammad Abdollahi's (2) direct addressing of the audience).

In sum, the visual performances of both parts of Stephanie's core story of dispossession (her identity 'on hold' and material dispossession of options to improve her living standards through, e.g., a driver's license), emphasize that performance is "the living tissue that connects story and event in tenuous processes of meaning-making" (Pollock 121). Through performing the troublesome situations that Stephanie deals with every day, she emphasizes the immutability of her status as she performs her dispossession previously negotiated verbally in her core story. The meaning created by visual (moving) images further complements her verbal narration of the story. Her digital *testimonio* provides a glance of 'what can really happen' and, hence, induces a glimpse of truth into the narrative world. The visuals shown in this YouTube clip also add a space for action to the narrator's storyworld that allows them to physically move in the world that, by norm, excludes 'illegal' immigrants by naming their being in the United States 'illegal' in the first place – train stations, buses, and university campuses. Further, the undocumented narrator's movement in this space adds to the viewer's common awareness that undocumented people are present in high numbers in all public spaces. Stephanie thereby gives undocumented status her personal name and identity (as portrayed in the video). This move acquires a postcolonial sense of subversion: Stephanie is, bluntly put, not *writing* back but '*showing* back' instead.

In this sequence of moving images, there is one instance which highlights a discrepancy between the verbal narration of the core story and the visual image. Stephanie claims that because of her undocumented status, she oftentimes feels "like a tourist" (00:03:33–00:03:36) on her very own university campus, because at times she cannot attend university for months due to the many jobs that she needs to finance her tuition. Instead of visualizing the emotional affect that this dispossession exerts, the visuals of this scene show Stephanie standing at a sunlit train station, waiting for her train to pick her up to go to university, smiling, resembling the cognitive image that the viewer most likely construes of a tourist. The contrast between the preceding verbal account of her dispossession and the performance of dispossession in this part of the narrative disrupts the serious tone that the digital *testimonio* maintains in most other parts, which could be interpreted as a form of sarcasm. Claiming that she is "pretending to have like the college experience" (00:03:33–00:03:36), while the viewer knows that Stephanie is working three jobs next to studying, it is apparent that Stephanie means the opposite of what she says. However, since the ride to campus, indeed, is a 'performance' that inhabits a pretending character, the most important indicators of this form of sarcasm are, indeed, the visual images. Sarcasm expresses that Stephanie has no other choice but to deal with it in a humorous way. Toward the end of 2009, hopelessness was predominantly spread in the Movement with regard to Comprehensive Immigration Reform (cf. Pallares, *Family Activism* 113). Redirecting immigration reform toward undocumented students, "a *partial* solution" rather than a wholesome one, became a source of hope especially among undocumented youth of that time (Pérez 149).

Stephanie Solis (1): performing offline activism: mock graduation ceremony (00:04:20–00:05:07)

The digital *testimonio* of Stephanie Solis, to begin with, embraces the most literal meaning of plural performativity which describes physical gatherings and protest. Toward the end her narrative, she has not only told her story of dispossession to us, the viewer, in multiple modes and media, she also moves through different settings 'on her way to UCLA campus', letting the camera (and hence the viewer) 'accompany her'. What follows are scenes depicting Stephanie telling her story to other participants of the event within the frame of a mock graduation event.[18] She introduces this event to us verbally on our (virtual) tour across campus, having the viewer head 'with her' to the event. While the camera in this scene becomes an observer that knows about Stephanie's state of dispossession caused by her undocumented status, during the event, the narrative places the audience virtually among the other audience members who are physically part of the audience on campus, listening to Stephanie's speech, not only showing her but also the audience in short scenes. Through this double mode of performance, however, the viewers feel they know the narrator better than the audience, as we have been exposed to Stephanie's immigration background earlier in the video. In contrast to the audience in the scene, the YouTube viewer has automatically become involved in the Movement as an 'insider' to the story of an undocumented immigrant. The ingenuity of this technical twist greatly affects the viewer's initial state of passivity.

What is more, filming the narrator speak to the audience – one, that is real and restricted, in contrast to the potentially unrestricted audience on the Web – creates yet another set of interesting effects. Calling it a 'two-fold modus of performance' here denotes the materialized performativity (Stephanie's enactment of the college graduate that she wishes to be) as it is materialized through a second instance of performance for the camera, and, thus, the YouTube audience. Hence, she realizes both instances of plural performativity, the performativity *of* as well as *in* plurality (cf. Athanasiou 176), to protest against her dispossession, which naturally fortifies the need to change her undocumented status. The close connection to the DREAM Act protests becomes further apparent in these scenes.[19] Positioning the narrative in the public political agenda of the Movement of that time (2007–2009), Stephanie is one of those undocumented students fighting for the DREAM Act (as indicated in the title of the YouTube video). The year of 2007 had not achieved any compromise bill on immigration, although it was invigorated by the massive protests in the year of 2006 against the Sensenbrenner Bill (cf. Pallares, *Family Activism* 112). However, "between 2007 and 2010 [...] the immigrant movement continued to pursue a relatively unified strategy for CIR"[20] (ibid) and in the years of 2009 and 2010 – close to the time of the narrative's publication on YouTube – experienced a "resurgence of youth activism" (113). Thus, at the time of production as well as publication of Stephanie's narrative, the DREAM Act was the major goal to fight for as an undocumented immigrant young adult and teenager, because it was seen as the only way to provide at least some kind of future to all those high school graduates every year. The preoccupation with this piece of legislative attempt is clearly evident in the title of Stephanie's digital story.[21]

Although the scenes shown do not record all of the story of dispossession as the YouTube viewer has learned it, a repetition of scenes from the very beginning of the narrative indicates a repetitive 'telling of the story'. Further, the first words the camera records for the viewer confirm that Stephanie has just told her (real) audience about the moment that her mother informed her daughter of their illegal immigration to the United States (Stephanie talks about her feelings up to that moment and the conflict arising from that). The scenes repeated from the first eight seconds of the video already show Stephanie at a 'mock graduation event' at her college, speaking to an audience through a microphone. From this speech, one sentence is used to introduce the video narrative as a whole: "And they never told me, because my family was, you know, ashamed and...and they didn't really know what to say" (00:00–00:08). This without even having been introduced to Stephanie as a person at that point, editing reveals the powerful impact that 'family' plays in Stephanie's decision to tell her story to the video team, the audience on campus, as well as the online audience. The final scene in this digital narrative, also, ends with the first sentence. However, this filmed graduation event reinforces a different rhetoric. To the postcolonial ear, the 'othering' in this statement is unmistakable: The first sentence contains a word, "they", which indicates estrangement from Stephanie's own family. During the second half of the narrative, these words make more sense, as the viewer knows about Stephanie's dispossession. In this speech, however, Stephanie further highlights her exceptionalism as an undocumented student, responding to the discourse in the Movement of that time. As Pallares explains, the 'innocence' of undocumented students (who were too young to decide against the illegal crossing of the border) was particularly stressed by politicians and youth advocates in the first years of lobbying for the DREAM Act (cf. *Family Activism* 109). Accordingly, Stephanie declares to her audience that "this is not a decision that [she] made" and that she feels like she is held "hostage" by dispossessing forces (as, for instance, the legislation) (00:04:46–00:04:50). The verbal component of this message clearly is greater than the visual, as Stephanie is merely performing a graduation ceremony rather than any of the visual implications that her statements might have. However, see Chapter 7 for the meaning that writing and the use of a common street sign adds to the former.

Angelica Velazquillo (5): community center

The filming device that Angelica uses in her digital *testimonio* clearly is a fixed camera, perhaps a webcam on the computer. The quality of the video itself is very good, clear, and audible. However, it is also noticeable that it is not a professional camera as used by a professional filming crew. The background setting in which the video is produced could be an educational institution, or even a community center. The fact that Angelica might record her video in a community center – and, hence, a space for offline activism – is illustrated by the gap in the door through which one can see people walk by occasionally.

It is not a homely place, but clean and simple. There is no extra detail in the background place, only what looks like a door and a wooden cupboard hanging on the wall. Its simplicity and functionality, however, also supports the impression that the video builds up: This type of personal visual narrative is produced for a specific purpose. There is, in contrast to many other videos one finds on YouTube (and also in this selection) and other participatory online networks, little staging around Angelica's personality or life, apart from her 'activist' identity. The narrative thus frames a strong political message that implies an urgent agency to act against 'the injustices' that dispossesses her, her brother, and her community.

Luis Maldonado (8): occupying space, fighting borders

In this section, Luis' body indeed becomes 'a turbulent performative occasion' in a literal sense (cf. Athanasiou 179), as undocumented narrators in digital *testimonios* renegotiate real and imagined spaces by means of their visual account. Accordingly, Luis Maldonado's digital *testimonio* addresses his dispossession, which is initiated by the deportation of his sister and discrimination that his LGBT community is facing under current immigration law. Luis employs a creative constellation of an interview-like situation, moving images as well as multiple static images in combination with his voice from the off. In comparison to the previous digital narratives, Luis more actively performs his dispossession by conquering 'real' space: Throughout the digital narrative, the moving image depicts the U.S.-Mexican border in Texas (Hidalgo) and Luis moving along it or looking at it while the viewer hears his voice narrating from the off.

The camera depicts the border and Luis' movement along it in a medium close-up that leaves more space to incorporate the border into the picture than there is for Luis himself, insinuating that Luis cannot 'overcome' it but that he is being 'dominated' by its presence. However, his movement along it symbolizes, most importantly, Luis' overcoming of his 'own precarity' that his undocumented status causes (cf. Butler and Athanasiou, *Dispossession* 101). He appears along it, "exercising in that way a 'right' (extralegal, to be sure) to existence" (ibid) along the side of the border that *he* ascribes a sense of belonging to – the United States – and actively legitimates his undocumented status.

On a verbal level, Luis explains that his coming out as an 'undocumented person' made him feel empowered even though it was a 'nerve-wracking moment'. While he speaks, the moving image films the ground and Luis' shoes, showing the footsteps that Luis takes presumably walking alongside of the border. The associative quality of this image lies in the metaphor of an *ongoing* and *active* struggle that is translated into visuals. At the same time, the combination of two independent 'topics' – the separation by the border transmitted via the visuals and the coming out as undocumented told verbally – are connected into one image. 'Coming out', here, could also be read as literally 'coming out': Luis shows that he is *unafraid* to leave the house and move into the public despite his precarious status.

Also in visual performances alongside the border fences, he connects his undocumented and homosexual identity to the topic of the ongoing separation of undocumented and mixed-status families. His narrative is published in September 2013 – a time when undocumented *students* had won some relief. This new narrative context becomes, literally, visible in Luis' digital *testimonio*: Luis includes his nephew in the visual image and moves along the border fence with him.

The fact that Luis' nephew does not interact with the camera, does not show much of his facial expressions and does not speak a word combined with the fact that the viewer does not know anything about the boy besides the deportation of his mother (Luis' sister) several years prior to the recording of the video, transforms this child into a representative for a family member who is immediately affected by deportation, even though he is *not* an active 'character' in Luis' *testimonio*. Thus, incorporating his nephew into his digital *testimonio* bears important meaning for Luis' narrative when glancing at its political context: "Since 2011", Pallares observed, undocumented youth "have been staging actions and coming out events in which they emphasize their relationship with their parents, have parents or siblings together speak at events, and are developing their relationship to the familial frame" (*Family Activism* 122). This incorporation of immediate family into undocumented youth activism that Pallares observed was partly caused by numerous personal experiences among the Movement's activists whose family members had been detained or deported, as Gaby Benítez, one of the undocumented youths that I interviewed during my research stay in Chicago in spring 2014, explains:

> It's not just about the youth. It's about the families. We can see that now in the Movement, right? And we have seen that change and shift. And I don't know if it's because it's happened to a lot of individuals, like it happened to me, but at least on a personal level, that's what made that shift for me.
>
> (personal interview)

Statistics show that there was a rise in deportation numbers during the Obama administration. "Deportation in the 2013 fiscal year increased by more than 20,000 over 2012 and by more than 51,000 over 2011", according to Preston (*Deportation* n.pag.).[22] Further, recent changes in immigration legislation such as "the creation of the DACA only justified even further the focus on parents and other older immigrants" (Pallares, *Family Activism* 125), an aspect which Gabriela Benítez describes as follows:

> And it's a very complex situation and I've spoken to other folks who have either adjusted through their visas, or have adjusted through and have LPR status and even to folks who have DACA at the moment, which is very temporary and it's not at all the same thing but it's still like saying 'Now I have this' and I will never forget while we were doing DACA, helping people apply for it, and after they got it, people were like 'I'm really excited, but I feel like I'm in a very cold room with my family. And I'm the only one who has a blanket.'
>
> (personal interview)

Even if youths eligible for DACA can now 'wear a blanket', this blanket is ominously thin, as Ellis and Chen stress, because the youth's "long-term opportunities in the United States remain limited" (252).

Connecting his nephew's lot to his own digital *testimonio*, thus, transforms the personal character of his 'immigrant story' on the Web into a collective one which links the Movement's politics to the media logic on YouTube, as it significantly moves away from personal issues discussed in the narrative.

Indirectly, the combination of border images and himself and his nephew provide yet another political theme that his *testimonio* addresses: 'Reentry' – the process of returning after a deportation – is a federal crime that exempts those returning to the United States from any form of relief or legalization in the future (cf. Pallares, *Family Activism* 31). Along the same lines, "a great majority of convictions that have eventually resulted in deportations are for unlawful reentry" (Wright n.pag.). These basically dictate that Luis' sister – if she returned illegally a second time – would be exempt even from any type of relief due to 'reentry' and banished forever from the life of her son, who is a U.S. citizen. Due to this 'crime', she would not even qualify for President Obama's recent deportation reprieve from 20 November 2014, whose "centerpiece [...] is a new program for unauthorized immigrant who are the parents of United States citizens" (Shear n.pag.), as she would have 'committed a significant crime', which is a disqualifier for this reprieve (cf. Badger and Elliott n.pag.).

How this situation affects many and leads to a new focus in the political agenda, Antonio Gutiérrez further explains in an interview:

S.Q.: And [...] how do you think 'reentry' is going to develop, the topic of 'reentry'?

A.G.: [...] As far as the organization that I'm part of, OCAD – Organized Communities Against Deportation, we have seen *many*, many cases. And a lot of the cases that are very, that they can go very public because they don't have any criminal record, except for the reentry, which ICE considers a [...] felony, criminal record, it is becoming something that we're seeing that they're [...] putting priority on these people and that is *unfair* because they don't have any other criminal, a natural criminal record, so we're really trying to focus on that campaign of 'reentry'. Overall, we want to stop *all* deportations, but we want to, at least, begin with that aspect, because it is very unfair, that somebody that has...they got caught when they were trying to enter the United States for the first time, and then they got sent back and eventually they were able to get in or whether [...] they were already here and then they got deported, they got sent back and then they came back because their family was here. I just, we don't feel that the need of 'reentry' just because you already have family here or because you're still looking for a better opportunity – that should be considered a crime. And that's where the big campaign right now, that is happening with these 'reentry'-cases that we're building up, here in Chicago, and we're starting to move nationally in another level with the 'Not One More'-campaign. But it really comes to play, that aspect, that we really, I mean, we're hoping that within time, within the next six months or something, we can really build up that momentum and really get that reentry policy to really change as far as how ICE treats it.

(personal interview)

While Antonio connects activism around reentry mainly to the incommensurability of reentry that the Movement perceives to 'other crimes', Marcela Hernandez focuses on the human struggle that deportations, in general, hold, arguing that "it's not fair" that those deported are used "as something that is disposable". Highlighting the "pain" that his nephew experiences through his mother's deportation and its consequential legal implications, Luis' speaks out against the treatment of family members (and others) as 'disposable' through performing his and his nephew's dispossession on YouTube.

Connecting the two 'modalities' of dispossession most immediate in his life, Luis' digital *testimonio* emphasizes the intersectionality of oppression at work in his life and further contextualizes his feeling that "there will always be a cause that [he] will feel attached to" and that "there will always be an injustice that [he] will need to fight for" (00:02:41–00:02:46). The intersections, including the struggle for his family's future (that of his nephew and sister, in particular), clarify why Luis talks about the ongoing struggle in which he is engaged. It is a struggle that includes the rights of undocumented gay people, such as the right to make your gay or lesbian partner a permanent resident or citizen, if you, yourself, are one. "I still feel that that's another battle of my identity, of my immigrant story" (00:01:28–00:01:33), he argues. Further, a university education, as he stresses by means of the visual pictures along the border with his nephew, is not enough to counter the inherent disposability that is imposed on whole populations (cf. Athanasiou 40) – populations like "his" community.

4.3. Performing props: symbolic objects in moving images

Stephanie Solis (1)

In the second half of her digital *testimonio*, Stephanie Solis attends a mock graduation ceremony, which highlights her activism in favor of the DREAM Act. In addition to the double modus of performance that we have detected earlier, the film's ability to fade another set of moving images into the current picture adds a property toward the end of the narrative that fortifies the political message of the digital testimonio. In addition to Stephanie's visually and verbally synchronous speech, wondering "what happens" to undocumented children when they grow up (00:05:04), a set of moving images first shown when she recounts the first part of her story of dispossession is blended in. This double visual is displayed until she has finished her sentence and is then blackened out. The combination of these modes and performances leads to her generalized speaking about an undocumented 'little girl' with Stephanie's own experience of dispossession (the loss of her baby pictures and the finding of them in a book). This, in turn, evokes the generalization that there are many more stories *like* Stephanie's, reinforcing the appeal to plurality that the narrative has made already by the performance of materialized performativity during the event.

The blending in of a book – the primary symbol for education – in addition to moving images of the mock graduation ceremony emphasizes the 'elite' status of undocumented students, which has not been uncontested in the Movement. Pérez, for instance, explains that "stories of high-achieving undocumented students" have been used to portray them "as the poster kids for legalization", which "forces the debate into a question of deservedness that pits superstar students against their lesser-achieving peers" (149). By emphasizing that books were not only common in Stephanie's household but that they were also appreciated *and* used, which is explicitly performed in the reenactment scenes showing a person skimming through the books, Stephanie's narrative aligns with this claim for excellence. However, her narrative also acts against the stigma of the 'uneducated' and 'working-class' immigrant' per se. In her story of dispossession, further, the books have symbolically turned into the savior of Stephanie's only childhood memories, as the DREAM Act would turn into the savior of undocumented immigrant students. If she felt the need to emphasize the symbolic quality of books in her family's household in the filmmaking process, *performing* the scene once more is an adequate way of giving the narrative a strong voice endorsing higher education of undocumented students. One of the four criteria that Baumann has established for performances as "site-specific interactions" is the "changing structures of social relations" that are evoked by the performance (in: Pollock 120). Her parents and she, herself, would then discredit the anti-immigrant, discriminatory reduction of the immigrant family as uneducated and illiterate. This perspective, thus, calls for a legislative change, and for a final passage of the DREAM Act.

The second instance in which Stephanie performs with a 'prop' is established through the frame of the moving image: Locking the door of what we assume to be her apartment, a sign reading 'bones' with an arrow pointing to the lock of the door and, through Stephanie's posture, to herself, creates an ironic picture. The humor lies in the fact that Stephanie's situation is indeed fatal – but not fatal in the lethal sense. She is not condemned to be 'bones' just yet. This humorous visual play with the written word and the moving image lightens up the serious situation portrayed in the narrative of dispossession that preceded the virtual ride to UCLA campus in Stephanie's digital *testimonio*. The frame of the moving image makes this possible, without the need for Stephanie to explicitly integrate a source for humor herself. Stephanie's 'comic relief' lightens up the tone of her video and might trigger the audience to watch the second half of the digital narrative as well. As Baym shows, the use of humor increases general likability in online communities (cf. 162), which might promise Stephanie more online support for her video on YouTube. In the performance of dispossession, mockery accentuates severe criticism of the situation that triggered the humor, as Chinn showed earlier (cf. 115). The performance with the bones sign criticizes those who dispossess Stephanie – those, who reduce her to her undocumented status and hinder her to *live* up to her fullest.

Mohammad Abdollahi (2): a setting for coming out: online participation in the movement

Throughout his video, Mohammad Abdollahi emphasizes the importance of activism in the offline Immigrant Rights Movement and explicitly connects his digital *testimonio* to other acts of coming out of the shadows, such as those in March of 2010. In the interplay of interacting with his cameraman, the setting, and to his words toward the end of his video, Mohammad further defines what coming out of the shadows may mean for the Web 2.0 generation and the audience of undocumented youths that he addresses directly. The setting incorporated in the frame of the moving images plays a major role in this redefinition of online activism, a form of participation that Mohammad explicitly projects to vlogging on YouTube. With reference to the many Coming Out of the Shadows events taking place in different states of the United States during the publication of his video, Mohammad reminds his audience:

> And, so, if you have some videos to share, if you have some stories to share, as you can see, you know, 'coming out' is not about 'coming out' in front of a press conference or 'coming out' in front of a big audience. (00:05:01–00:05:09)

Instead, he changes his posture for the first time in the video, bends sideways, and addresses his cameraman directly, whom we then hear laughing at this sudden shift in his stance. Making the audience aware of the production processes, as if confiding that "the only thing around me is just some weird people that are taping this video right now", Mohammad downplays the potentially huge audience for his video online. We sense he wants to embolden other youths who are too afraid to publish their coming outs online.

Mohammad adds humor to his digital *testimonio*, countering the peril produced in outing himself by explicitly performing that triviality and normality are also part of his everyday life. Turning away from his audience (and the camera) for the very first time, Mohammad points to a poster on the wall of his room that portrays major characters from the popular TV series *The Office*. Since these characters have no connection whatsoever to his bleak story of dispossession, their uncanny appearance here evokes humor that loosens up the serious political context in which Mohammad's digital *testimonio* is produced and published. Through this move, the end of Mohammad's video accommodates the media logic of YouTube. As Baym finds in her study of cognitive functions in online communities, a "strong emphasis on humor" in online communities shows the great extent "to which emotive elements can be essential to shaping and negotiating a community's core values" (217). Through humor, Mohammad attempts to trigger not only sympathy and popularity on the part of his audience but also to revalue the political message he wants his audience to understand, which might entice them to publishing their coming out videos online as he has done. His humorous performances, hence, evoke the sense of "power to shape the perceived group consensus" – a strategy which Baym finds to work well in online communities (162).

Luis Maldonado (8): a DREAMer's props and belonging

Since the state of Texas was the "first state to offer in-state tuition to undocumented immigrants in 2001" (Foley), Luis' *testimonio*, published in September 2013, does not directly fight for a state DREAM Act like many of these narratives. However, he recounts at the beginning of his narrative that he joined the "DREAM movement" during his early years of college (00:00:24–00:00:29). Through the quick filming of medals, report cards, and certification, which are artistically spread on a table and pinned onto the walls of what we assume is Luis' room, he establishes and reinforces a connection to undocumented students who are still 'phase one' DREAMers – those who identify with each other via extraordinary student achievements (cf. Anguiano 77) – by letting the camera sway over the carefully spread out and, for this occasion 'prepared' school and college records.

The moving image visually documents Luis' success and eligibility for the DREAM Act. Filming the medals and certificates that Luis has earned in an educational institution visually validates being a 'DREAMer'. This aspect does not highlight his undocumented status but rather the path that he could still take in his life toward legalization, and the qualifications he has earned. Since this image is far from depicting dispossession, the moving image performs a sense of belonging to this part of the Movement without having to repeat the Movement's early rhetoric in words by, for instance, blaming his parents for migrating to the United States. Thus, in contrast to narratives such as Stephanie Solis', Luis' establishes 'student excellence' but also shows that he is not 'apologetic' – which Anguiano describes as the third phase of the Movement: The 'unapologetic DREAMer', who confronts the public with protest tactics such as the civil disobedience tactics (cf. Anguiano 78). This, newest phase of the Movement is depicted through pictures and sound, as the succeeding chapter of this investigation will show.

A second set of 'props' appears at the very ending of the video. Through montage, two separate moving images are blended – a big close-up shot of Luis' head and a row of international flags, presumably filmed at the Hidalgo border as they represent Texas, Mexico, and the United States. Through the blending in of the images, the 'new' image plays with spatial metaphors of belonging as well. The new image distributes the three flags over Luis' face and, for the first time, we see Luis laughing. His smile serves as a device to leaven the mood of his *testimonio*, providing the note of entertainment that YouTube narratives incorporate in their logic. The sound of his voice, however, is muted. This strategy connects his narrative to beginning of the revived Immigrant Rights Movement as it reminds us of the massive marches in 2006 when marchers waved "Mexican flags to express ethnic pride, and carried U.S. flags as a symbol of patriotism and loyalty to this country" (Flores-González and Gutiérrez 4). Luis' smile expresses confidence and happiness, which is an open sign for belonging. It shows that he is fighting against dispossession but, as the core story showed, is not the only one dispossessed in his *testimonio*. Rather, his smile shows that dispossession can take more tragic turns than his and that he needs to fight for his community and *their* dispossession as well, which thus becomes *his*.

5. The other narrator: framing narrative through montage and zooming

Although there are great differences between oral and written narrative, one can compare "literary texts to [...] 'natural discourse'" (Ryan, *Face-to-Face Narration* 42). Characteristics of the latter are, for instance, "omniscient narration, stream of consciousness, jumping back and forth between different plot lines" or the "disruption of chronological sequences" (43). While all these techniques can be used in recorded speech as well, the recording frames and finishes off the narrative. It then becomes unalterable once it is on the Web, resulting in the same product to be listened to/viewed many times.

Another significant feature of oral storytelling is the fact that undocumented youth, when using recorded speech narrative, cannot be interrupted – only by cutting and deleting parts of their recording. This 'interruption' into the narrative is voluntary and enables the producer to focus on the things that are most important to be communicated to the listeners/viewers. The affordances of video editing, thus, have a major impact on the narration in the digital form of the oral *testimonio*: "Camera angle and movements, transitions, montage", according to Ryan, can create "the ghostly figure of the cinematic narrator" (*Moving Pictures* 196), as the final section of this chapter shows.

Carlos Roa (3)

Throughout his roughly three-minute-long digital *testimonio*, Carlos does not allow for much negative emotion to be expressed visually (through, for instance, crying or changes in posture). The combination of cutting the moving image and proceeding with quick camera shots closer to the narrator in a relatively short period of time symbolizes how 'close' the viewer can get to Carlos' emotions. In such an episode, Carlos briefly recounts the year his family immigrated to the United States and his grandfather's immigration background. Carlos cannot understand how his grandfather could be a citizen for "over 40 years" while his own father could not, although the latter apparently tried "year after year to get [the family] legalized" and spent "tens of thousands of dollars for lawyers" (00:00:34–00:00:43).

Shortly before the family's struggle for legalization comes up, the moving image is cut and Carlos is filmed in a medium close-up, signaling that he is going to recount more intimate detail than before. After a second cut, a close-up follows in which he dispels what he finds to be a common misbelief about undocumented immigrants: He rejects the notion that in order to get legalized, "people think it's as easy as getting behind a line" (00:00:43–00:00:45). The final shot is introduced with Carlos' recount of how he feels about the legalization struggle of his family. The close-up makes him look very sad, especially compared to before, when Carlos still smiles as he tells us how long his family has been in the United States, in effect decriminalizing their unlawful immigration to the country. This effect, however, is produced primarily by our closeness to his face, enabling us to study his sad look in more detail. Due to the plain background and Carlos' plain black shirt, there is also no other visual 'distraction'. Therefore, the viewer almost *has* to look into Carlos' face. 'Looking somebody in the eyes', in personal conversations, is also a way to deduce candor.

This is particularly important for what Carlos says, as some people in the debates on undocumented immigration reinforce the belief that undocumented immigrants receive social services but do not pay taxes (and therefore do not 'contribute'). Performing their protests against this perception, many undocumented immigrants in the Immigrant Rights Movement since 2006, like Carlos, "frequently describe themselves as model citizens", emphasizing that they are "law-abiding, paid their taxes, worked to support their families, did not receive welfare, and were not a burden to the state", and this way contribute to "discourse of morality and responsibility" (Pallares, *Representing 'La Familia'* 226). The visual reinforcement of candor and sincerity, in this instance, thus also conveys a political message. A candid performance implies that Carlos, in fact, materialized this part about his undocumented immigrant identity and shows how Carlos had to deal with stigma attached to the label of the 'undocumented'. Through this naming of the stigma attached to his identity, he has the chance to counter it by the means of audiovisual narration. In sum, this narrative intervention through montage just introduced conveys that the affective level of dispossession is particularly relevant. The zoom here shows how the production processes of videos on YouTube tend to respond to the publication of intimate details such as Carlos' struggle for legalization and personalize them in visual terms as well. The zoom diminishes literal and symbolical 'distance' between the viewer and the dispossessed.

Ivette Roman (7): cutting down to the 'gist' (00:00:00–00:02:05)

The most significant difference between Ivette's digital *testimonio* and the other *testimonios* in this selection is its separation of two narrative foci: The first revolves around her undocumented status (00:00:00–00:02:05), while the second recounts the moment she came out to her mother as gay (00:02:06–end). While both parts are strictly separated, the first part shows frequent cuts of the moving image that essentially shape what is being said, and, more importantly, *how long* this utterance is going to be. In detail, the cuts occur at the following passages:

1 (00:00:14): The video is cut after the introduction to her name, country of origin, age, immigration status, and sexual orientation.
2 (00:00:51): The video is cut after introduction to her arrival in the United States and the process of settling-in.
3 (00:01:04): The video is cut after reporting the bullying she experienced in school due to language problems.
4 (00:01:19): The video is cut after summarizing that school was "just really hard".
5 (00:01:47): The video is cut after introducing the financial demands imposed by her college of choice.

All these cuts signal changes in the topic of the story. Cut 2, for instance, marks the transition from the story of immigration and announces the beginning of an entirely new scene in which Ivette recounts how she was bullied in school. Cut 5 moves the narrative away from the financial and other demands confronting Ivette and transits to Ivette's hard working and studying. However, as most cuts are blended in and, thus, become almost invisible, they are designed to cause as little disruption as possible, as if trying to vanish as a narrative intervention in the narrative completely, thus setting together a puzzle of narrative pieces to form a *testimonio*.

The first part of the narrative introduces us to her family's immigration history, and most importantly, her migration from Peru to the United States at the age of nine. Ivette likely experienced a great deal of responsibility in her childhood years and the topic of 'illegal border crossing' must have been very present to her at a young age already. In addition to that, travelling without papers all the way from Peru to the United States also meant crossing all of Central America first, which is a long and dangerous journey. By means of shortening this set of data with frequent cuts, all topics that Ivette addresses in the short pieces of moving image gain as much attention and narrative time as the border-crossing itself – or the period of transnational motherhood that Ivette experienced – which leads to a de-emphasis on the individual situations of dispossession connected to undocumented status in this first half of the narrative – and certainly to a de-emphasis of Ivette's immigration background. The original video material seems cut into little pieces to produce a narrative the editor desired to be told. Further, the cuts that occur in this section do not only keep the narrative short – in accordance with many other videos YouTube – but also set the tone for the following parts of the narrative: Since there is not much room for elaboration, the narrative conveys the impression that there are yet more 'relevant' issues to follow, which is a paradox because the situations that Ivette describes in the first part already show the major implications that illegal immigration has for the family. The dominance of the producer in determining the tone and topic for the narrative thus stands out as unique in this section of the narrative.

Ivette Roman (7): zoom: framing the dispossessed body (00:02:06–end)

The second half of Ivette's digital *testimonio* – in contrast to the first – is framed by zooming rather than by cuts. Most notably, the first zooming-in occurs right at the beginning of this sequence and films Ivette's body from there on not in a medium close-up but in a close-up shot. In contrast to the cuts in Carlos Roa's digital *testimonio,* for instance, the camera zooms in significantly during Ivette's narration *without* making further cuts. Through this, the image moves repeatedly during the recording process, making the viewer more aware of the fact that he/she is getting to know more intimate details of Ivette's life than before. This is a paradox as Ivette has experienced many potentially traumatic events in her young life already. Finally, through this type of camera movement, Ivette's face is positioned as the most important element of the visual picture and the sole focus of the narrative. Through the zoom, the viewer is not able to see her use of gestures but rather the moving elements in her face, conveying performances of affective influence of dispossession on her, which she communicates through a change in facial expression.

The core story, which dominates the second half of the narrative, is introduced by another page with captions, posing a question about Ivette's coming out as a lesbian to her mother (see Chapter 7 for an elaboration on the captions). The zoomed-in camera frame signalizes that an important and emotional part is following and that the audience should pay closer attention. This emphasis is a direct intervention into Ivette's digital *testimonio* that she does not make by herself but that the *other* narrator imposes freely on the digital *testimonio.* The coming out story is not interrupted as much as the first part of the narrative, yet the frequent zooming between the cuts causes movement. While Ivette recounts the situation in which she comes out to her mother at home, the camera films her in a close-up shot, zooming out to a medium close-up once that scene is over and Ivette reports how she and her mother dealt with the new situation. The following cut interrupts the narrative as Ivette recounts that her mother would not even look her in the eye for months (00:03:09), signaling a stagnation in their relationship. A second cut (00:03:15), however, introduces a more emotional narrative episode, shortly after Ivette recounts that the rejection by her own mother made her consider suicide: Ivette turns her gaze away from the 'eye' of the viewer, while the camera undertakes a second major zoom on her face, displaying the emotional impact of her mother's rejection. The zoom, most significantly, focuses on Ivette's sexual dispossession; her tears signaling that the dispossession mapped on to her body (cf. Athanasiou 18): The place Ivette finds herself in when her mother rejects her for being homosexual, is a place of 'non-being' and 'desubjectification' (cf. Athanasiou 27): Ivette's closing of her eyes shows her sadness and her earlier confirmation that she wished to 'not live' anymore reinforces the impression that she feels essentially worthless in her society. In the eyes of her mother, who would not "speak" to her "in months" and did not "even look" her "in the eye", she did not exist anymore (00:03:05–00:03:08). In the narrative performance of her dispossession, the camera approaches Ivette's face – *looks* directly *at her* – through a stark zoom, which is the zoom closest to her face in the whole narrative. Through this device, the digital narrative breaks Ivette's 'proper place of non-being' ascribed to her by the multiple workings of dispossession (cf. Butler and Athanasiou, *Dispossession* 19) by performing the opposite – her physical *being* – online and allowing her audience to acknowledge her being by watching her video clip.

Notes

1 It needs to be stressed that the analysis follows the media logic of YouTube videos and their socio-technological, hence, semiotic idiosyncrasies and hence not 'classical' film analysis.
2 I understand 'indigenous', here, as a more incorporating term that defines as not exclusively the 'First Peoples' – "original inhabitants of areas later colonized by settler states" (Ginsburg 582) – but also as peoples in dispossession, as undocumented immigrants. I ascribe this freedom to the legal 'homelessness' that the latter experience in the United States, which questions decisions of the 'right to a home' altogether.
3 Beats are known to be looking rather insignificant: The hand moves with the rhythmical pulsations of speech, accentuating "single propositional elements and mark them as important" (Hübler 46).
4 For orientation, in the analysis Chapters 5–7, I use these kinds of headings to indicate which narrative I am specifically analyzing for the next few paragraphs. The narratives are numbered as introduced in Chapter 4.
5 We hear the cameraman laugh a little towards the end of the video, revealing him as a man.
6 More specific detail is discussed in Chapter 6.
7 The legal situation changed remarkably since the publication of Carlos' digital *testimonio*. Not only might Carlos be eligible for the DACA (Deferred Action for Childhood Arrivals) but also might the DACA open up a path to the military for him. Since 25 September 2015, "undocumented young people who have been granted deportation deferrals by the Obama administration" are "eligible to apply for the military under a recruitment program for immigrants with special language and medial skills", according to Preston (*Military Path* n.pag.). Carlos does not specify the state he is from in his narrative. However, the fact that on a picture that he uses in his digital narrative, his father wears a 'Florida' sweater and in the description it says that Carlos, by now, attends a college in Miami, one can assume that he lived in the state of Florida during the time of the publication of his digital *testimonio*. A state-level DREAM Act for Florida was signed into law on 9 June 2014 (Lee n.pag.).
8 Other types of gestures are included in this discussion of abstract pointing in order to correctly grasp the context in which Mitzy uses the latter.
9 See Chapter 7 for an elaboration on the use of still images to portray the American Dream.
10 Anguiano distributes the Movement into three phases, of which Stephanie's digital *testimonio* belongs to the first. The first of these phases stresses "*the exemplar student identity*", a collective identity among the so-called 'DREAMers' that

identifies through hard, academic and other work and attempts to appeal to the opposition in that way (77). The second phase, "*undocumented unafraid*", is characterized by "public disclosure efforts" that seek to "get national visibility for the Movement" (78). In the third phase, which Anguiano calls the phase of the "*unapologetic DREAMer*", activists "escalate the mobilization efforts by modeling civil disobedience tactic of previous civil rights movements" (ibid). The later two phases are presented by some of the other narratives chosen for this study.

11 Similar to other state DREAM Acts, Rusin reports that the Illinois Dream Act allows certain undocumented youth to "pay in-state tuition when attending public universities in Illinois" (6). When doing so, they are provided with "trained counselors" to be informed on career options as well as "savings programs so that parents can invest and save for their children's education" (ibid).

12 Yet, change has come. Recent executive action in November 2014 grants about four million undocumented parents with citizen children relief from deportation if they "pass background checks and pay taxes" (Shear n.pag.), "have lived in the United States for at least five years" (Shear and Pear n.pag.) "and allow many to work legally, although it offers no path to citizenship" (Shear n.pag.).

13 Through a request for voluntary departure, if "facing deportation (removal) from the United States", one may leave the country on one's own "without receiving an order of deportation on your immigration record" (Gearty n.pag.).

14 Apart from a few occasional beats and one instance of pointing (referring to a far-away state in the United States upon the pronouncing of the word 'Georgia'), David does not use clearly recognizable and gestures that produce significant meaning for the narrative.

15 As Chapter 7 will explain in more detail, David's digital *testimonio* was published within the frame of a civil disobedience action that fought against the incident that "the Georgia Board of Regents recently voted to ban undocumented youth from the state's top five public universities" (Lozano n.pag.).

16 When I asked Uriel Sánchez in a personal interview in Chicago how he thought the year (2014) was going to end, he confirmed the enforcement of political pressure by the Movement: "We've been escalating through our own means" but "they're gonna be escalating in response to the pressure that they're feeling", he answers (personal interview).

17 By the beginning of 2015, California is one of the 11 states (and Washington, DC) which grant driver's licenses to undocumented immigrants. Students granted DACA can also apply for a driver's license nation-wide.

18 One strategy of political campaigns in the Movement are 'mock graduation ceremonies' which ought to demonstrate the value of education in the immigrant community and the latter's demand for access to higher education (cf. Anguiano 106).

19 See also: Chapter 7 on the written language of the signs in the creation of political meaning.

20 Comprehensive Immigration Reform.

21 In California, the DREAM Act passed in 2011, allowing for in-state tuition to those students that go to Californian universities. It seems to be fitting that Stephanie is one of the earliest narratives published on YouTube with regard to the issue and, obviously, with the rewarding 'success' politically (cf. McGreevy and York).

22 There is need to contextualize this quote further. According to Preston, these figures also show a "pronounced shift away from removals of immigrants living in [...] the country, toward a focus on swift expulsion of those caught crossing the border illegally, particularly along the border with Mexico" (*Deportation* n.pag.).

References

Abdollahi, Mohammad. DreamActivist. "My name is Mohammad and I am Undocumented." Online video clip. *YouTube*. YouTube, 19 Mar. 2010. Web. 22 Dec. 2014.

Anguiano, Claudia A. "Undocumented, Unapologetic, and Unafraid: Discursive Strategies of the Immigrant Youth Dream Social Movement." Diss. U. of New Mexico, 2011. Web. 15 May 2013.

Ashcroft, Bill, Griffiths, Gareth, and Helen Tiffin, eds. *Postcolonial Studies. The Key Concepts*. 3rd ed. Routledge Key Guides. New York: Routledge, 2013.

Bacallao, Martica L., and Paul R. Smokowski. "The Cost of Getting Ahead: Mexican Family System Changes after Immigration." *Family Relations* 56 (2007): 52–66. Web. 8 July 2013.

Badger, Emily, and Kennedy Elliott. "Flow Chart: Who Qualifies for Obama's Immigration Offer?" *The Washington Post* 22 Nov. 2014. *The Washington Post*. Web. 24 Nov. 2014.

Baym, Nancy K. *Tune in, Log on: Soaps, Fandom, and Online Community*. Thousand Oaks, CA: Sage Publications, 2000.

Benítez, Gabriela. Personal interview. 13 March 2014.

Benmayor, Rina. "Digital 'Testimonio' as a Signature Pedagogy for Latin@ Studies." *Equity & Excellence in Education: Univ. of Massachusetts School of Education* 45.3 (2012): 507–524.

Beverley, John. "Testimonio, Subalternity, and Narrative Authority." *Handbook of Qualitative Research*. Ed. Norman K. Denzin and Yvonna S. Lincoln. 2nd ed. Thousand Oaks, CA: Sage Publications, 2000. 555–565.

Butler, Judith. *Excitable Speech: A Politics of the Performative*. New York: Routledge, 1997.

———. *Gender Trouble: Feminism and the Subversion of Identity*. New York: Routledge, 1990.

Butler, Judith, and Athena Athanasiou. *Dispossession: The Performative in the Political*. Cambridge: Polity Press, 2013.

Calderón, Mitzy. SUDDENmovementDotOrg. "I am No Longer Hiding! I am No Longer Afraid!" Online video clip. *YouTube*. YouTube, 13 Nov. 2010. Web. 22 Dec. 2014.

Campbell, Neil, and Alasdair Kean. *American Cultural Studies: An Introduction to American Culture*. 3rd ed. New York: Routledge, 2012.

Chinn, Sarah E. "Performative Identities: From Identity Politics to Queer Theory." *The SAGE Handbook of Identities*. Ed. Margareth Wetherell and Chandra T. Mohanty. Los Angeles, CA: SAGE, 2010. 104–124.

Elam, Harry J., and Michele Elam. "Race and Racial Formations." *The SAGE Handbook of Identities*. Ed. Margareth Wetherell and Chandra T. Mohanty. Los Angeles, CA: SAGE, 2010. 186–200.

Ellis, Lauren M., and Eric C. Chen. "Negotiating Identity Development among Undocumented Immigrant College Students: A Grounded Theory Study." *Journal of Counseling Psychology* 60.2 (2013): 251–264. Web. 6 Aug. 2013.

Esser, Frank, and Jesper Strömbäck, eds. "Mediatization of Politics: Towards a Theoretical Framework." *Mediatization of Politics: Understanding the Transformation of Western Democracies*. New York: Palgrave Macmillan: 2014. 3–28.

Flores-González, Nilda, and Elena R. Gutiérrez. "Taking the Public Square: The National Struggle for Immigrant Rights." *Marcha! Latino Chicago and the Immigrant Rights Movement.* Ed. Amalia Pallares and Nilda Flores-González. Urbana, IL: University of Illinois Press, 2010. 3–36.

Gearty, Lauren. "Voluntary Departure: Who Is Eligible?" *NOLO: Law for All.* N.p. n.d. Web. 27 July 2015.

Gianettoni, Lavinia, and Particia Roux. "Interconnecting Race and Gender Relations: Racism, Sexism and the Attribution of Sexism to the Racialized Other." *Sex Roles* 62 (2010): 374–386. Web. 25 Oct. 2015.

Gilroy, Paul. "Urban Social Movements, 'Race' and Community." *Colonial Discourse and Post-Colonial Theory: A Reader.* Ed. Patrick Williams and Laura Chrisman. New York: Columbia University Press, 1994. 404–420.

Ginsburg, Faye. "Indigenous Counterpublics: A Foreshortened History." *Sensible Politics: The Visual Culture of Nongovernmental Activism.* Ed. Meg McLagan and Yates McKee. New York: Zone Books, 2012. 563–588.

Gugelberger, Georg M., ed. "Introduction: Institutionalization of Transgression: Testimonial Discourse and Beyond." *The Real Thing: Testimonial Discourse and Latin America.* Durham: Duke University Press, 1996. 1–19.

Gutiérrez, Antonio. Personal interview. 25 March 2014.

Herman, David. "Word-Image/Utterance-Gesture: Case Studies in Multimodal Storytelling." *New Perspectives on Narrative and Multimodality.* Ed. Ruth Page. New York: Routledge, 2010. 78–98.

Hernandez, Marcela. Personal interview. 27 March 2014.

Hübler, Axel. "The Role of Electronics in the Perception of Everyday Narratives." *Narrative Revisited: Telling a Story in the Age of New Media.* Ed. Christian R. Hoffmann. Amsterdam: John Benjamins B.V., 2010. 39–55.

Jagger, Gill. *Judith Butler: Sexual Politics, Social Change and the Power of the Performative.* Abington, Oxon: Routledge, 2008.

Jewitt, Carey, ed. Glossary. *The Routledge Handbook of Multimodal Analysis.* London: Routledge, 2009. 293–308.

Kaindl, Klaus. "Multimodality in the Translation of Humour in Comics." *Perspectives on Multimodality.* Ed. Eija Ventola, Cassily Charles and Martin Kaltenbacher. Document Design Companion Series 6. Amsterdam: John Benjamins Publishing Company, 2004. 173–192.

Kavoori, Anandam. *Reading YouTube: The Critical Viewers Guide.* New York: Peter Lang, 2011.

Kim, Gooyong. "The Future of YouTube: Critical Reflections on YouTube Users' Discussion over Its Future." *InterActions: UCLA Journal of Education and Information Studies* 5.2 (2009): 1–30. Web. 21 Aug. 2014.

Kress, Gunther. "What is Mode?" *The Routledge Handbook of Multimodal Analysis.* Ed. Carey Jewitt. London: Routledge, 2009. 54–67.

Langellier, Kristin M., and Eric E. Peterson. "Shifting Contexts in Personal Narrative Performance." *The SAGE Handbook of Performance Studies.* Ed. D. Soyini Madison and Judith Hamera. Thousand Oaks, CA: SAGE, 2006. 151–168.

La Rose, Tara. "Digital Media Stories Through Multimodal Analysis: A Case Study of Erahoneybee's Song about a Child Welfare Agency." *Journal of Technology in Human Services* 30.3–4 (2012): 299–311. Web. 16 Apr. 2015.

Lee, Esther Yu-Hsi. "Florida Governor Signs In-State Tuition Bill for Undocumented Students." *ThinkProgress* 9 June 2014. Web. 22 July 2015.

Lozano, Pepe. "Immigrant Youth Arrested in Georgia after Civil Disobedience." *Peoplesworld.* n.p., 07 Apr. 2011. Web. 09 Mar. 2015.

Maldonado, Luis, and Sheridan Lagunas-Aguirre. "Luis Maldonado: A Brief Look into the Life of an Undocumented Immigrant." Online video clip. *YouTube.* YouTube, 20 Sept. 2013. Web. 9 Sept. 2014.

Manuel, José, et al., eds. Foreword. *PAPERS: Stories by Undocumented Youth.* Portland, OR: Graham Street Productions, 2012. iv–vii.

"Maryland Dream Act." *Montgomery College.* 2015. Web. 30 July 2015.

Mauk, David, and John Oakland. *American Civilization: An Introduction.* 5th ed. New York: Routledge, 2009.

McGreevy, Patrick, and Anthony York. "Brown signs California Dream Act." *Los Angeles Times* 9 Oct. 2011. *Los Angeles Times.* Web. 14 July 2015.

Mittell, Jason. "Film and Television Narrative." *The Cambridge Companion to Narrative.* Ed. David Herman. Cambridge: Cambridge University Press, 2007. 156–171.

Pallares, Amalia. *Family Activism: Immigrant Struggles and the Politics of Noncitizenship.* New Brunswick, Canada: Rutgers University Press, 2015.

———. "Representing 'La Familia': Family Separation and Immigrant Activism." *Marcha! Latino Chicago and the Immigrant Rights Movement.* Ed. Amalia Pallares and Nilda Flores-González. Urbana, IL: University of Illinois Press, 2010. 215–236.

———. "The Chicago Context." *Marcha! Latino Chicago and the Immigrant Rights Movement.* Ed. Amalia Pallares and Nilda Flores-González. Urbana, Chicago, and Springfield: University of Illinois Press, 2010. 37–61.

Patton, Cindy. "Sexualities." *The SAGE Handbook of Identities.* Ed. Margareth Wetherell and Chandra T. Mohanty. Los Angeles, CA: SAGE, 2010. 360–378.

Pérez, William. *Americans by Heart: Undocumented Latino Students and the Promise of Higher Education.* New York: Teachers College Press, 2012.

Pollock, Della. "Moving Histories: Performance and Oral History." *The Cambridge Companion to Performance Studies.* Ed. Tracy C. Davis. Cambridge: Cambridge University Press, 2008. 120–135.

Preston, Julia. "Deportation Up in 2013; Border Sites Were Focus: Deportation Surged in 2013, Data Shows." *The New York Times* 1 Oct. 2014. *The New York Times.* Web. 14 Oct. 2014.

———. "Military Path Opened for Young Immigrants." *The New York Times* 25 Sept. 2014. *The New York Times.* Web. 14 Oct. 2014.

Ramirez, David. Thedreamiscoming2011. "David Ramirez, Immigrant Youth Justice League." Online video clip. *YouTube.* YouTube, 5 Apr. 2011. Web. 22 Dec. 2014.

Roa, Carlos. Cccvideovault. "Carlos: The Story of an Undocumented Student." Online video clip. *YouTube.* YouTube, 21 July 2010. Web. 22 Dec. 2014.

Roman, Ivette. MsKYYoung. "Maryland's Undocumented Immigrant Students – Ivette." Online video clip. *YouTube.* YouTube, 5 Jan. 2013. Web. 22 Dec. 2014.

Rusin, Sylvia. "Addressing the Elephant in the Room: Understanding the Daily Life of Undocumented Latino High School Youth." *Honors Projects 41.* n.p.: Illinois Wesleyan University, 2013. Web. 8 July 2013.

Ryan, Marie-Laure, ed. "Part 1: Face-to-Face Narration." *Narrative across Media: The Languages of Storytelling.* Lincoln: University of Nebraska Press, 2004. 41–46.

———. "Part 3: Moving Pictures." *Narrative across Media: The Languages of Storytelling.* Lincoln: University of Nebraska Press, 2004. 195–201.

———. "Part 5: Digital Media." *Narrative across Media: The Languages of Storytelling.* Lincoln: University of Nebraska Press, 2004. 329–335.

Sánchez, Uriel. Personal interview. 24 March 2014.

Segal, Lynne. "Genders: Deconstructed, Reconstructed, Still on the Move." *The SAGE Handbook of Identities.* Ed. Margareth Wetherell and Chandra T. Mohanty. Los Angeles, CA: SAGE, 2010. 321–338.

Shear, Michael D. "Obama, Daring Congress, Acts to Overhaul Immigration." *The New York Times* 20 Nov. 2014. *The New York Times.* Web. 23 Nov. 2014.

Shear, Michael D, and Robert Pear. "Obama's Immigration Plan Could Shield Five Million." *The New York Times* 19 Nov. 2014. *The New York Times.* Web. 23 Nov. 2014.

Sipe, Dan. "The Future of Oral History and Moving Images." *The Oral History Reader.* Ed. Robert Perks and Alistair Thomson. London: Routledge, 1998. 379–388.

Solis, Stephanie. UndergroundAtBrown. "Lost & Found (Story of a DREAM Act Student)." Online video clip. *YouTube.* YouTube, 12 May 2009. Web. 5 Nov. 2013.

Stöckl, Hartmut. "In Between Modes: Language and Image in Printed Media." *Perspectives on Multimodality.* Ed. Eija Ventola, Cassily Charles and Martin Kaltenbacher. Document Design Companion Series 6. Amsterdam: John Benjamins Publishing Company, 2004. 9–30.

Velazquillo, Angelica. Mercy Sister. "An Undocumented Immigrant, Angelica, Tells Her Story." Online video clip. *YouTube.* YouTube, 2 Mar. 2012. Web. 22 Dec. 2014.

Wetherell, Margaret. "The Field of Identity Studies." *The SAGE Handbook of Identities.* Ed. Margaret Wetherell and Chandra T. Mohanty. Los Angeles, CA: SAGE, 2010. 3–26.

Wildfeuer, Janina. *Film Discourse Interpretation: Towards a New Paradigm for Multimodal Film Analysis.* New York: Routledge, 2014.

Wright, Tequan. "Immigration Reform Laws and Deportation 2014: Pew Research Study Reveals Most Deportations of Undocumented Immigrants are Due to 'Unlawful Reentry'." *Latin Post.* 20 Mar. 2014. *Latin Post.* Web. 3 Aug. 2015.

Yoshikawa, Hirokazu. *Immigrants Raising Citizens: Undocumented Parents and Their Young Children.* New York: Russell Sage Foundation, 2011.

6 Activism in soundscape

Voice, noises, and music in digital narratives

1. Introduction: orality, sound, and the performance of resistance in digital *testimonios*

The production of a 'traditional' *testimonio* "generally involves the tape-recording and then the transcription and editing of an oral account by an interlocutor who is a journalist, ethnographer, [...] literary author" (Beverley, *Narrative Authority* 555–556). Crucial to the political context is the fact the interlocutor could also be called a "social activist" (Beverley and Zimmerman in: Ashcroft et al. 259). The digital *testimonio*, too, is created by the recording of the narrator's voice in a one-on-one conversation between the narrator and the "facilitator" (Benmayor 510). Thus, the production process of the digital *testimonio* is similar to that of the traditional *testimonio*, yet moves a step further away from other forms of 'oral history': This genre is often linked to the *testimonio* but relies strictly on the "research methodology" that the researcher defines for his/her purposes (Abrams 2). In the production of *testimonio*, the interlocutor's role in the production is diminished. In addition to the verbal narrative of the undocumented narrator, other possible participants or voices and noises from the immediate surroundings need to be recognized as important constituents of meaning in the narratives. The analysis of this aspect in one narrative, that of Ivette, that demonstrates the role that other 'voices' play in the videos and the meaning they might play in digital *testimonios*.

A central distinction between the two *testimonios* is the retention of the actual, physical voice in the final story. Apart from the dominance of the visual moving image, the digital *testimonio* generally produces a spoken account – not a written (published by the interlocutor).[1] The digital *testimonio* thus reestablishes the connection to the original form of oral history, as the latter "deals with the spoken word" and rigorously defines itself by this "character of orality" (Abrams 19). Digital *testimonios*, too, relate the spoken word "to social action" and represent "oral narrative[s] of personal experience as a source of knowledge, empowerment, and political strategy for claiming rights and bringing about social change" (Benmayor et al. 153). The following sections investigate the effect of 'orality' and voice and which role they play in the creation of political meaning in the selected digital *testimonios.* Yet, which effect does digital editing, including the combination of voice and music, have on the orality of a *testimonio*?

While the narrator of the traditional *testimonio*, as also in other forms of oral history, is excluded from 'crafting' and publishing the final version of the *testimonio*, the narrator of the digital one is not as strictly excluded from the 'crafting' process, as his/her spoken voice *literally* always *remains* in the final product. There is no (language) transcription and editing process on part of the interlocutor. In the digital *testimonio*, the spoken voice enters into a production process prior to the recording of the video, which includes practicing, editing, and performing 'the story' of dispossession. In the Center for Digital Storytelling in California, for instance, the students make sure to follow "oral speech patterns" despite the preparation and practice (Benmayor 513). While the production steps she traces are parallel to those of the traditional *testimonio*, her account also rekindles one of the most heated debates in testimonial discourse: How are truth, authenticity, and reliability of historical fact 'guaranteed' in a production process characterized by so many performative elements? Instead of falling back into this interminable debate, one that vexes all online narrative genres, the question for this chapter will be posed in reverse: How do vocal features, sounds, and music add a level of performative meaning to the spoken account, and what conclusions can be made about an explicit political agenda?

Regarding digital *testimonios* as performances that consist of materialized (performative) utterances emphasizes the unique semantic functions of verbal modes of communication in the creation of political meaning and power through the medium of voice. According to Pollock, performance studies theory distinguishes, in particular, "between the narrated event (what is *told* of the past) and the narrating event (the *telling* of it in the present)" (120). She further stresses that performance is "the living tissue that connects story and event in tenuous processes of meaning-making" (121), instead of reading the distinction between narrated and narrating event "as a conventional distinction between content and form, text and performance" (120). Theory from the field of Sound Studies on the effects of music and sounds in narratives similarly asserts that power dynamics lie in orality itself, assigning political value to the narrator's physical voice. Sterne explains that "voice has long been conflated with ideas of agency" (9), underlining the idea that performative verbal utterances actually *do* something, shifting the generic understanding from narrative as descriptive to performative.

In digital *testimonios*, it is the voice that gives them their power, not the image, compelling the viewer to 'listen' (cf. Benmayor 513). Likewise, Portelli finds that spoken narrative voice more emphatically "reveal[s] the narrators' emotions, their participation in the story, and the way the story affected them" (65). He argues that "this often involves attitudes which speakers may not be able (or willing) to express otherwise, or elements which are not fully within their control" (65–66). He says of oral narrative transcriptions, "by abolishing these traits, we flatten the emotional content of the speech down to the supposed equanimity and objectivity of the written document" (66). Thus, "in the search for a distinguishing factor, we must [...] turn in the first place to form" (65).

In her analysis of accounts of oral history, Pollock finds that "what is said is inseparable from the saying of it"; "indeed, understanding 'what is said' would be sorely compromised without understanding the complexities and complicities entailed in saying it" (127). As West shows, "sound", in particular, "has an ability to bypass the linguistic system of awareness and stimulate emotions in ways that we are less verbally conscious of" (285). In the analysis of the meaning of voice in spoken (testimonial) narrative, Abrams, however, demands "close attention to orality" – *how* something is said – such as "the shape and rhythm of the speech act, because these are taken to be capable of revealing important attributes of the story, the contents, the practice of telling and the culture which produces it" (19). Further, "orality comprises the rhythms and cadences, repetitions and intonations, the use of particular speech forms such as anecdote or reported speech, the use of dialect, as well as the volume, tone and speed" that are all crucial for the interpretation of the oral tradition of narrative (ibid). According to Stöckl, "volume, intonation, timbre, rhythm, speed or pausing, [...] are design features of language in its spoken form and are often termed para-verbal" (11) or "vocal gestures" (Hübler 46). As with all gestures, "meaning potentials" are also "metaphor potentials", according to Van Leeuwen, which are "very broad" in their interpretation (70).

In two of the eight *testimonios*, music is part of the multimodal ensemble.[2] Current findings in brain research on the effects of emotion on voice and music indicate that "similar mechanisms support emotional inferences from vocalizations and music and that these mechanisms tap on a general system involved in social cognition" (Escoffier et al. 1796). Klüppelholz also stresses the inherent kinship of the sound of voice and music in its interpretation, calling not only for a similar but also inclusive method for interpretation that incorporates both – the sound of music and that of the voice – in one, coherent analysis.[3] Stöckl adds to this perspective that language, in contrast to music, for example, works on the "denotative" levels of meaning, while the latter is "strong on associative meaning" (26; see also Lexmann 55). In the two narratives, for instance, music takes the shape of a 'leitmotif'. The latter, according to West, defines as a "distinct musical theme[...] associated with characters, places or ideas within a particular work of music", which "is usually a short melody, a certain chord progression, or a rhythmic pattern", and which can "supplement or extend the plot" (286).

Lastly, because of 'synchresis', the automatic forging and mental fusion between sound and visual images when being played at the same time, it is mostly impossible to separate the sound level from the visual level in any type of film. In this context, we must stress that in digital *testimonios*, meanings created by the "multimodal ensemble" are "corresponding, complementary and dissonant as they harmonize in an integrated whole" (Jewitt 301). Therefore, this chapter mostly presents "interrelationships between co-present modes" – the sound *in combination* with the visual images – rather than the solitary creation of meaning of individual modes. In the narratives, voice and visual recordings are mostly congruent (although voice-overs and, thus, the exclusive recording of the voice of the narrator also take place). Along the same lines, the socio-technological format of YouTube video clips affords the montage of the moving image and its original soundtrack. It offers multiple ways of adding or subtracting original verbal language and sound, as well as sounds from the off, to the video. Benmayor considers the montage of image and sound to be crucial for producing meaning in digital *testimonios*. The digital medium encourages the 'staging' of 'the voice' with a musical soundtrack or visual esthetics (cf. Benmayor 521). Taking these attributes into consideration, analyzing the creation of political meaning in the use of voice in the soundscape of the digital *testimonios* on YouTube appears particularly promising in the assessment of the mediatization of politics. This analysis will focus upon the mediatization of voice; its 'power' and its potential to 'protest'; and the individual voice as a sense of signature, ritual, and personalization of the Movement given to the dispossessed.

2. Connecting traditions: collective ritual in digital *testimonios*

Despite the fact that "each individual *testimonio* evokes an absent polyphony of other voices, other possible lives and experiences" (Beverley, *Narrative Authority* 557), the narrative voice in traditional *testimonios* assumes the form of "the voice of a singular subject" (*Testimonio* xii). This voice is meant to be experienced by the reader as that

> of a *real* rather than fictional person, is the mark of the desire not to be silenced or defeated, to impose oneself on an institution of power or privilege from the position of the excluded, the marginal, the subaltern. Hence the insistence on the importance of a personal name or identity evident sometimes in titles of *testimonios*, such as *I, Rigoberta Menchú*. (*Narrative Authority* 556)

This personal pattern of introduction like Menchú's can be found in six of the eight digital *testimonios*. This introduction, however, does not take the form of a word-for-word imitation. Rather, the emphasis lies on the positioning of the name to the undocumented status. The connection to the *testimonio*'s introductory pattern, in particular, lies in the 'coming outs' of undocumented youth. Here, the synthesis of the original, physical voice with the narrative voice in digital *testimonios* is made possible precisely through the mediatization of the physical voice. Just like Menchú who, according to Yúdice, "clearly conceives of her testimonial as [...] a performative speech" (55),

On a content level, Menchú not only communicates her name and 'age', she also classifies her account as a testimony of her life as well as that of a whole nation of people, as the quote from her book shows:

> My name is Rigoberta Menchú. I am twenty three years old. This is my testimony. [...] I'd like to stress that it's not only *my* life, it's also the testimonio of my people. [...] My story is the story of all poor Guatemalans. My personal experience is the reality of a whole people.
>
> (1)

The introduction to her *testimonio* fuses personal, autobiographical detail with the political representation of her community *through* the act of telling the narrative, which makes it, inherently, a testimonial statement. It requires, on the one hand, "that these writers *stage* themselves" (Hunsaker 8). With regard to *testimonio*, Menchú, however, embeds her narrative "in the life of the community, just as her 'I' is embedded and absolutely tied to a 'we'" (Zimmerman 113). Thus, if understanding digital narratives of undocumented youth as *testimonios*, it is necessary to stress that the stories of dispossession play with the blending of "the *personal self*", and "individuated self-concept", with the "*collective self*, which corresponds to the concept of social identity", according to Brewer and Gardner's distinction (84).

Further, the oral form of narrative voice in digital *testimonios* adds perceived authenticity to the narrative's outing of 'undocumented status' to an unknown audience because, as Sterne argues, "voices are among the most personalized and most naturalized forms of subjective self-expression" (491). Hearing "embodied, sonorous" voices, "belonging to real people", confirms "for us, in vital ways, who we are, where we are, and what it is we are going about doing", Kimbrough adds (264). As undocumented youth rise from the despised underground – the shadow that is illuminated through this very act – the combination of the physical and narrative voice represents a "'humanising element'", as Murphet explains, an "aspect of narration that seems to proceed directly from a human consciousness" (76). The digital *testimonio* humanizes its narrator through the use of the narrator's *own*, unique voice. In combination with the visuals, the voice, the name, autobiographical data, and the declaration of the undocumented status serves as an individual signature: a ritual that all undocumented youth can reproduce yet completely individualize in the spirit of individual output on platforms such as YouTube.

Undocumented youth transform a reference to tradition or ritual, one could claim, through the performative use of their voice, which ascertains their recognition as a coherent Movement by means of their digital *testimonios*. This 'ritual' is, as indicated above, performative in nature. Through the pattern, undocumented youth ascribe a sense of collective identity (within and outside of the Movement), belonging *to each other*. As Albiez et al. explain, "the performative dimension of *belonging* [...] raises the issue of social representations that result from repetitive practices". (15). Likewise, in *Excitable Speech*, Judith Butler wrote:

> The performative is not a singular act used by an already established subject, but one of the powerful and insidious way in which subjects are called into social being from diffuse social quarters, inaugurated into sociality by a variety of diffuse and powerful interpellations. In this sense the social performative is a crucial part not only of subject formation, but of the ongoing political contestation and reformulation of the subject as well. The performative is not only a ritual practice: it is one of the influential rituals by which subjects are formed and reformulated. (160)

Linking their story to a common practice, thus, forms their identity *in* and belonging *to* the Movement that then results in the reformulation of their dispossessed identity, as it becomes 'recognizable'. Forming a common 'body' of dispossession through this introductory pattern, undocumented youths produce a common ground for recognition, claiming their places as 'human' in current discourse (cf. Butler and Athanasiou 90).

The logic of YouTube fortifies the struggle for recognition – a process that is again highly regulated by norms – led by undocumented youth through the personalization in online communities. As Baym found, users in autobiographical online forums "generally use real names, which create congruence between on-and offline identities" and "a good deal of self-disclosure, which is one of the main ways in which they let other people know who they are" (152).[4] Having a 'ritual' to establish a sense of community, further, assumes "a highly social integrative function" (Hjarvard 18). Through performing common affiliation, in sum, undocumented youth shift the "contexts of bodies, situations, and discursive forces" (Langellier and Peterson 166).

As stated before, six of the eight narratives employ an introduction resembling Menchú's. Six of the eight narrators state their name as the first aspect in their narrative (all but Stephanie Solis (1) and Luis Maldonado (8)); the following sentences introduce the "undocumented" status (again in six of the narratives; not in Stephanie Solis (1) and Carlos Roa's (3) narratives).[5] Frequently, age (in three of the narratives), country of origin (in six of the narratives), age at migration (in six of the narratives), and sexual identity (in two of the narratives) are also revealed within the closely following sentences. During this performance, all narrators focus on the camera and do not use any other intermedial storytelling devices besides their voice, underlining the importance of this act of 'outing oneself'. The idiosyncrasies of the individual performances add further levels of meaning to the performance of the testimonial introduction, which the following section shows in detail by means of four of the narratives. The 'double' sense of outing – disclosing their sexuality in addition to the undocumented status – that can be found in Ivette Roman (7) and Luis Maldonado's (8) narratives will be discussed in Section 3 of this chapter.

Mohammad Abdollahi (2): guidelines for coming out online

Among the eight digital *testimonios*, Mohammad Abdollahi's (2) performance of the 'meta-level' of offline and online organizing is unique. Right at the beginning of his video, he announces that there are guidelines in the *DreamActivist* online network for other undocumented youth to follow when creating a personal 'coming-out' video, claiming that "the most important thing for [them] to say is 'my name is' and 'I'm undocumented'" (00:00:22–00:00:25). These guidelines subordinate individual freedom in producing and publishing narratives of undocumented youth on YouTube. However, the performative act of 'coming out' itself necessitates mentioning the name and the undocumented status together at some point in the narrative.

Setting up these guidelines puts Mohammad in a leading position in the undocumented online community (whom he imagines watching his video and whom he addresses frequently). This is possible, as Baym explains, because "any group can take new directions at any time because of the influence of a single contributor" (201). This aspect forms a strong parallel between Mohammad's envisioning and addressing of his audience and Menchú's *testimonio*: As Menchú addresses her reader with 'you' occasionally (cf. 20), according to Sommer, "she implies both the existing relationship to other representative selves in the community and the potential relationships that extend her community through the text" (152). The effect of this address is that 'we readers' "identify with the narrator's project and, by extension, with the political community to which she belongs" (ibid). Mohammad, too, stresses that the community that watches his video is like-minded and supportive of the cause, idealizing YouTube as a public space for their political output and participation. This, Baym reminds us, essentially locates "the romance of Internet community in a nostalgia for the homogenous small town" (206).

Moreover, after explicitly repeating the guidelines for online storytelling, Mohammad repeats his introduction, explaining that he intended to not only give the guidelines but also that this was "how [he] was gonna start off [his] video" (00:00:27). Performing his story according to the guidelines emphasizes that undocumented youth like him, dispossessed by their undocumented status, can come out online and be actually *recognized* as belonging to the Movement, which, in turn, triggers a nationwide support as Mohammad stresses toward the end of his *testimonio*. Applying Athanasiou and Butler's concept at this point, 'recognition' is based on established identity categories. By building essential elements for a new, *recognized* identity – that of undocumented youth – Mohammad counters the regulation of recognition in his society. At the same time, Mohammad also performs according to these 'new rules' to secure the association with this identity. Further, Mohammad individualizes digital coming out narratives on YouTube by marking them as belonging to the newly found activism that he is part of.

A further important political move that Mohammad performs through spoken word describes the work he did in activism as a realization that there were so many other undocumented students in his situation, stressing the interstate cooperation and the "amazing" work of this organization. By presenting himself as one of the founders of this organization, he, again, empowers himself over the other undocumented students, although, a few seconds earlier, he had just told his audience how he felt like there were many like him 'out there'. This impression is rendered, in particular, by naming the names and states of other who started organizing in the year of 2010. Selecting particular states that are far away from each other, his list of names and states conveys a sense of nationwide support just by naming them (00:04:12–00:04:20). His speech act, hence, is performative. By locating the activism of undocumented youth across the whole United States on an imaginary map, Mohammad stresses unity and mutual support of each other across all boundaries. His online *testimonio* is, after all, a prominent example for organizing via social (and new) media and for *naming* this support.

Carlos Roa (3): a voice from the off

Carlos Roa's narrative is one of those two *digital testimonios* in this selection that does not perform the collective testimonial introductory tradition introduced above. Instead, a voice-over introduces *his* spoken narrative,[6] saying: "My name is Carlos Roa and I am America" (00:00:16–00:00:19), while a black-and-white moving image appears on the screen. Since the viewer is introduced to Carlos via the voice from the off, the visual, which shows Carlos smiling and only slightly nodding but otherwise not producing any further narrative action, creates the effect that the spoken word is much more important than the visual image in this sequence. Through the black-and-white image, the voice seems much closer and more full of life than the visual. While Carlos does not state that he is undocumented until later in the narrative, this technique connects his narrative to the oral tradition of the *testimonio* and thus de-emphasizes the visual turn that YouTube reinforced.[7]

David Ramirez (4): the ritual

While introducing his digital *testimonio*, David's voice makes notable changes, compared to the rest of this speech. Toward the end of the short sentence, his intonation rises significantly and a pronounced break follows. The features indicate that David lists these individual elements and is careful not to forget any of them, as they represent and determine the 'emergency' state that he finds himself in. Further, 'listing' these elements denotes that many an undocumented student has 'come out' this way to the public prior to his own *testimonio*. Repeating these words, hence, in form of a 'sonic' list symbolizes yet another act of plural performativity in the digital *testimonio*.

Mitzy Calderón (6): outing oneself

Mitzy's greeting of the viewer is cheerful. Her head is bent slightly toward one side and she smiles, appearing as a self-confident narrator with an upbeat beginning of her video. Most notably, the paralinguistic features of her voice do not change, nor do her facial expressions, when she introduces herself and her immigration story. After introducing her name, age, and undocumented status (00:00:00–00:00:04) in the familiar structure that we have already established, she nods her head in confirmation as she claims that "a lot of people can relate to [her] situation" (00:00:08–00:00:11). The viewer can further see a slight smile in her face when she enunciates this sentence; however, she moves on very quickly, signaling that the focus in her video does not lie on her family and immigration background and history. The introduction seems rehearsed, as it leaves out many natural pauses, sounding dispassionate. Considering that within the first four seconds, Mitzy has 'outed' herself to millions of potential viewers, she indeed seems to feel self-confident and 'unafraid'. We assume that this personal online narrative is not Mitzy's first disclosure of her status. In any case, the viewer senses that this introduction represses emotional events in Mitzy's life, perhaps her immigration story and introduces another focus of the story to follow.

3. A voice for all?

3.1. The appropriation of voice: naming

Undocumented youth narrators humanize the struggle of 'the dispossessed' with their personal narrative, while they, at the same time, form a performative ritual that serves collective identification and recognition processes. Undocumented youth narrators further establish connections to the Movement and their 'community' via the spoken word by means of 'naming', one aspect of the 'politics of performativity' (cf. Butler and Athanasiou 99).Due to the multiplicity of different struggles nowadays, the process of naming connects dispossession back to identity politics. "In the face of the proliferation of modes, names, occasions, or social ontologies of dispossession (of refugees, immigrants, exiles, expatriates, LGBTQ persons)", Athanasiou explains, "we are venturing a return to identity politics, through precisely performative forms of naming" (134). "If we are always named by others" – a condition that Butler and Athanasiou advocate – "then the name signifies a certain dispossession from the start. If we seek to name ourselves, it is still within a language that we never made" (Butler and Athanasiou 137).

According to Butler's earlier work on the performative, "name-calling may be the initiating moment of a counter-mobilization", because "the name one is called both subordinates and enables, producing a scene of agency from ambivalence, a set of effects that exceed the animating intentions of the call" (*Excitable Speech* 163).[8] Since the language we use to address our political dissent has been created (be)for(e) us, this speech act becomes a 'performative occasion' itself (cf. Butler and Athanasiou 143). This act, nevertheless, causes confusion and a search for 'the right name' for something we wish to be replaced.

Through the politics of performative, "recalls, norms, names, signs, practices, and regulatory fictions can be invoked, cited anew, and challenged at once" (Butler and Athanasiou 99). Because of the provocative power of performative acts, as Chinn notes, they often elicit severe criticism as "inappropriate" forms of mockery (115).

In conclusion, Athanasiou argues, "naming is not only a site of trauma, but also potentially a strategy of subversive mimesis" (139). The potential of the testimonial tradition here lies in the resistant self-determination that does not seek "recourse to the grand narrative of the self-contained, self-sufficient individual" but rather "within and against this normative narrative" (Butler and Athanasiou 99). Likewise, Yúdice argues that *testimonio* "gives a personal specificity to those marginalized and oppressed elements of which she [Menchú] herself is one" (57). "Self-naming", thus, becomes crucial when "people struggle with what to name themselves, how to change the name, how to petition that others use the name that they wish" (Butler and Athanasiou 137). The examples in this section will show not only how undocumented youth narrators name themselves in their digital *testimonios* but also how they name 'others' within and outside of the Immigrant Rights Movement since 2006. The narratives of Ivette Roman (7) and Luis Maldonado (8) serve as examples for the connection of the Movement to the gay rights movement in the United States.

Stephanie Solis (1): materializing voices for the undocumented

The most significant contribution that sound makes to Stephanie Solis' (1) otherwise very visually animated digital *testimonio* is the moment in which the visual space portrayed in the video is completely empty (all we see is a black screen). One can only hear Stephanie's voice from the off saying: "Stephanie is eighteen years old and I don't exist" (00:00:33–00:00:36). This statement of course is a contradiction. More contradictory, however, is the combination of the existence of a voice with the lack of any type of corporeality and materiality visible in these seconds of the clip. Other than explicitly pronouncing the materiality and existence of the dispossessed body, this moment portrays Stephanie's dispossession as no other medium could. Written or face-to-face *testimonios* would not be able to show a 'non-existing' body as well as a dark screen and a voice from the off could. The voice itself denotes an existence of the undocumented that is very 'close' to the viewer – an impression created by the sole focus on the auditory channel. The lack of the visual channel, however, creates even more effectively a non-existence that relates to the meaning of being 'undocumented' or 'in the shadows'. The technological affordances of video-making, hence, are crucial to the expression of dispossession among undocumented immigrants like Stephanie, while the media logic itself stresses visual culture and the visualization of the personal. Therefore, this emphasis on the voice distinguishes her *testimonio* from other YouTube clips, in which the visual performance and meaning is always most prominent.

Angelica Velazquillo (5): emphasizing political logic

Angelica Velazquillo's digital *testimonio*, most notably, does not use any interactive linguistic features (such as the pronoun 'you') to address her audience. However, the narrative ends with a short "thank you". The impression that this ending creates is that Angelica was indeed a 'witness' who would not be interrupted during her speech, requesting undivided attention from her viewer. In this respect, Angelica actively breaks with the media logic of YouTube, which uses its video and text functions on the website to "include a notion of an interactive audience" (Lange 23). By not 'speaking' to the audience throughout her video, Angelica does not invite response either. Further, thanking her audience for listening to her purports a voice – as in the traditional *testimonio* – that is "not to be silenced or defeated" throughout her speech (Beverley, *Narrative Authority* 556). At the same time, Angelia, however, ensures to establish "narrative contract with the reader" (557).

Mitzy Calderón (6): "our" movement: undocumented, unafraid, unapologetic

As we have seen earlier in this chapter, Mitzy's outing as 'undocumented' and her consistent use of vocal features, in particular, reveal that her core story of dispossession is not being undocumented but rather the dispossession she experiences as she is being 'moved by others', highlighting her dependency on a social security number as that criterion which determines whether she is considered an American in the eyes of the Other.

Toward the end of her narrative, Mitzy establishes a link to Freedom University in Georgia, which she describes as an alternative college that accepts students "no matter of [their] sexual orientation, you know, [their] race, [their] status" (00:05:33–00:05:37). In this speech act, Mitzy positions all other universities (at least in Georgia) as discriminatory of all these groups and confirms, as we have seen in Chapter 5, that to her, the intersections between race and undocumented status are very tight. Also toward the end of her digital *testimonio*, Mitzy performs the motto of that year in very clear words, as she claims:

> I can actually now sit here and tell you that I am no longer ashamed, I am no longer living in the shadows, I am no longer hiding. And I can tell you I am undocumented and I am proud to say it.
>
> (00:05:44–00:05:57)

The confidence displayed in these sentences performs the message of the revived Immigrant Rights Movement in very clear terms. What is clearly recognizable in this narrative is the change in confidence with which undocumented youth around 2012 came out as undocumented. With reference to the California DREAM Act, Pérez observes an increased likelihood for students to come out of the shadows with "high confidence" and "in stark contrast to the stigma they all felt prior to the law" (82). Moreover, "these findings suggest", according to Pérez, "that laws have the potential to transform social identities and encourage political mobilization" (ibid).

Likewise, I suggest here, Mitzy performs not only her current confidence but also the affective dimension of her dispossession that she felt prior to her coming out of the shadows and, possibly, the announcement of the DACA (roughly five months before the publication of her digital *testimonio* on YouTube). She argues not only that she is not afraid or hiding, but also that she is not doing that *anymore*, implying that up to that point, she had been afraid and hiding her whole life. With her statement, Mitzy refers to other *testimonios* of undocumented youth and establishes a solid link to the Immigrant Rights Movement since 2006. By 2011, "the motto of this new undocumented youth movement ha[d] become 'Undocumented & Unafraid'", according to (Pérez 88; Anguiano xi) and in the year of 2012 would further develop into 'unapologetic'. Since both of these phrases originated from members of the Immigrant Youth Justice League (IYJL), I personally asked Antonio Gutiérrez, one of the active organizers, about the origin of those words:

A.G.: [...] The 'undocumented – unafraid – unapologetic' is a symbol, or the phrase that IYJL got known for nationwide. And now, it's like a *national* thing. I mean, I just remember, one of the first trips that I was able to be part of is, I went to a conference in D.C. where I was part. NDLON was organizing it. [...] It was really the first conference to really unite all the best organizations, all the organizations that wanted to come and be part of the discussion to really talk about these deportation issues. [...] And I just remember, after we had our conferences and discussions and stuff, we also wanted to go out and we went to a bar, a couple of us and stuff, and I just remember, there was some other group there that was also undocumented and it was odd. I think at one point, we started chanting like "undocumented – unafraid!" and *every*body in that bar, whether it was maybe four of us that were from IYJL, everybody in that bar starting chanting with us. Because it became something that is well-known nationally. And that's how we reconnect with other people and so the Movement becomes national, I believe.

S.Q.: And the 'unapologetic' – that came a bit later, right?

A.G.: Yes. So, that came a little later and that's when we were really just frustrated with the situation, I think. I think it was, really that was when the 'DREAM Act', the national 'DREAM Act' failed. And that's

> when people started getting really kinda upset about the whole situation. It wasn't about, anymore, about saying that you were undocumented, and you were also not scared to put yourself on the line, or to show yourself, so to come out of the shadows but it was also to this point of like they really wanted us to say that we were sorry and that it was our fault that we were here. And that was not the case.
>
> (personal interview)

What Antonio's account shows particularly well is the level of frustration that played into the formation of those performative motto words for the Movement. Reiterating the words "undocumented" and "unashamed" in her narrative strongly connects her *testimonio* to a common cause, a common identity within the Movement, and, thus, transforms it into a counter-discursive strategy against the dispossession of undocumented youth due to their status not only in Georgia, but nationwide.

3.2. 'Undocu-queer' performances

What needs to be stressed is, first and foremost, the intersectionality of dispossessed identities. Therefore, what really unites the gay liberation movement with Luis Maldonado's, Ivette Roman's, and Mohammad Abdollahi's *testimonios* is the shared history of oppression that their community has encountered through identifying as gay/lesbian. Outing themselves as undocumented and gay[9] in their *testimonios*, thus, transforms the latter into a performative act that unites both struggles against dispossession.

Frequently observing the intertwinement of the gay and the Immigrant Rights Movement, Pallares highlights that undocumented "youth have openly articulated the ways in which their coming out strategy was inspired by [...] the gay liberation movement, and the civil disobedience strategy from the civil rights movement", realizing "their relationship to these traditions" (*Family Activism* 123; see also Pallares, *Representing 'La Familia'* 225). As briefly introduced in Chapter 2, with the Coming Out of the Shadows Day, the IYJL "clearly drew on the rhetorical strategies of gay and lesbian politics in calling on undocumented migrants to 'come out' about their migration status and march for legalization" (White 990).

This, first reference is connected to the performative speech act of 'coming out of the closet'. Sedgwick's *Epistemology of the Closet* (1990) defines "'closeted-ness'" as "a performance initiated as such by the speech act of a silence – not a particular silence, but a silence that accrues particularity by fits and starts, in relation to the discourse that surrounds and differentially constitutes it" (3). Further, coming out of the closet also counters 'shame', although, as Sedgwick shows, "there are psychological operations of shame, denial, projection around 'ignorance' that make it an especially galvanizing category" (7–8). Thus, a great number of undocumented students are actually 'coming out' in a twofold sense: They do not only 'come out of the closet' with regard to their status but also testify to potentially everybody who has access to the Internet or print media that they are also gay/lesbian. These narrators seem to bring themselves in a dual danger: that of deportation in addition to processes of moralization on the part of mostly conservative individuals in our society. This 'dual danger', inherently at work at the intersection of identities, has only more recently, according to Pallares, become more popular in the Movement. The author finds that "the 'undocuqueer' identity becomes increasingly politicized", expanding the definition of the 'worthy' immigrant family (*Family Activism* 127).

Judith Butler's *Gender Trouble*, according to Segal, called for queer theorists "to expose the linguistic mobility, or performativity, of both sexed bodies and gender categories", meaning that "the human body was seen as acquiring its sexed makings through the range of discourses available" (329). The "active/passive binary (or 'heterosexual matrix') for distinguishing male from female performance" was disrupted (ibid). An important discourse parallel between the political struggle of undocumented youth and that in the queer movement, hence, is that both movements disrupt established notions of binaries on the part of the queer rights movement and American/not American as paradigms of protest in the Immigrant Rights Movement. One could argue that the 'national matrix' is disrupted in the latter. In Ivette Roman and Luis Maldonado's narratives, the 'coming outs' break 'the norm' in similar ways. The contrast between both is that for Ivette, the coming out as a lesbian was many times more traumatic than the undocumented 'coming out', making the former the core story of dispossession in her narrative. To Luis, in contrast, the coming out as 'undocumented' was a lot more "nerve-wracking moment" (00:00:49–00:00:53). Both narrators, however, actively connect their homosexual identity to the undocumented Immigrant Rights Movement.

Ivette Roman (7): a voice for acceptance

In the end of her narrative, Ivette Roman explicitly triggers a connection to the gay rights movement, claiming:

> I'm just here, trying to get a future. I want the same … I want the same rights as they do. I'm still just like them. Looking for something better to do with my life. And … so my mother could be proud of me.
>
> (00:04:09–00:04:30)

In this statement, Ivette positions her *coming out as undocumented*-narrative into her *coming out as homosexual*-narrative, by combining her mother's sense of pride for her daughter (and Ivette's work in activism) with a general fight for 'a better future' – an endeavor that necessarily needs to be connected to the context of undocumented immigrant student activism, in which Ivette clearly positions herself. As Ivette narrates her story of dispossession, revealing her coming out to her mother, with strong, visible emotional impact, she emphasizes the fact that she belongs to 'more vulnerable groups' in the Movement. The latter, according to Pallares, include, in particular,

> undocumented families with no citizen children; LGBT immigrants who are not married or whose marriage is not recognized by the federal government for immigration purposes; immigrants not eligible for the military, immigrants not able to study; and adults who have aged out of DREAM.
>
> (*Family Activism* 130)

Offering the viewer a resolution that stresses how she and her mother are now "working together", highlights the intersections of and unites Ivette's struggle in undocumented youth rights activism with her lesbian identity. Yet, the viewer does not know whether the two are now working together professionally, on a personal relationship basis, or for the 'undocu-queer' movement. Nevertheless, this resolution in the form of the mother's accepting of her daughter is necessary for the viewer to understand that Ivette's resistance against the sexual dispossession and the dispossession caused by her undocumented status, is a struggle that works only on the basis of its intersections. However, the 'resolution' of the mother-daughter conflict also signals that the social acceptance of homosexuality can be 'resolved', while undocumented immigration status cannot. Thus, Ivette highlights the need for a collective and united struggle against the norms that dispossess undocumented immigrants in the United States. Antonio Gutiérrez, an undocu-queer leader in the IYJL, describes the crucial need to continue this struggle:

> I feel like, in both situations, in both groups, I have found myself in situations where one of my identities is not well-taken in that space. Or that they don't wanna support that side of me. [...] They're definitely connecting a little more now and interconnecting and working together a little more but I feel that there's still a big distinction between the immigration movement and the human rights movement and that's unfortunate because we could be *so* much stronger if we just unite them both at the same time.
>
> (personal interview)

Luis Maldonado (8): verbal naming: positioning and resistance

Within the frame of the introductory testimonial pattern that we have established for the digital *testimonio* in the previous section, Luis introduces his video and himself by affirming: "I'm undocumented and unafraid, queer and unashamed. My name is Luis Maldonado" (00:00–00:07). The order in which Luis makes claims about his identity suggests that among his multiple identities, the undocumented identity comes first, and his queer identify comes second (even before his first name). With regard to immigration, and his *immigration* story, as the narrative is named, it makes sense that the undocumented identity comes first. But why, then, did Luis not name any other parts of his identity? To answer that question, it is evident that these two parts of his identities are the ones that 'struggle with the norm' in Luis' fight against dispossession. Further, the political connection between the two emphasizes the united struggle between the gay and the Immigrant Rights Movement, as explained earlier.

Luis shows, first of all, how his queer identity is a solid part of himself, giving the term 'unashamed' an additional meaning: In the current Movement, 'unashamed' is used by undocumented youth (now most likely to have DACA) to refer to their parents – taking away the blame and guilt that was thrust upon them in an early phase of the Movement in order to demand a national or federal legalization of the DREAM Act. Luis now actively uses this term to establish the link between his two identities: his homosexuality and his undocumented status. Through its history of oppression and discrimination, homosexuality is connected to 'shame', as Sedgwick has shown earlier, much more than 'shame' can be connected to Luis' parents' decision to migrate to the United States illegally.

In turn, Luis also appropriates the discourse strategy of being 'unashamed' from the gay rights movement to his undocumented immigrant rights activism. As Athanasiou explains, "naming is not only a site of trauma, but also potentially a strategy of subversive mimesis" (Butler and Athanasiou 139). Using naming to counter dispossession "implies a performative which is necessarily interwoven in the fabric of propriation that authorizes it, while at the same time it remains somehow capable of exposing and exceeding its prescribed limits" (138). Appropriation is, in particular, also performed in Luis' definition of the 'undocumented person'. Talking to the viewer about first coming out as an 'undocumented person', he repeats this term three times in a short sequence of roughly 20 seconds (00:00:43–00:01:07). In this speech act, he not only renames the major agents of the Movement from 'immigrant' to 'student' but he also does so repetitively, materializing the creation of himself – and his Movement – as an*other* identity in his performance.

Compared to initial years of youths 'outing themselves' as undocumented (and some, gay), online and offline, the 2013 Movement had already gained immense momentum. Because of the legislative shift implicated by the DACA in 2012 from undocumented students to a focus on families, many undocumented youths today are moving away from the DREAMer's Movement focusing on undocumented students' access to college and university, to a more unified Movement claiming the rights of undocumented immigrants. There is a noticeable change in narratives published in the 'early' years of the Movement around 2007 and those published from 2012 until today. Manuel, editor of *PAPERS: Stories by Undocumented Youth*, observes:

> As we listened to these stories over the last five years, we have noticed the tone and content change. Several years ago, undocumented youth

> were much more isolated. Some of those who were the most 'out' only knew each other by first names or aliases on social media. Now these activists have begun to deliberately use methods and language from the civil rights, women's rights and gay rights movements.
>
> (x–xi)

Manuel et al. see the effects of this change in "the social activism and political organizing led by youth activists", as it apparently "added to the pressure that brought the DREAM Act to a vote in 2010 and to President Obama's June 15, 2012 announcement of Deferred Action for Childhood Arrivals (DACA)" (xi). Nonetheless, these benefits are still not available to most of undocumented youth, which leads the editors to "believe that if only they [the narrators of the stories published] were known and understood by their neighbors, their request for legal inclusion into American society could not be denied" (Manuel et al. xi). This shift, from a very desperate situation of dispossession for undocumented youth to at least some limited options for undocumented students with certain qualification leads to a shift of focus in the Movement to anti-deportation campaigns that Luis also serves in his core story, which emphasizes the effect of deportation on family members.

Considering this political context, Luis' synthesis of both the physical and the narrative voice, serves as an important device for identification and personification. For instance, the soaring number of deportations, which narratives of the past two years increasingly address, are impalpable to the viewer. Being an afflicted 'witness' to family separation himself, Luis' core moments of dispossession, exclusion, and marginalization are humanized through his act of outing himself as 'undocumented'. At this point, the fact that 'undocumented' immigrants are often called 'illegals', or even 'illegal aliens', as well as many other derogative terms, his attempt to 'humanize' the immigration debate seems to make great sense. Butler's and Athanasiou's discussion of this form of 'dispossession' captures the need that is central to the undocumented narrators: "The human", they argue, "is always the event of its multiple exposures – both within its relatedness to others and within its exposure to the normative forces that arrange the social, political, and cultural matrices of humanness" (32). Because undocumented youth understood their relation to the public debate, part of the campaign they led within the frame of the Drop i-word campaign stands up against derogative terminology to which they are subjected and which dehumanizes them. In this context, Luis connects the activism of undocumented youth to the very literal understanding of 'voice'. He construes a meta-level, in which he consciously 'signs' his name, his identity, his story, and his voice to the collective Movement, justifying this by asking: "If we don't speak up, who will be our voice?" His voice and the use of drum beats that inspire political activism serve what has been determined as a crucial device for the projection of (sociopolitical) attitudes (cf. Klüppelholz 57).

4. Paraverbal features: identities in change

4.1. Speech tempo, loudness, and pitch

Mohammad Abdollahi (2): De-emotionalizing narration in monotonous language

Just as paraverbal features of the voice such as rhythm or volume might create the impression that digital *testimonios* can have an activating effect in the viewer, paraverbal features that do not change can create the impression that the story 'has been told before' or the video is merely an imitation of others. In two of the eight narratives, this feature is especially distinct. Monotony and similarity in phrasing the verbal output, first of all, conveys the impression that the production of digital *testimonios* grows steadily and, hence, makes the issue seem important. Secondly, while personalizing the video with biographical data, a similar style and order of narrating it, at the same time, de-personalizes the accounts.

Mohammad Abdollahi uses monotony in his speech for his narrative. His speech tempo, to begin with, is much higher than that of the other undocumented narrators. Making the 'guidelines' for testimonial storytelling explicit, he professes that digital *testimonios* of undocumented youth contain similarities in their production and are not produced completely independently. Mohammad is the only narrator of those chosen for this study who adds this meta-perspective to his narration. At the same time, he hints at the universality in processes of dispossession, which incorporate, as he claims, "the same thing that we hear from everybody" (00:00:57). The introductions to the digital *testimonios* thus become repetitive speech acts that secure a sense of recognition by the viewer. Within this act, as Madison and Hamera describe, words "are reiterative in [...] speech, meaning, intent, and custom" and thus "become communicative and comprehensible because they are recognizable in their repetition" (xvi). I maintain that Mohammad monotonously performs his *testimonio* in order to enhance recognition and to de-emphasize the personal. By doing so, he counters the media logic of YouTube, which generally fetishizes "the *idea* of celebrity, of being/becoming famous" and illustrates an "important element of why people put up their videos" on YouTube (Kavoori 13).

Angelica Velazquillo (5): setting the 'tone'

The narrative of Angelica Velazquillo provides an excellent example of how "in speech, the somatic and the semiotic intertwine", as Van Leeuwen would argue (69). While pitch is individual (cf. Klüppelholz 56), a change in pitch and other prosodic features such as speech tempo or loudness (cf. Hübler 46) create meaning (cf. Klüppelholz 56–57; Van Leeuwen 70–71).

When Angelica finishes recounting the arrest of her brother and the emotional struggle that Angelica and her mother went through during that night he spent in jail, she signals by a change in intonation that she drew her conclusions from this event and decided to 'fight' from that moment. "This was a turning point for me" (00:00:53–00:00:55) she says after a short break, and in a clearly, audibly raised pitch of the voice. Instead of going down with intonation, her voice now sounds unnaturally high, almost incongruous with the negative implications of the event that are really in play. Indeed, Angelica does not seem very emotional about the turning point itself, nor the history of 'problems' that her undocumented status had brought her all her life, but rather about the moment she realized that her brother was gone. In similar manner, Angelica also confirms her growing role in undocumented youth activism: Half way through the narrative, Angelica explains that an offline organization helped to save her brother from deportation. She recounts that she "got in touch with a group of young advocates", who, again "recommended making his case public" (00:01:52–00:01:57). "And we did", Angelica says with a very high pitched voice. This pitch also stresses that the only solution was to keep her brother with her, and removes, one could argue, negative associations that anti-immigrant viewers have with the term 'advocate', which conservatives often associate with revolutionary 'troublemaking'. Moreover, her voice in that sentence is so high that it does not seem possible that it could go any higher, symbolizing that her family had no alternative to activism in order to defend the brother.

What is striking in this narrative about her brother is that although we do not know that the brother that Angelica is talking about is her younger brother, we always have the impression of this teenage boy, just about able to drive a car, forgetting to leave his high beams on. This effect is created, in parts, by Angelica's high-pitched voice. When recounting 'that night he spent in jail', she is barely able to fully pronounce 'jail' – a term that is usually associated with 'criminals'. The sound that Angelica makes when she pronounces 'jail' is so high-pitched that it sounds like a different word (a phonetic transcription of the sound could look something like: "djil"). This disassociation with the original term, 'jail', further paints the picture of a law-abiding little brother who should, in turn, be disassociated with crime. Through pitch, thus, Angelica counters views of undocumented immigrants as 'criminals' – views that are rigorously fought in the Movement (cf. Pallares and Flores-González xxvi).

4.2. Dramatic silences

One of the distinct affordances of audiovisual videos on YouTube, in contrast to, for instance, radio, is the possibility to add silence and pauses to the narrative without making silence a threat to 'destroy' narrative integrity (cf. Dunn 193–194). However, as with radio, "there is an important distinction between the use of dramatic silence and 'dead air'" (195). Technically, also, these moments are also "not silence at all" but "atmospheric or ambient noise" and is "whatever sound is left in the recording environment when people stop talking" (ibid). Dramatic silence, to sum up, is "the silence of a pause for thought, of reaction, of an action that interrupts the flow of sound", which "can be filled with anticipation, expectation, wonder" (ibid). In the construction of meaning, Portelli reminds us that in interpretation of spoken voice, the "velocity of speech" is not universal (65). He shows that "slowing down may mean greater emphasis as well as greater difficulty, and acceleration may show a wish to glide over certain points, as well as a greater familiarity or ease" (ibid).

David Ramirez (4): dispossession as silence

David Ramirez uses silence in combination with a cut of the moving image as a stylistic device that breaks with the style that Benmayor described for digital *testimonios*. In the middle of the narrative (00:01:04), the recording is openly disrupted, as David discontinues his narration, glances away, and exhales a long and clearly audible sigh. As if it had been, literally, 'strenuous' for him to having to 'dig that hole', as if all this had taken away his strength, he exhales a big, clearly audible amount of air from his mouth, looks in another direction, and shakes his head. David is exhausted, we understand immediately, without his having to say so. All it takes to convey this impression is to contextualize the sounds and the metaphor he gives verbally.

This narrative silence simulates the natural process of interpersonal communication. The meaning that this performance of silence expresses is that either the person does not know what else to say or that he/she feels a sense of boredom, exhaustion, or emptiness. By not cutting this scene from the final version of David's digital story, he distinguishes his narrative from those personalized video accounts on YouTube that seem rehearsed and staged to gain a bigger audience. Through performing that he does not have the means to continue with his narration, David demonstrates that he does not seem to be interested in what the viewer thinks about his wordlessness and performs a stark contrast to the "ideal poster children" in other campaigns (Pallares, *Family Activism* 124). Further, the verbal context that this silence appears in is important for understanding it. Previously, David argued that he felt like he was "digging himself further into a hole" (00:00:53–00:00:55) whenever he tried to 'reconcile' his undocumented identity with stigmatization, prejudice, and hate (see Chapter 5 of a discussion of this aspect). Using silence here performs exactly this moment of dispossession – the feeling of aporia described in the metaphor of 'digging oneself further into a hole'. David performs how dispossession "marks the limits of self-sufficiency" (Butler and Athanasiou 3). Since David overcomes this aporia through his activism (which the YouTube video is a part of), his performance of silence materializes his core moment of dispossession.

Angelica Velazquillo (5): dramatic silence, increasing awareness

In the introduction to herself, Angelica Velazquillo pauses clearly after giving her name. Then after claiming she has a university degree, she pauses again, before telling us that she is "also undocumented" (00:00:21). With the most clearly audible sigh, a gasp for air, and a gulp, she informs her audience that she "cannot work in [her] field" or "renew [her] drivers license" (00:00:21–00:00:24). The 'dramatic pauses' and sighing that continue throughout the whole narrative serve as audible devices to express distress or sorrow about a certain situation or circumstance. The affective dimension of dispossession can, thus, be transmitted through paraverbal means and do not have to be transcribed by an interlocutor, as with the traditional *testimonio*. This makes the moment of dispossession narrated in digital *testimonios* more lively accounts. Further, Angelica's pauses and sighs work on a subconscious level, producing meaning by themselves that lies, like an imaginary frame, on the whole narrative: Her sighing and pauses communicate that Angelica is conscious that she is telling intimate details about likely the most distressing problem in her life – undocumented status – to a large audience online.

Mitzy Calderón (6): pausing

One of the most significant aspects of Mitzy Calderón's digital *testimonio* is that she seems to have recorded it all by herself. This assumption originates the fact that there is no form of montage, hence, no zoom, and not even cutting of the moving image prior to posting the video online. Mitzy further confirms this impression by addressing the camera as her sole 'audience' whenever she talks. The fact that the camera does not move except for when she moves the table where she sits further away shows that there is no interlocutor with Mitzy but rather that the narrator uses a camera that is connected to or integrated into her computer (perhaps a webcam). We can see this in 00:01:00, when she moves her hands strongly, letting them drop to the table, which the camera records as a faint banging sound at the same time as the recorded moving image jolts a little. The elementary production style conveys the message that Mitzy does *not need* to perform a high technical knowledge in order to participate in the Movement with an online story. This relates her narrative to Burgess and Green's understanding of participatory culture on YouTube as "the apparent link between more accessible digital technologies, user-generated content, and some kind of shift in the power relations between media industries and their consumers" (10). Mitzy demonstrates that all she needs is a webcam – and while this is connected, of course, to material means and the possession of a computer – the use of her voice and her face are the only narrative devices needed for her digital *testimonio*.

The 'amateur production' of content on YouTube is further emphasized by narrative time: Instead of cutting her narrative significantly in moments in which she pauses as she searches for words, Mitzy looks at the notes that she seems to have lying next to her computer or straightens her hair.

During these pauses she hence lets narrative time pass until she has found a 'right' way to proceed, expressing, at the same time, narrative authority that the *testimonio* purports (cf. Beverley, *Narrative Authority* 556). Further, as Lundby and Hertzberg argue,

> Digital Stories, as a genre, is a strictly defined form of multimodal expression which is *up to the individual narrator* to fill with content connected to an authentic personal experience. This means that the authenticity inherent in this genre will depend more on how, and under what circumstances, the story is told than on the references to the life story of the narrator, that is the autobiographical evidences.
>
> (119, *emphasis added*)

Assuming this authority to fill the narrative time as she pleases, pausing, Mitzy demonstrates her understanding of the intertwinement of the media logic with the political logic of the *testimonio.* The fact that Mitzy stops reading from what seems to be a piece of paper with her *testimonio* on it, underlines the fact that in traditional *testimonios,* the voice of the narrator is the "centerpiece" of the story, no matter how often the actual telling (recording) of the story has been practiced (Benmayor 521; 513). Mitzy's narrative, thus, becomes one example for digital *testimonios* in the Movement which center the speech act, the 'voice' in combination with the 'face', as the most important element of the whole narrative. Mitzy and Angelica Velazquillo (5), who do not use any additional media devices, understand the video as a 'space for appearance' and transform it into a 'media event across time and space' (cf. Butler and Athanasiou 197), as they *speak*. Both narrators show that they do not need to use any other modes to communicate their messages, adding a sense of authenticity in spite of the fact that both accounts seem to have been 'prepared' prior to the recording. It is the voice that is most important, bearing witness to ills that happen in the communities of the dispossessed.

4.3. Acoustic space

Ivette Roman (7)

Ivette Roman includes background noise in her digital *testimonio* that displays the production context, recalling the traditional context of production of the *testimonio.* Background noise, to begin with, produces another dimension in the space that the video displays. West explains that "aural space, also known as auditory space or acoustic space, is a term used by soundscape designers to describe a lack of noticeable sound" (286). However, he notes that "moments of aural space are used to redirect the attention of the listener, to build tension or to simply let the ear rest from sound" (ibid). The 'surrounding sound' thus, according to Dunn, creates space "acoustically" (196).

The appearance of background sound in Ivette's narrative has a strong effect on the frame of her digital *testimonio.* At about minute 00:01:09, one can hear a woman's voice responding with an affirmative, nonverbal sound to Ivette's narration (at this moment, she recounts that some kids in her school spread lies about her). The sound comes from the direction in which Ivette is looking, which tells us that there must be at least one other person (besides the camera) in the room, having an interview-like conversation with Ivette. This sound thus serves as a confirmation of what the bodily posture that Ivette displays, as she does not look directly into the camera but instead centers her eye on an abstract point to her left. The background sound gives the viewer an idea of what (or whom) Ivette is focusing on: a woman who must be Ivette's interlocutor. At the same time, through the creation of acoustic space, as explained above, the woman is closer to *us*, the viewer, which establishes an interview-like situation.[10] The fact that a woman is interviewing Ivette exemplifies the opening up of the testimonial tradition to females in the current Latin American literature after the 1970s (Logan 199). The inclusion of women gives topics of gender and sexual difference more significance (cf. Maier 2), as Ivette's digital *testimonio* shows.

Further, through this acoustic space, Ivette's agency is reduced and transferred to at least two other people involved in the production of her *testimonio* – the female interlocutor and camera (wo/)man. Since Ivette's posture does not 'face' the audience directly, she emphasizes that there is some distance between the narrator, herself, and the receiver, the audience on YouTube. Along these lines, the audience further assumes the role of a witness *to* the digital *testimonio* that Ivette gives. (Interaction in form of comments, hence, would probably not directly address Ivette, but rather the producers of the *testimonio*.) By means of this active distancing, there is a focus on the interest that others might have in Ivette's story of dispossession, implying a general demand for the story and its implications. The vocal intervention by another person in the *testimonio* thus becomes immediately associated with a caption that contains the organizational logo of *Equality Maryland* at the end of Ivette's video clip. The cause that Ivette speaks for becomes a resistance to multiple, intersectional instances of dispossession framed by an organization in which Ivette is only one in many affected individuals.

5. The sound of music: extra-diegetic instrumental music

As already noted in the introduction to this chapter, only two of the eight digital *testimonios* appropriate the meaning potential of music for their narratives. In both narratives, the music is instrumental and extra-diegetic – that is, the music does not belong to the storyworld (cf. Ryan 267).

Carlos Roa (3)

Carlos' digital *testimonio* was created within the frame of the WeareAmerica-campaign (see Chapter 7 for more details). The more professional filming is evident in the official campaign ad that introduces the narrative, consisting of an audiovisual collage of voices and photographs which symbolize different stories to be told within the same campaign. While the voices exclaiming 'I am America' at the beginning of the introduction are audibly very different, the background music remains the same throughout the whole narrative, thus symbolically uniting Carlos' narrative with all the other narratives taking part in the campaign. Thus this music, in Kalinak's words, has an 'additive function' in the creation of meaning rather than serving in "the construction of the narrative" itself (21). Additive music, she explains, lends "coherence or unity to a film", bridging "a sequence to smooth over gaps in time", for instance (ibid). As Carlos' narrative revolves around different aspects in is life – his father's immigration background, his plans for the future, and his mother's fight against cancer – this function creates the impression of a narrative that unites its topics into one, coherent story that, one could argue, also serves one, coherent political goal: the fight against the dispossession of undocumented immigrants in the United States.

The background music in Carlos' digital *testimonio* could be termed as 'classical', instrumental music, consisting of piano and flute sounds that are consistently repeated. According to Klüppelholz, the use of classical music serves an associative function in the creation of meaning, as it has its origins in church, aristocracy, and the upper class, and it remains that cultural symbol up to today (cf. 62). Applied to Carlos' narrative, the use of classical background music elevates the status of his family and, likewise, *all* immigrant Americans (included in the audiovisual introduction of the 'WeareAmerica'-campaign), without the use of words. It introduces a deep sense of narrativity as a "metaphorical phenomenon", possessing "narrativity without being a narrative" (Ryan 267), as it implicitly refers to the discourse of 'worthiness' proclaimed by pro-DREAM Act students, especially in the earlier personal narratives originating in the Immigrant Rights Movement since 2006. Since the piano (and later the flute) repeats the musical theme frequently throughout the narrative, the theme serves as a 'leitmotif', a "distin-guishing characteristic of tonal music" that plays "a series of notes [...] in a memorable and recognizable order" (Kalinak 11). However, since the theme is simple, it does not distract the viewer from the verbal and visual input – a choice which thus eventually bestows more meaning potential upon all other modes in the narrative.

What is more, the leitmotif is harmonious, meaning that the music does not create tensions or frictions. "*Harmony* has to do with the coordination of notes playing simultaneously", Kalinak explains, which is "often less immediately recognizable than melody, but its effects are powerful and discernible even by those without the language to describe them" (12).[11] The theme in Carlos' background music essentially *reminds* the listener/viewer constantly of the political message that the associative function of the theme forms (as explained above), and adds, through its harmonious sound, an effect that symbolically reduces the potential stress or irritation that Carlos' narrative could cause in the viewer.

In sequence (00:01:28–00:02:17), when Carlos recounts the death of his mother, a different flute-like instrument (which sounds like an oboe or clarinet) is added to the piano music. The instrument also plays the leitmotif, though the theme sounds darker through the change from the piano music to the flute, more muffled and sad.[12] The flute, then, adds an emotional level to the moving image that "can also create and resonate emotion between the screen and the audience", which eventually leads to the viewer to "become more invested" in the "characters or events" (Kalinak 4), no matter whether the listener enjoys that music or not, according to Klüppelholz (cf. 60).

Luis Maldonado (8): rhythm and loudness

Luis Maldonado's digital *testimonio*, in difference to Carlos' narrative, is a valuable example of how the narrator uses rhythmic musical sounds to accompany his rhythmic use of voice and, by doing so, calls attention to his narrative and promises an 'ongoing' struggle against the dispassion that he experiences as an undocu-queer whose immediate family got deported.

The rhythmic sounds provide an additional layer of meaning to the verbal elements in the digital narrative, as, according to Lexmann, it is "one of principal attributes of music *per se* and [...] shapes up its meaning" (29). In Luis' initial words of his *testimonio*, his outing as "undocumented" is accompanied by the sound of regular rhythmic drum beats consisting of two components: Three slow drum beats and three maraca sounds in seven successive rows. The drum beats are high in volume and low in pitch compared to the rattle sounds. However, Luis' voice is even higher in volume. This causes his voice to drown the drum beats, or for the drum beats to merely 'accompany' the voice. This renders a supportive effect for his voice in the sense that the musical sounds summon the viewer's attention upon the words the narrator is articulating. In view of the message that Luis sends in his first words – 'outing' himself as undocumented and gay, "unashamed" and "unafraid", it is crucial that the musical sound does not drown the voice of the narrator. This would cause a hiding of the voice, and hence, a hiding also of the undocumented narrator. Further, the choice of the instrument – producing simple, non-synthetic drum beats – implies a naturalness and historical reference associated with the stereotypical yet not unrealistic picture of indigenous activism in the fight against colonial powers. In Luis' digital *testimonio*, it thus mediatizes the spirit of ongoing activism once associated with Chicanismo in the United States.

According to Klüppelholz, changes in prosodic features[13] such as the rhythm or loudness of voice and music are patterns which human beings instinctively interpret on the basis of ancient experiences with threat:[14] Anything unexpected would or could potentially create a source of danger (cf. Klüppelholz 61). Kalinak adds that especially "Western music is characterized by a high degree of regularity in terms of rhythm, and deviations from established patterns [which] can be very potent" (Kalinak 13). For audiovisual narrative, Lexmann anchors this feature in the "sensitivity of audition to the perception of rhythm [which] is many times higher than sensitivity of vision"

(29). In music and sounds today, changes such as a sudden high volume still create a sense of 'tension', 'suspense', 'excitement' or threat (cf. Klüppelholz 61). For spoken narrative, this theoretical basis implies that changes in rhythm and volume can cause perceived threat as a reaction in the listener, such as the release of emotions that, potentially, could lead to an action on part of the listener. Sudden sounds at least provide a call for undivided attention to the subsequent sounds, no matter what the consequential 'action' outcome might be (cf. Klüppelholz 55). Due to this activating effect caused by changes in rhythm, Portelli ascribes a greater sense of power to the narrator of oral accounts over the narrator *and* the reader of written accounts, because it is for the narrator to decide who implements changes in, for instance, duration and rhythm in the narrative account. Theory on the effects of rhythmic music and sounds in audiovisual narrative asserts these power dynamics that lie inherently in orality itself. The power of the narrator is further connected to agency. Sterne argues that "voice has long been conflated with ideas of agency in political theory" (9) and lately, "not only [has] the metaphor of voice become the sine qua non of 'being' online, but it has been charged with all the political currents of democratic practice" (Crawford in: Sterne 9).

What does this mean for the shift of textuality from the written testimonial narrative voice to the oral one? The option to create changes in rhythm, duration, intonation or volume of voice, sounds, and music illustrates an inherently powerful tool reserved only for the digital *testimonio*, not the traditional, as these performative features of the narrator's voice can only be partly translated into written text – a process by which much of the original rhythm gets lost. Certainly, there are many ways of creating rhythm in written narrative, too. Yet, the task of 'editor' of the spoken account in the traditional *testimonio* is precisely *not* to create but to 'record' the account of the interviewee. The beat of the drums, in sum, does not only indicate a clear beginning and end of the narrative itself; the highly regular beats also suggest a stringent sequence that is likely to continue, thus indicating ongoing activism on a symbolic level. Moreover, the sound of the drums again gets louder only when Luis is finished speaking. These attributes, in sum, reflect the importance of the narrative context: the increased loudness of his voice and the digital addition of the drum beats serve as physical and literal amplifiers of a political voice and resistance. They become the "*leitmotif*" of Luis' *testimonio* through the "identifiable and recurring musical pattern" (Kalinak 11).[15]

The rhythm of the drum music, which becomes even louder when Luis has finished speaking, accompanies, in the same composition as detected before, Luis' verbal declaration of his ongoing fight for his idea of justice (00:02:37–00:02:59) framed as follows:

> So, to me that means take action, and through that there will always be a cause that I will feel attached to. There will always be an injustice that I will need to fight for, because if we don't speak out against these issues, then, who will be our voice?
>
> (00:02:37–00:02:59)

The rhythm not only announces activism, it also gives a temporal dimension to the narrative. As Kalinak argues, "through rhythm, music's ordered articulation of time is transferred to film itself" (24). She explains further: "Rhythm refers to the organization of music through time; its basic unit is the beat, a discernible pulse that marks out the passage of time" (12–13). Thus, the music metaphorically and literally *prolongs* Luis' announced, ever-continuing activism. The drum beats, hence, symbolize a "forward movement" and a "desire-for-something-to-come" (Ryan 268).

Notes

1 Beverley explains that in *testimonio*, "the narrator is someone who requires an interlocutor [...] in order first to elicit the oral account, then to give it textual form as a testimonio, and finally to see to its publication and distribution" (*Testimonio* 36).

2 The two narratives are those of Carlos Roa (3) and Luis Maldonado (8).

3 Neben den Geräuschen ist eine andere wichtige Quelle für die Wirkung von Musik die Sprache. Gesprochene Sprache besteht aus Melodik, Tonhöhenbereich, Lautstärke, Rhythmus, Tempo, ganz wie die Musik. Eine Kombination dieser Eigenschaften kommuniziert über die sprachliche Semantik hinausgehend emotionale Bedeutungen (Klüppelholz 61).

4 "This stands in contrast to the dominant discourse on online identity", Baym nevertheless concedes, "which emphasizes how anonymous users switch genders, appearances, sexual orientation, and countless other usually integral aspects of the public self as well as taking on multiple identities" (154).

5 In these two narratives, the status and further information is revealed clearly within the stories of dispossession.

6 For a detailed account on the image- and sound-collage added to the beginning and end of Carlos' digital *testimonio*, see Chapter 7.

7 The voice from the off could also be understood more metaphorically. Associating the black-and-white image as something that 'is past', Carlos' voice stands for a 'voice in the Movement' that *has* been significant in the process of *becoming* America. Indeed, Carlos is well-known in the Movement for having participated in the so-called 'Trail of Dreams'. Along with three other undocumented students, he walked from Miami to Washington DC to "advocate for the passage of the DREAM Act" (Pérez 86).

8 Originally, Butler insists on the idea of the performative as a tool for opposition, as it can re-appropriate the contexts in which speech acts are produced and create (potentially political) meaning. She argues that

> the possibility for the speech act to take on a non-ordinary meaning, to function in contexts where it has not belonged, is precisely the political promise of the performative, one that positions the performative at the center of a politics of hegemony, one that offers an unanticipated political future for deconstructive thinking.
>
> (*Excitable Speech* 161)

9 The term 'undocu-queer' is used by undocumented Chicago youth leader Antonio Gutiérrez in a personal interview in which he highlights the intersections of dispossession, and of undocumented and the homosexual identities.

10 This effect is fortified by the use of written captions in the format of a question, which Ivette 'answers' and which introduce the topic of the subsequent narrative episode. For a detailed discussion, see Chapter 7.

11 Harmony is created, in detail, by "stress points built upon dissonance and resolutions that dissipate dissonance. The farther harmony moves from the tonal center, the more associations of disorder and instability will be activated; the closer to the tonal center, the more associations of order and stability" (Kalinak 12).
12 Kalinak shows that "associations of happiness and brightness are often attached to the major mode while associations of melancholy and ominous are attached to the minor" (11).
13 Prosodic features "include lexical and rhythmic stress, lexical tone and intonation" (Ashby and Maidment 154).
14 "Eine spezifische emotionale Wirkung von Musik, die über eine allgemeine Aktivierung hinausgeht, dürfte vor allem in den Erfahrungen liegen, die die Menschheit mit Bewegung, mit Größenverhältnissen und der Lage im Raum gemacht und in einem kollektiven Gedächtnis gespeichert hat" (Klüppelholz 61).
15 Although Luis' *testimonio* does not use a specific melody, the drum beats can be called a leitmotif, as the latter "can consist of any kind of musical material – a distinctive rhythm, for instance", Kalinak explains (11).

References

Abdollahi, Mohammad. DreamActivist. "My name is Mohammad and I am Undocumented." Online video clip. *YouTube*. YouTube, 19 Mar. 2010. Web. 22 Dec. 2014.

Albiez, Sarah, et al., eds. *Ethnicity, Citizenship and Belonging: Practices, Theory and Spatial Dimensions*. Madrid: Iberoamericana, 2011.

Anguiano, Claudia A. "Undocumented, Unapologetic, and Unafraid: Discursive Strategies of the Immigrant Youth Dream Social Movement." Diss. U. of New Mexico, 2011. Web. 15 May 2013.

Ashby, Michael, and John Maidment. *Introducing Phonetic Science*. Cambridge: Cambridge University Press, 2005.

Ashcroft, Bill, Griffiths, Gareth, and Helen Tiffin, eds. *Postcolonial Studies. The Key Concepts*. 3rd ed. Routledge Key Guides. New York: Routledge, 2013.

Baym, Nancy K. *Tune in, Log on: Soaps, Fandom, and Online Community*. Thousand Oaks, CA: Sage Publications, 2000.

Benmayor, Rina. "Digital 'Testimonio' as a Signature Pedagogy for Latin@ Studies." *Equity & Excellence in Education: Univ. of Massachusetts School of Education* 45.3 (2012): 507–524.

Benmayor, Rina, Torruellas, Rosa M., and Ana L. Juarbe. "Claiming Cultural Citizenship in East Harlem: 'Si Esto Puede Ayudar a la Communidad Mía…'." *Latino Cultural Citizenship: Claiming Identity, Space, and Rights*. Ed. William V. Flores and Rina Benmayor. Boston: Beacon Press, 1997. 152–209.

Beverley, John. "Testimonio, Subalternity, and Narrative Authority." *Handbook of Qualitative Research*. Ed. Norman K. Denzin and Yvonna S. Lincoln. 2nd ed. Thousand Oaks, CA: Sage Publications, 2000. 555–565.

———. *Testimonio: On the Politics of Truth*. Minneapolis, MN: University of Minnesota Press, 2004.

Burgess, Jean, and Joshua Green. *YouTube: Online Video and Participatory Culture*. Digital Media and Society Series. Cambridge: Polity Press, 2009.

Butler, Judith. *Excitable Speech: A Politics of the Performative*. New York: Routledge, 1997.

Butler, Judith, and Athena Athanasiou. *Dispossession: The Performative in the Political*. Cambridge: Polity Press, 2013.

Calderón, Mitzy. SUDDENmovementDotOrg. "I am No Longer Hiding! I am No Longer Afraid!" Online video clip. *YouTube*. YouTube, 13 Nov. 2010. Web. 22 Dec. 2014.

Chinn, Sarah E. "Performative Identities: From Identity Politics to Queer Theory." *The SAGE Handbook of Identities*. Ed. Margareth Wetherell and Chandra T. Mohanty. Los Angeles, CA: SAGE, 2010. 104–124.

Dunn, Anne. "Structures of Radio Drama." *Narrative and Media*. Ed. Helen Fulton et al. Cambridge: Cambridge University Press, 2005. 191–202.

Escoffier, Nicolas, Zhong, Jidan, Schirmer, Annett, and Qiu, Anqi. "Emotional Expressions in Voice and Music: Same Code, Same Effect?" *Human Brain Mapping* 34.8 (2013): 1796–1810. Web. 25 Oct. 2015.

Gutiérrez, Antonio. Personal interview. 25 March 2014.

Hjarvard, Stig, ed. "The Mediatization of Religion: A Theory of the Media as Agents of Religious Change." *Northern Lights Film and Media Studies Yearbook*. Vol. 8. Bristol: Intellect, 2008. 9–26.

Hübler, Axel. "The Role of Electronics in the Perception of Everyday Narratives." *Narrative Revisited: Telling a Story in the Age of New Media*. Ed. Christian R. Hoffmann. Amsterdam: John Benjamins B.V., 2010. 39–55.

Hunsaker, Steven V., ed. "Introduction: National Identity and the Autobiographical Self." *Autobiography and National Identity in the Americas*. Charlottesville, VA: The University Press of Virginia, 1999. 1–12.

Jewitt, Carey, ed. Glossary. *The Routledge Handbook of Multimodal Analysis*. London: Routledge, 2009. 293–308.

Kalinak, Kathryn. *Film Music: A Very Short Introduction*. Oxford: Oxford University Press, 2010.

Kavoori, Anandam. *Reading YouTube: The Critical Viewers Guide*. New York: Peter Lang, 2011.

Kimbrough, Andrew M. *Dramatic Theories of Voice in the Twentieth Century*. Amherst, NY: Cambria Press, 2011.

Klüppelholz, Werner. "Audioanalyse: Werner Klüppelholz." *Medienwissenschaft hörbar. Eine akustische Einführung*. Ed. Rainer Leschke. Siegen: Universis Verlag Siegen, 2006. 54–64.

Lange, Patricia G. *Kids on YouTube: Technical Identities and Digital Literacies*. Walnut Creek, CA: Left Coast Press, 2014.

Langellier, Kristin M., and Eric E. Peterson. "Shifting Contexts in Personal Narrative Performance." *The SAGE Handbook of Performance Studies*. Ed. D. Soyini Madison and Judith Hamera. Thousand Oaks, CA: SAGE, 2006. 151–168.

Lexmann, Juraj. *Theory of Film Music*. Series of Slovak Academy of Sciences 2. Frankfurt am Main: Peter Lang, 2006.

Logan, Kathleen. "Personal Testimony: Latin American Women Telling Their Lives." *Latin American Research Review* 32.1 (1997): 199–211.

Lundby, Knut, and Birgit Hertzberg. "Mediatized Lives: Autobiography and Assumed Authenticity in Digital Storytelling." *Digital Storytelling, Mediatized Stories: Self-Representations in New Media*. Ed. Knut Lundby. New York: Peter Lang, 2008. 105–122.

Madison, D. Soyini, and Judith Hamera. "Introduction: Performance Studies at the Intersections." *The SAGE Handbook of Performance Studies*. Ed. D. Soyini Madison and Judith Hamera. Thousand Oaks, CA: SAGE, 2006. xi–xxv.

Maier, Linda S. "Introduction: The Case for and Case History of Women's Testimonial Literature in Latin America." *Woman as Witness: Essays on Testimonial Literature by Latin American Women*. Ed. Linda S. Maier and Isabel Dulfano. New York: Peter Lang, 2004. 1–17.

Maldonado, Luis, and Sheridan Lagunas-Aguirre. "Luis Maldonado: A Brief Look into the Life of an Undocumented Immigrant." Online video clip. *YouTube*. YouTube, 20 Sept. 2013. Web. 9 Sept. 2014.

Manuel, José, et al., eds. Foreword. *PAPERS: Stories by Undocumented Youth*. Portland, OR: Graham Street Productions, 2012. iv–vii.

Menchú, Rigoberta. *I, RIGOBERTA MENCHÚ: An Indian Woman in Guatemala*. London: Verso, 1984.

Murphet, Julian. "Narrative Voice." *Narrative and Media*. Ed. Helen Fulton et al. Cambridge: Cambridge University Press, 2005. 73–85.

Pallares, Amalia. *Family Activism: Immigrant Struggles and the Politics of Noncitizenship*. New Brunswick, Canada: Rutgers University Press, 2015.

———. "Representing 'La Familia': Family Separation and Immigrant Activism." *Marcha! Latino Chicago and the Immigrant Rights Movement*. Ed. Amalia Pallares and Nilda Flores-González. Urbana, IL: University of Illinois Press, 2010. 215–236.

Pallares, Amalia, and Nilda Flores-González, eds. "Introduction." *Marcha! Latino Chicago and the Immigrant Rights Movement*. Urbana, IL: University of Illinois Press: 2010. xv–xxix.

Pérez, William. *Americans by Heart: Undocumented Latino Students and the Promise of Higher Education*. New York: Teachers College Press, 2012.

Pollock, Della. "Moving Histories: Performance and Oral History." *The Cambridge Companion to Performance Studies*. Ed. Tracy C. Davis. Cambridge: Cambridge University Press, 2008. 120–135.

Portelli, Alexander. "What Makes Oral History Different." *The Oral History Reader*. Ed. Robert Perks and Alistair Thomson. London: Routledge, 1998. 63–74.

Ramirez, David. Thedreamiscoming2011. "David Ramirez, Immigrant Youth Justice League." Online video clip. *YouTube*. YouTube, 5 Apr. 2011. Web. 22 Dec. 2014.

Roa, Carlos. Cccvideovault. "Carlos: The Story of an Undocumented Student." Online video clip. *YouTube*. YouTube, 21 July 2010. Web. 22 Dec. 2014.

Roman, Ivette. MsKYYoung. "Maryland's Undocumented Immigrant Students – Ivette." Online video clip. *YouTube*. YouTube, 5 Jan. 2013. Web. 22 Dec. 2014.

Ryan, Marie-Laure, ed. "Part 4: Music." *Narrative across Media: The Languages of Storytelling*. Lincoln: University of Nebraska Press, 2004. 267–273.

Sedgwick, Eve K. *Epistemology of the Closet*. Berkeley, CA: University of California Press, 1990.

Segal, Lynne. "Genders: Deconstructed, Reconstructed, Still on the Move." *The SAGE Handbook of Identities*. Ed. Margareth Wetherell and Chandra T. Mohanty. Los Angeles, CA: SAGE, 2010. 321–338.

Solis, Stephanie. UndergroundAtBrown. "Lost & Found (Story of a DREAM Act Student)." Online video clip. *YouTube*. YouTube, 12 May 2009. Web. 5 Nov. 2013.

Sommer, Doris. "No Secrets." *The Real Thing: Testimonial Discourse and Latin America*. Ed. Georg M. Gugelberger. Durham: Duke University Press, 1996. 130-157.

Sterne, Jonathan, ed. "Sonic Imaginations." *The Sound Studies Reader*. London: Routledge, 2012. 1–17.

Stöckl, Hartmut. "In Between Modes: Language and Image in Printed Media." *Perspectives on Multimodality*. Ed. Eija Ventola, Cassily Charles and Martin Kaltenbacher. Document Design Companion Series 6. Amsterdam: John Benjamins Publishing Company, 2004. 9–30.

Van Leeuwen, Theo. "Parametric Systems: The Case of Voice Quality." *The Routledge Handbook of Multimodal Analysis*. Ed. Carey Jewitt. London: Routledge, 2009. 68–77.

Velazquillo, Angelica. Mercy Sister. "An Undocumented Immigrant, Angelica, Tells Her Story." Online video clip. *YouTube*. YouTube, 2 Mar. 2012. Web. 22 Dec. 2014.

West, Tore. "Music and Designed Sound." *The Routledge Handbook of Multimodal Analysis*. Ed. Carey Jewitt. London: Routledge, 2009. 284–292.

White, Melissa A. "Documented the Undocumented: Toward a Queer Politics of No Borders." *Sexualities* 17.8 (2014): 976–997. Web. 25 Oct. 2015.

Yúdice, George. "Testimonio and Postmodernism." *The Real Thing: Testimonial Discourse and Latin America*. Ed. Georg M. Gugelberger. Durham: Duke University Press, 1996. 42–57.

Zimmerman, Marc. "*Testimonio* in Guatemala: Payeras, Rigoberta, and Beyond." *The Real Thing: Testimonial Discourse and Latin America*. Ed. Georg M. Gugelberger. Durham: Duke University Press, 1996. 101–129.

7 Intermedial spaces

Written language, static image, and props

1. Introduction: commonalities

From an intermedial and multimodal perspective, this chapter investigates the combination of the logics of space and time on the basis of two core modes, static written language and static image (photographs). This fusion is motivated by the analogy of the two in their creation of meaning and interpretation through the logics of space. In contrast to writing and image, Kress points to the stark differences in the creation of meaning between speech and writing (cf. 56). Sound, for instance, is received in the form of "hearing" and not "sight" (55). Writing then utilizes different modes to visually express 'emphasis', too. Size, spacing, and bolding, for instance, indicate and imitate certain modes of speech such as loudness. Most importantly, Kress finds general "socially shaped" differences between the production and reception of two core modes (cf. 56).

One focus of this chapter is that writing is understood as mimicking speech by using the affordances of space (cf. Kress 56). Even more than Kress, Stöckl stresses that "written language [...] wields strong pictorial powers" (9). On the other hand, just like written language, "visual images are also abstractions" that rely on a grammar, only that they "are realized through a visual grammar network" and "expressed through visual systems of *graphics*, such as *form*, *perspective*, *layout*, and *strokes*" (Lim 55; see also Kress 55). These aspects compose the "display stratum" (Lim 55) that stands in contrast to the "expression plane", in which "the system of *colour* and *form* [are] used to make meaning" (56). In particular, "meaning", again, "is made by the arrangement of entities in the framed space; by the *kinds* of relations between the depicted entities" (Kress 56). Thus, both planes are subject to 'graphic rhythm', which – in addition to the content plane (the elements and persons depicted) and the combination of photos with other media of narration (intermediality) – is a focus in the analysis of static images and written language in this chapter. "Graphic rhythm" has been defined as "a virtual category", relating to "a distribution of expressive elements in space or on surface, a distribution of the segments of spatial artefacts, lines, colours, etc." that includes "the regular or irregular repetition of the elements in space" or "the symmetry of the elements" (Lexmann 86; see also Hickethier 106).

In the interpretation of written language and static images (photographs) with regard to the aspects listed above, the context of the moving image is nevertheless prominent because often, "the verbal and the visual version blend in the mind of the reader-spectator into one powerful image, each version filling the gaps of the other" (Ryan, *Moving Pictures* 139). The analysis of the different modes in their combination in the context of the multimodal *ensemble* in the videos, hence, shall provide an answer to the question of how political meaning is created in the digital *testimonios* of undocumented youths.

2. Captions

The first section of the chapter focuses on written language in the form of captions, which are digitally implemented into the videos. This means, most importantly, that all the videos in this section needed to have been edited by a video editing program. This, in turn, poses important questions concerning the agency of undocumented youth in the production of their digital *testimonios*, as the viewer cannot tell who edited the video in the first place. As Benmayor proposes, the production of digital *testimonios* takes the form of a "collaborative practice [...]" (523). Through the use of this 'perspective' in written text, the captions provide a glimpse of 'who is speaking'. Indeed, in all of the videos, the captions signify another person speaking, essentially de-personalizing the content portrayed in these episodes of the digital *testimonios* but also offering 'perspectives' that assert the production of the video in communality, and in the (undocumented) immigrant community.

2.1. Written interpellations: digital **testimonio** *as interview*

As introduced in Chapter 3, the *testimonio* directly addresses an interlocutor, whom the narrator "exploit[s] in order to have her [or his] story reach and influence an international audience, something that, as an activist for her [or his] community, she [or he] sees in quite utilitarian terms as a political task" (Beverely, *Testimonio* 38). Benmayor understands the setting for production of digital *testimonios*, too, as a conversation between the narrator and the interviewer, not a solitary practice (cf. 510). In such a setting, the narrative is interrupted frequently by conversational attributes such as questions from the interlocutor, to which the narrator responds (cf. Ryan, *Face-to-Face Narration* 44).[1] As the *testimonios* in this selection are digital, Ryan reminds us that "no amount of hyperlinking can match the oral narrator's freedom to adapt his tale to the particular needs of the audience" (41). Therefore, we can conclude that although some of the narratives might seem like 'face-to-face narrations', we cannot view them as such in their final product, although during the production process they might well be. This means that the interaction between the interviewer and interviewee has been cut out of the narrative. While some of the narratives seem to be produced by the narrator themselves (Angelica Velazquillo (5) and Mitzy Calderón (6)), interaction in this analysis shows in the written captions that formulate the questions that are posed to Carlos Roa (3), for instance, simulating the interview situation in which the production of his digital *testimonio* presumably originates.

Carlos Roa (3): the interview

While the four narratives[2] integrate captions into their video clip, only one of them, Carlos Roa (3), integrates a caption that forms a question directly addressing Carlos, which he answers immediately.

At minute 00:02:21 of Carlos' *testimonio*, the written question: "What about the American Dream?" appears on the screen. After the question is blended in, Carlos' reaction is shown, as if he had just been asked this precise question. After a reflecting pause he redefines the American Dream, although he already did this in the prior episodes of his narrative, having explained what the American Dream means to his family. Using an impersonal, written interview question eliminates any impression that he is actually repeating himself, because the question is there to be 'blamed' for any type of repetition or renewed emphasis on the 'American Dream'. Carlos, for his part, is just dutifully answering that he was posed. His facial expressions show that he is taking this question seriously and that he is thinking hard to express himself correctly, due to which the viewer assumes that Carlos really has something to say about the topic. Through these visual devices, the otherwise *invisible* part of thinking and knowing and 'having something to say' is, indeed, emphasized by the simulation of the interview situation, the visuals portraying Carlos' countenance, body posture, hand gestures. Because viewers can 'witness' all of these 'natural' components of a one-to-one interview, they become part of the original interview-situation.

2.2. *Meta-functions in captions and links*

In addition to Carlos Roa's (3) digital *testimonio*, the narratives of Stephanie Solis (1), Ivette Roman (7), and Luis Maldonado (8) utilize written captions on (black) title screens that are edited into and interrupt the moving image. While the written captions appear, there is no additional sound. As the semantic production and functions of the captions are very similar in the latter three digital *testimonios*, dividing the different captions according to their structures emphasizes the meta-functions of the written language used in all three narratives.

Stephanie Solis (1), Ivette Roman (7), and Luis Maldonado (8): textual functions

As Stöckl reminds us, "any mode is – to varying degrees – able to depict states-of-affairs (ideational), design some social interaction between the communicators (interpersonal) and contribute to organizing and structuring the text (textual)", mostly "distributed across the modes present" (25). All three narratives begin with a black title screen depicting mostly the title of the YouTube video: In Stephanie Solis' narrative, small white letters appear that say "lost and found"; in Ivette Roman's video the captions "Maryland's LGBT Undocumented Immigrant Students" are blended in; and in Luis Maldonado's video it says "Luis Maldonado: A Brief Look Into the Life of An Undocumented American."

It is noticeable that in these narratives, the blending in of the titles at the beginning of the videos establishes a textual connection of the *testimonios* to more professionally produced videos on YouTube. This additional artistic dimension positions the narrative closer to the 'short film' or the 'documentary film' than to the political dimension of the *testimonio*. This, however, this is not the only meaning: The blending in of the title after an episode of moving images, in Stephanie Solis' (1) narrative, for instance, marks everything played before as introductory, and, thus, central to understanding the meaning of the entire narrative. As the episode before shows Stephanie speaking at a mock graduation ceremony, this structure gives further importance to mock graduation events and other offline protest actions, which, reinforcing the importance of such action in the 'real' world of the Immigrant Rights Movement. This move illustrates that offline actions such as marches, for instance, depict "the movement's main muscle" (Pallares, *The Chicago Context* 54).

Likewise, the corresponding closing credits of these three digital narratives document the artistic production of the videos but, what is more, also stress the cooperative production process, giving the sponsors and/or professional producers and supporters of the production process of the YouTube videos a name. However, there is a crucial difference between the closing captions and the introductory ones. While the 'style' – color and form, for instance – remains the same, Stephanie Solis (1) and Ivette Roman's (7) title screen de-centers the captions from the middle of the screen to the outer bottom on the right. Luis Maldonado's 'credits' appear in non-bold, less capitalized, and less colorful letters. In accordance with the traditional *testimonio*, the act of de-centering and de-emphasizing the 'other' participants in the production process, on the one hand, shows that all narrators assume the prominent role in their *testimonios* – even more prominent than those who essentially produce and publish the videos. However, all *testimonios* take care to include these participants in their videos and, thus, point to the importance of community in a *united* struggle against the dispossession of undocumented immigrants (youth).

Stephanie Solis (1) and Ivette Roman (7): Interpersonal: the narrator and 'othering'

Burgos-Debray notes in the introduction to Menchú's *testimonio*, "projects depend to a large extent on the quality of the relationship between interviewer and interviewee" (Burgos-Debray xiv). While the viewer knows potentially very little of the relationship between the interviewer and the interviewee in digital *testimonios*, written captions reveal a perspective to the content. In both Stephanie and Ivette's video, the written text implies the additional presence of a narrator who aligns him/herself with the two undocumented youth and their cause. (In Stephanie Solis' video, the words "Help Stephanie and other college students gain a path to legalization"; in Ivette Roman's video it says "Why support Maryland's LGBT Undocumented Immigrant Students?"). At the same time, however, this narrator also 'others' the two youths, as he/she marks their situation of dispossession in difference to his/her own. This step indicates that the narrator is not directly involved in the Movement and even establishes a 'dependency' of undocumented students on the viewer. Dependency, we know, is a major part of dispossession described as the "heteronomic condition for autonomy, or, perhaps more accurately, as a limit to the autonomous and impermeable self-sufficiency of the liberal subject" (Athanasiou 2).

Toward the end of her *testimonio,* Ivette confirms her dependent and, thus, dispossessed position by answering, indirectly, to the question posed in the caption. She claims that she is just "trying to get a future", stressing that she is "just like them", *deserving* of this future (00:04:07–00:04:22). In combination with this caption, the viewer is, once again, prompted to act upon Ivette's dependency. It is apparent that Ivette feels less privileged than 'other' people, such as the viewer, for instance. Thus, it is the viewer who is being 'othered' this time. The crucial difference is that this time, othering originates in Ivette's spoken word instead of that of the other narrator, leaving her the 'final word' in her *testimonio* after all, to speak for "Maryland's LGBT Undocumented Students".

Stephanie (1) Carlos Roa (3) and Ivette Roman (7): Political (inter) action: 'interpersonal' links

Three of the narratives selected for this study further provide links at the end of the video clip. These incorporate the links (inactivated) to the organization that the undocumented narrator is part of and the emblem of the sponsor/producer of the video clip. Instead of viewing their layout as meaningful, for our purposes, the link itself conveys an important message: Electronic (though inactivated) links prompt the viewer to become active in the Immigrant Rights Movement. The viewer's activity will be triggered by viewing *more* stories like Carlos' or by comprehending the organizations' political goals and undertakings. This gives an additional layer of 'activist agenda' to the individual *testimonios*, implying that the Movement is united in the struggle (which it not always is, as we have seen in Chapter 2). Further, through the interactive function of the captions that is established through the links, the digital *testimonios* connect to the tradition by describing, in Gugelberger's words, a "genre with the hope for solidarity and community" (11).

2.3. The other narrator: ideational functions and framing

Like an editor of film, Burgos-Debray describes how she edited the transcripts of the interviews she conducted with Rigoberta Menchú, essentially becoming "Rigoberta's listener": "I allowed her to speak and then became her instrument, her double by allowing her to make the transition from the spoken to the written word", she explains (Burgos-Debray xx). While some of the narrators, including Angelica, Mitzy, and Mohammad, seem to make the decisions of what to explain themselves, the narrators of the stories in this section indeed must have had a listener such as Burgos-Debray, who was making changes with them, proposing topics to talk about, and even asking questions. In most cases, written captions *during* the video clip *describe* information on the narrators' diverse backgrounds and dispossessed identities. These reveal information that the undocumented narrator must have recounted in the process of "in-depth interviewing", as Randall terms the production process of *testimonios* (61). In form of 'explanations', then, the interviewer assumes the role of an 'other' "potential storyteller" in the stories (cf. Ryan, *Face-to-Face Narration* 41).

The use of captions that are blended in in-between the interview scenes are mostly ideational, giving details about her 'story', is particularly prominent in Ivette Roman's (7) digital *testimonio*. (The text reads: "Three years later Ivette travelled to the US to live with her mother. She made the trip with only her younger brother. She was nine." and "When Ivette was fifteen she made the decision to come out as lesbian to her mother…").

When recounting her family's immigration story, the moving image of Ivette's narration is cut frequently, as we saw in Chapter 5. This process of cutting is particularly evident at one point: Shortly prior to a caption, Ivette takes in another breath, as if wanting to say something more; however, she is then cut off from what she is about to say. The captions take over, providing the viewer with further, condensed information about Ivette's family history. This editing procedure signifies that the emotional details about this immigration background are not as important as 'carrying on' with the narrative of dispossession connected to Ivette's coming out to her mother as a lesbian. The difference between Ivette's captions and that of the other narratives, then, is that they co-narrate the story. Without them, the viewer would not be able to understand what she is saying. Thus, they serve a contextualizing function but at the same time de-personalize Ivette's 'voice', reducing it to the 'most important' parts – her dispossession.

This voice reappears in the caption that expresses the shocking conditions of unaccompanied child migration – an aspect which taps into a very recent discussion within the Movement but appearing also in more general and international media coverage. As of spring 2014, countless newspaper articles reported on the "surge of young illegal migrants traveling by themselves" from the Central American countries of "El Salvador, Guatemala and Honduras", which "has been building since 2011" (Preston n.pag.; see also Hennessy-Fiske 14). The trends posed a major humanitarian crisis, because it "has been so rapid that U.S. officials have been scrambling to find housing and medical care for the young immigrants" (Hennessy-Fiske 14). This situation triggered a major uproar in immigrant communities, who saw their task in ensuring that the children have access to legal services "because they won't know what they're entitled to" (Mackler in: Mueller n.pag.). It is possible that "one might object here that the interlocutor is manipulating the material the informant provides to suit her [or his] own metropolitan political, intellectual, and aesthetic predilections", as Beverley formulates the critical concern directed at Menchú's editor (57). I argue, however, that through the connection to inherently prominent topics in the Undocumented Immigrant Rights Movement, the 'other' narrator's 'voice' in the captions essentially unites with Ivette's in her political activism against her *multiple* dispossessions.

Carlos Roa (3): De-emotionalization

The captions in Carlos Roa's narrative assume a textual and ideational function, not only providing information on his immigration background but also creating a structure, framing the narrative in different episodes. In contrast to the captions in Ivette's video, the captions in Carlos' video are preoccupied with informational content that is highly emotional: Two of the three captions used in his narrative inform the viewer of the 'fight' that Carlos' mother led against cancer, framing (through opening and closing) Carlos' descriptions and associations with the topic in narrative time (00:01:28–00:02:17). (The captions read: "After the birth of his sister in 1993, Carlos' mother was diagnosed with breast cancer. After a decade long battle with cancer, Carlos' mother passed away in 2006.")

While the captions appear, the music becomes louder and, employing stringed instruments, suggests emotional meaning. It is, however, the subtitles that tell us of his mother's death in 2006, not Carlos himself. Leaving this piece of information to an 'outsider' (the 'other' narrator), suggests two possible meanings: Either Carlos is still grieving too much to talk about his mother's death, or the other narrator *wants* us to assume that Carlos feels this way, 'taking over' this task for him, leaving the viewer wondering. As a major function of the multimodal ensemble, the music evokes emotion, filling possible 'gaps' in the narrative.

David Ramirez (4): undocumented, unafraid

The use of written language in David's digital *testimonio* reveals the closeness between the oral and the written form of a *testimonio* not only in structure but also in content. As David already introduced himself in the tradition of the *testimonio* (see Chapter 6 for detail), he uses only one written caption that is blended in as we see David's upper body during the interview, seemingly for the purpose of adding to the repetitive character that a ritual on the web assumes in order to be noticed by the fast-clicking audience. Hence, the caption would assume a 'textual function', contributing to the emphasis on certain information in the 'text'. (The caption reads: "David Ramirez, Undocumented and Unafraid, Illinois, 21 yrs old"). However, the captions add another piece of information to David's biographical data: "Undocumented and Unafraid" – two capitalized adjectives – that appear right beneath his name. As the two words are included in the list of biographical data on David, they assume an implied importance for David, more so than the fact that he is from Illinois or his age. I discovered during my research with the Immigrant Youth Justice League (IYJL) in Chicago that it was David who originated the slogan "Undocumented, Unafraid, Unapologetic". The phrase "undocumented and unafraid", according to Pérez, became "the motto of this new undocumented youth movement" in that year (88). Adding the motto of the Movement literally *onto* David's narrative thus contextualizes his digital 'coming out' into the Immigrant Rights Movement, connecting it to campaigns and actions taking place during that time and after. The motto itself is also highly performative in nature: In spatial combination with 'undocumented', the adjective 'unafraid' – a mental state and feeling – the phrase acquires an attitudinal character which describes an important part of the identity of an undocumented youth in the Movement. However, since David does not pronounce the words himself, the motto is de-personified and adds another narrator to the narrative. In connection to the motto of the Movement, the viewer thus assumes that other members of the Movement have added the written words to David's narrative, making the latter's *testimonio* an act of plural performativity that expresses a mental state which is ready for further acts of resistance.

3. Rearranging space: written language on props and static images

Stephanie Solis (1): Visual (de)criminalization

As we have learned prior to this section, Stephanie belongs to those undocumented students who learn of their status in late adolescence, right before transferring into adulthood. With regard to her identity development, she then has to face the lack of opportunities in higher education. Further, she also learns that she is different in this regard from most of her U.S.-born peers. In her story of dispossession, hence, Stephanie defines herself as being "a child forever" and being a "tourist, pretending to have … like … the college experience" (00:03:32–00:03:36).

The following paragraph shows how Stephanie manages to 'decriminalize' herself in order to fit the qualifications for the proposed version of the DREAM Act, which would essentially "allow individuals to apply for legal permanent resident status" (King and Punti 236). The most important eligibility criterion of the DREAM Act is that youths must not have any criminal record. As discussed before, Stephanie connects blame and shame to her parents and, in the same moment, determines the idea of her dispossessed self as innocent; claiming the wrongfulness of the dispossession that conflicts with her plans for the future.

The technical devices of video-making, at this point, open up a second plane of meaning production that underlines the undisguised political message of the video. This message is emphasized more strongly than ever before in the narrative, impressing the viewer with the powerful association of personal memories and the story that the narrative has told up to this point. While the soundtrack of the mock graduation ceremony is played, the visuals are replaced by a photo of a famous street sign: The yellow street sign in the foreground of the photo illustrates a family running in one direction together, symbolizing an illegal migrant family's crossing of a freeway close to the Mexican-American border. The border as well as the freeway is included in the background of the photo, which serves this particular construction of meaning. We hear Stephanie's voice from the off reminding us that:

> Nobody remembers the children whenever they see the sign. You know, the famous sign that you see around San Diego of, you know, the mother and the father and they're pulling their little girl along. Nobody looks at the little girl and thinks 'What happens to her when she grows up?'
> (minute 00:04:49–00:05:24)

The combination of Stephanie's voice and photo establishes a sense of personal identification with the girl in the photo. Thus, she visually underlines her feelings of how "it was not [her] decision" to immigrate to the United States illegally and simultaneously places the blame on her parents. Through this visual, also, Stephanie implies that she was *dragged* to the United States without her consent. However, as her background is a Filipina and not Mexican, this sign is clearly used as a symbolic device, not a literal depiction of the migration to the United States. This relation becomes more explicit when she cries out: "This is not a decision I made. You're holding children hostage!" (00:04:46–00:04:49). By blaming her parents for 'dragging' her into the United States on the one hand, and blaming the U.S. legal system for denying her possibilities to do something with her life on the other, Stephanie manages to *decriminalize* herself. This is necessary because in order to address U.S. legislative powers who are in charge of passing the DREAM Act, Stephanie needs to free herself from any charges against her so that she can call for protection from the law.

Making the DREAM Act one of the narrative's main political goals leads to a de-emphasis of the family and ascribes a special, *deserving* role to Stephanie. This understanding of youth was, further, inherently inscribed in the version of the DREAM Act in 2009 and 2010 – the time Stephanie's narrative was published: Youth applying were regarded as "innocent", "exceptional" and "already American" (Pallares, *Family Activism* 105). Logically, underlining innocence is only possible by actually denying any active partaking in the 'illegal' migration to the United States. Thus, Stephanie places the blame on her parents for having put her in this situation.

Through the criminalizing/decriminalizing rhetoric that Stephanie applies, she challenges the "anti-immigrant rhetoric" that establishes undocumented youth as 'lawbreakers' and depicts herself as a "law-abiding" yet unauthorized resident (Pérez 32). Stephanie's self-decriminalization helps her cope with societal perception of the criminality of undocumented immigrants like her family, without ever explicitly – meaning *verbally* – blaming her parents in the first place. This is crucial because 'blaming' becomes an injurious speech act, as Judith Butler shows: "When the injurious term injures [...], it works its injury precisely through the accumulation and dissimulation of its force" (*Excitable Speech* 52). In contrast to the current campaigns of the Immigrant Rights Movement, through this type of visualization and verbal narration, the blame remains within the undocumented family and community.

As we have seen in earlier chapters, the tendency to 'blame' the parents in public campaigns has diminished in the recent years. In a personal interview, Chicago activist Marcela Hernandez summarizes how she perceived this change in the Movement. Her words shall serve, at this point, to contextualize the shift perceived in the stories since 2006, which rediscovered, in particular, the role of the family and family unity in the Movement:

> But then we realized that a lot of the messaging was actually hurting the immigrant community because one of the big issues was that it was blaming parents for bringing youth here [...]. So, for a lot of youth, sharing their stories meant also being able to control their own messaging and putting their family first, instead of, you know, putting where a lot of politicians were just trying to keep their jobs or were trying to appeal to mainstream media.
>
> (personal interview)

Clearly, Stephanie Solis' digital *testimonio* does not embrace this political logic – a fact that strongly highlights the meaning of 'political' as defined for this investigation: The stories are political in the sense that they offer a public face of the group they 'speak for' that attempts to gain attention but that is also sensitive to quick and strategic change in order to do so.

Other voices: plural performativity

The visuals in Stephanie Solis' video combine two important core semiotic resources: moving image and written language on props. As noted in Chapter 5, through the recording of Stephanie's 'mock graduation speech', she realizes both instances of plural performativity, the "performativity *of* plurality and performativity *in* plurality" (Athanasiou 176), to protest against her dispossession that is caused by her undocumented status. The audience becomes a party in the Movement that not only 'also' listens to Stephanie's speech, as the viewer does in this moment of the narrative. Now the audience also has 'a voice of its own' – enabled through the use of written language: In the scenes that we see, a group of protesters is assembled in a park area in front of what seem to be university buildings. The woman in the foreground of the visual frame holds a poster with her own hands symbolizes that she is also the creator of the poster. The message that the poster sends can be interpreted by the meaning of the words but also the capitalization of one word in the sentence, which reads 'Education NOW'. Thus, through typographical idiosyncrasies and the combination of a voice from the off and, at first glance, 'voiceless' participants in the video clip, the poster embeds Stephanie's fight for the DREAM Act in a context that emphasizes urgency, as the capitalized 'NOW' expresses. It also transforms Stephanie's struggle into a collective one, enabled through the public gatherings and enacting "a performativity of embodied agency, in which we own our bodies and struggles for the right to claim our bodies as 'ours'" (Athanasiou 178), yet marking them with a postulation, as it is written on the poster. Although the second image works in the same way as the first, it is important that it follows, as this order reveals an important semantic implication: Through the preceding image, the viewer associates the smaller written posters with members of the Movement that take part in the mock graduation event as well. The difference in color and handwriting on the posters also indicates multiple agencies. The postulations on the posters – calling for driver's licenses of undocumented immigrants and for the DREAM Act – again support Stephanie's cause.

Mohammad Abdollahi (2): coming out in written word

One of the most significant aspects about Mohammad Abdollahi's (2) digital *testimonio* is the fact that he 'comes out' as undocumented not only in spoken word but even earlier, in written form: The words 'I am undocumented' are printed on his t-shirt in big, white letters. While the t-shirt is black and the rest of the room and Mohammad himself are poorly lit, the letters are clearly visible. Further, because Mohammad faces the camera during most of the taping process, the viewer can see the words constantly. Through this, Mohammad performs his 'coming out' as undocumented throughout the whole narrative time, without explicitly (verbally) having to express it.

Further, the closeness of written language and spoken language becomes literally visible, since the words 'I am undocumented' are phonetically transcribed right beneath them. Phonetics as well as the stress-marker (in form of dots between the syllables), as Stöckl reminds us, are attributes of typography, which is to writing "what intonation, speed and rhythm are to speech" (11).[3] This linguistic play highlights the tight relation that the viewer is to understand between a spoken 'coming out' and a written one, as the use of paraverbal means explains. The crucial difference between the person who wears the shirt and the person who speaks his 'coming out' is that the former cannot escape his/her dispossession by others, since he/she marked his/her body as 'undocumented' in a permanent and clearly visible way. The written words on Mohammad's t-shirt are not merely constative language, but they actually *do* something, constantly marking his body as undocumented, and highlight their active character through the link to spoken language. His t-shirt thus also symbolizes a continuous state of resistance to his dispossession; by means of the performance of his 'undocumented status' that the (written) performative speech act inscribes 'on' his dispossessed body. A second interpretation implied by this performative speech act is that of 'naming'. Instead of having *others* call him names that are derogatory, Mohammad shows that he can choose what to call *himself*. As Athanasiou showed, "naming is not only a site of trauma, but also potentially a strategy of subversive mimesis" (139). Mohammad rejects the naming of others, making the originally official term 'undocumented' something personal and, hence, his *own*.

David Ramirez (4): "the DREAM is coming": plural performativity on t-shirts

When trying to understand the narrative within the political logic of David's digital *testimonio*, the written words on his t-shirt provide the most reliable link to the campaign for which David performs his narrative. As his t-shirt reveals, David participated in "the DREAM is coming"-campaign that performed an offline civil disobedience action with a group of seven undocumented youth in Georgia, fighting against "the Georgia Board of Regents" vote "to ban undocumented youth from the state's top five public universities" in early 2011 (Lozano n.pag.). All seven participants eventually got "arrested" and had "prepared videos and testimonies on The Dream is Coming project website", a "national student and immigrant advocacy network that organized the action" (ibid). It thus seems as if this online video is an important part of the civil disobedience. This aspect highlights the 'new' political strategy – or media-informed strategy – that follows and is a major part of the creation of his online video. The fact that David talks about 'his' situation shortly before taking part in an offline, civil disobedience action, and that his online narrative is not the only one seemingly spontaneously created at that time, suggests that offline activism, in fact, is the solution to his personal struggle in search of a community, against being dehumanized, and for the DREAM Act.[4]

As a result of this activism, David does not seem to feel alone anymore, as he claims: "I feel like I've finally made it. I have a community" (00:01:22–00:01:25). This sentence stands out as he is part of a collective civil disobedience action. Finding undocumented youth to fight 'the hate' together with, gives David support. Likewise, having this offline (and online) community back-up, publishing his coming out to a potentially even wider audience seems to be no further problem. The best protection against criminalization and threatening detention after a failed civil disobedience seems to be precisely the accumulation of community support and collective belonging. As David waited until this particular moment to publish his video, it is obviously part of the action, which will, if watched by other undocumented youth, collect even further community support, only in 'online' form. David Ramirez understood that undocumented students need to 'come out', get active – both online and offline – to get protective support from their community.

Hence, using language in a mode other than the dominant one (the dominant social shaping of affordances on YouTube has formed spoken language rather than written) can also provide a significant link to the contextualization of the video. The written words on David's t-shirt reveal much information on his offline activism and popularity in the Movement. One could argue, here, that David inscribed his activism on his very own body. The body thus becomes "the occasion of situated acts of resistance, resilience, and confrontation with the matrices of dispossession, through appropriating the ownership of one's body from these oppressive matrices" (Athanasiou 22). Aware of this, the precariousness described earlier, assumes even more weight and makes us read David's constant smiling and playfulness as a clear outlet for the likely pressure that he experienced in the production process of the video. Not only does his t-shirt provide a link to an important campaign in the Movement (in Georgia), in connection with David's personalized core story and the fact that at least the other six participants in the campaign probably wear a similar shirt in their *testimonios*, the written words on his t-shirt also serve as a sight for plural performativity of resistance against dispossession, in the offline *as well as* the online context.

The performative context further invokes the danger of getting arrested and perhaps even deported at offline civil disobedience actions. Performing this danger online in YouTube videos like David's, makes explicit use of the medium's fast distribution channel with potentially unlimited audience as a means of protection and resistance to this danger. Pallares heralds the liberating benefits of this type of defensive disobedience:

> Since the acts of civil disobedience started, no youth who has participated in these actions has been deported, even when deportation proceedings haven been initiated. This led one youth to comment shortly after the Georgia arrests in spring 2011 that it seemed like the best protection against being deported was to engage in civil disobedience.
>
> (*Family Activism* 123)

Ivette Roman (7): spatial prominence

With medium close-up shot, the viewer can see the background setting more closely. The frame of the video reveals one and a half words written on a poster of the wall as well as half of a photo depicting a woman with long hair reaching up her arm in front of a wall to write something on a surface attached to the latter.

The constellation of the moving image's frame points out, through the use of color, the relation between Ivette's body, the woman in the photograph, and the poster on the wall of Ivette's film setting. All three 'media' consist of a heavy use of red in combination with very dark color or a strong contrast of the red color. The similarities in color constellation indicate a connection between Ivette and the woman on the photo, even possibly depicting herself. Since the photo shows a woman painting a big object which could be a poster, the poster in Ivette's film setting establishes a mutual relation with the photo. What is more, the photo could unite Ivette's body and the poster by depicting the act of painting the very poster on the wall of the video's setting. To be clear, this connection exists merely by color, not by spoken word. The 'additional' narrative that this act creates, hence, emphasizes Ivette's offline activism in the unification of the undocumented immigrant with the gay and lesbian movement, as the words on the poster presumably say 'no more abuse' in Spanish. The word 'más' connects to campaigns such as the 'Not One More Campaign', a campaign by Organized Communities against Deportation, which organized multiple "acts of civil disobedience against deportations" in addition to "civil disobedience against [...] state laws in Arizona (2010) and Alabama (2012), and educational policies in Georgia (2011)" – the latter of which David Ramirez (4) also participated in (Pallares, *Family Activism* 124). This aspect further highlights the current trend in the Movement to distance itself from exclusively youth to incorporate entire families. In a 2014 interview, Antonio Gutiérrez explains:

> Right, so, I mean I think IYJL has changed within the year-and-a-half that I've been part of it. We used to be very oriented as far as just working with youth, and dealing with youth as far as the development. Now we're really focusing on this whole aspect of families and working with the whole community, whether that means stopping individuals' deportations or saying 'Not One More' or saying 'stop deportations' in general.
>
> (personal interview)

Thus, while Ivette's digital *testimonio* at first glance seems to focus on Maryland's undocumented gay and lesbian students, through her use of an office-like setting and a poster, she nonverbally manages to include the current campaigns that the Movement leads.

The word 'abuso' can refer to the abuse of the rights of undocumented immigrants but also imply sexual abuse. 'No more abuse' is a performative expression thus actively *resisting* abuse. This performative is materialized through the co-presence of the photo in the video's setting space which presumably depicts Ivette painting the words on the poster herself. This example shows how performative speech acts need not be speech acts at all but can be articulated through other media and modes – as it is color and visual image in Ivette's digital *testimonio*.[5]

Luis Maldonado (8): online participation in offline activism

In his narrative, Luis Maldonado uses photos to be blended in during his narration to demonstrate his previous activism and affiliations. The photos illustrate scenes from his offline activism, often involving activists holding banners and posters which depict written language – names of organizations, mottos, and also longer texts that resemble political 'manifestos'.

All these photos are integrated into the video, yet Luis' voice from the off still continues narrating, making the digital *testimonio* the ne plus ultra intermedial narrative. Most notably, all the photos' content plane shows Luis, literally, 'in action' with or in front of a crowd of people. In "Photo 5" and "Photo 6", the crowd is symbolized through the technological devices – a recording device/microphone and a megaphone – that can provide an even larger audience for his messages than the crowds captured on the photos. Hence, the photos enhance the value and status of Luis as a leader of the 'Dream Movement', as he calls it, claiming an active belonging to it without having to verbally elaborate on his activism.

The "multiple frame technique", which the constellation of successive photos in the digital video resembles, tells "more complex stories [...] than single-frame pictures", Ryan claims (*Still Pictures* 142). It is due to this technique that the viewer perceives an image of Luis as active in the Immigrant Rights Movement. Further, through the different 'real' people clearly depicted in each photo, the sum of people in the end forms a small yet visible community in the viewer's mind. We are made to feel that no matter what the outcome of Luis' undocumented status and his public activism, and no matter how much more active he would become, the community would be there to support and protect him. As Pallares observed,

> Since the acts of civil disobedience started, no youth who has participated in these actions has been deported, even when deportation proceedings have been initiated. This led one youth to comment [...] that it seemed like the best protection against being deported was to engage in civil disobedience.
>
> (*Family Activism*, 123)

The people in the photo seem to provide a protective shield over the activist. The mere use of photos, hence, mitigates the precariousness that Luis' dispossessed state positions him in.

Further, the people depicted in the photos who carry t-shirts and posters spelling out the Movement's motto of that year, 'undocumented, unafraid, unapologetic', engage in a process of plural performativity in and of the

Movement's political campaigns. Here, the "dynamic moments" in images, which suggest "a new departure" (Baetens and Bleyen 168) particularly comes to the fore through the activism performed in the photos. Static images in digital *testimonio*, hence, are much more than simply 'static'. The role of the verbal narration, in combination with the photos, has only one important function: It contextualizes Luis' story of dispossesion *in* the resistance against this dispossession depicted in the photos. Verbally, Luis recounts "how much" he is fighting for his nephew's and his sister's reunification ever since the latter got deported (00:02:18–00:02:22), while the "Photo 5" illustrates Luis giving an interview. Thus, the photo provides the viewer with the information that 'fighting' automatically means 'going public' with the problems that he and his community face due to undocumented status.

4. Photos: personalizing dispossession

Because of 'synchresis', the automatic forging and mental fusion between sound and visual when being played at the same time, it is almost impossible to separate the sound level from the visual level in any type of filmic material. Consequently, meaning in digital *testimonios* is created not only through its various media representations, but with regard to the visual and auditory level, through the fusion of the images and sounds. However, multimodal elements penetrate the purely visual and auditory distinction, including the use of photos in narration. In the examples chosen for this section, not only do we continue to hear the narrator's words relating to the content of the photo but we also see the narrator relating to the photo in some way, as Stephanie Solis' (1) narrative shows, creating at least three media streams that unite in the moment of meaning-making.

When there is no written language to contextualize and create political meaning, only spoken language supports the potential meaning-creation of images that are used. This section explores the use of static images, digitally integrated into the narrative by a video editing software, in "semiotic combination" with verbal language (*Still Pictures* 143). Pictures, "left by themselves, lack the ability to articulate specific propositions and to explicitate causal relations" (*Moving Pictures* 139). Thus, the level of meaning that sound adds to the narration, according to Ryan, is, in the first place, "vastly superior in narrative versality" to the combination of static images by themselves (*Still Pictures* 143), always and necessarily 'manipulating' the interpretations of the viewer, giving them, literally, another perspective (cf. Hickethier 103). Pointing to the multidimensionality of narration that combines verbal language and static or moving image (cf. Hickethier 96), most visual signs are symbolic, iconic, or index signs, while the visual image brings the sound to life (cf. 97).

On the other hand, Dunn argues that "sound is epistemologically unreliable", since "we cannot know the true nature of things as reliably through our hearing as we can through sight" (193). Of course, she adds, our eyes can deceive us too, but not quite to the same degree as our ears" (ibid). This aspect challenges the voice-over (or 'voice from the off') that the three narratives[6] avail in their video clips. Thus, all narratives add a visual component to the video clip, either in moving or static form, in order to validate the element of sound. This visual component is the focus of this section.

This dependence on the visual prompts us to ask whether the producers' distrust in the narrative potential of sound *alone* comes from what one can term the 'pictorial turn', which has fully integrated into the visual dominance of YouTube material. The 'pictorial turn' confronts "the rise of the image in today's society and communication" with such questions as the one posed above (Baetens 181). This perspective questions "the changes of visual culture in terms of old and new" media and the reinterpretation of "the image in terms of *imageness*", "hovering not only between the representable and the unrepresentable, but also between the sayable and the unsayable" (182). The following analysis of photographs in digital *testimonios* proposes that "the selection of formal devices and thematic subjects does not reflect a world view but literally reshapes the world", carrying inherent "political power" (183). Thus, in the creation of meaning, in combination with voice-overs, photographs enliven the sound, while sound lends the images their credibility. Another narrative level is added to the multimodal ensemble when visual images are "amorphous and ambiguous", thus "open to multiple interpretations" (Kalinak 17).

4.1. The immigrant story in photographs

Stephanie Solis (1): humanizing immigration

The sequence of the video clip which shows photographs from the past creates a time frame in Stephanie Solis' story of dispossession. By introducing an explanation of her family's immigration background, Stephanie interrupts her story of dispossession. This is clearly noticeable as her tone lightens up, making voice the primary marker of this change in topic. However, the photos have another function in her narrative: Stephanie recounts that her father initiated the family's move to the United States in the 1990s. Apparently, he could not earn enough money by "installing and maintaining the sounds system for all discos" in her hometown in the Philippines (00:01:39). The slightly faded photo blended in at this point shows a party photo of young Filipino men in front of a discotheque. As, according to Lehtimäki, "we need to acknowledge that what distinguishes the photo-image from other forms of representation is its material link to reality" (188), the viewer immediately understands the connection between the father, Stephanie, and the photographs. The choice of the photo is ambiguous, however, and if unaccompanied by the verbal narrative, the viewer would not understand that the family was getting so poor that it had to emigrate from the Philippines. Thus, it serves a different function: Through the choice of this photograph,

Stephanie reveals her father's 'love of life', as it depicts him partying with his friends, and internal wish for success – revealed by the 'celebration'. Thus, the first photograph mainly serves the purposes of "visualizations, emotional coloring", in Ryan's words (*Moving Pictures* 139).

The second photo shows a little girl in front of a shiny Mercedes. The story Stephanie tells at this moment identifies the little girl as herself and frames the time in which the photograph was taken. Further, Stephanie reveals that it was her father who took the photograph. This piece of information triggers the viewer to identify with the father, assuming the latter's perspective during the moment of taking the picture. The fact that the viewer sees 'through the eyes of the father' instantly humanizes him, as all the viewer gets to see is the laughing daughter and a shiny car that unite in a moment which seems to have been precious enough to document. Again, instead of showing the economic hardship that Stephanie's family must have experienced before and upon immigration, the photograph plays with bright and happy emotions that connect the viewer's understanding of the father's decision to migrate (unlawfully) to the 'will' to strive for happiness, peace, and family well-being.

Through their additional meaning, the photographs become a literal illustration of a core feature of the American Dream in Stephanie Solis' digital *testimonio.* There is no trace of the problems that she encounters upon her 18th birthday visible in the photographs. They rely on the verbal narrative to be revealed. In connection to the latter, the photographs add Stephanie's judgment to the multimodal narrative. The father's 'good intentions', which the photographs reveal are, in combination, playfully challenged by Stephanie's amusement over the naïve faith that a Mercedes Benz car parking on the street proves that there are "millionaires everywhere" in the United States. The contrast between photographs and verbal narration further shows that the father's intentions – which so impact his daughter's happiness – have not been fulfilled: It is Stephanie who needs to live with the consequences of her father's move and who has no other option but to fight them, if she wishes to be happy. Through the photographs, in sum, the viewer learns about intimate wishes of Stephanie's father for a good life in the United States, assuming a performative dimension of the family's version of the 'American Dream'.

Carlos Roa (3): mediatized melting pot

Carlos Roa's video is the least self-produced of all the videos in this selection, as evidenced by the use of multiple editing devices such as black-and-white images, captions, and pictures. The video is further shot in a professional studio with a 'seat' for the narrator. Further, the video is edited several times and, in contrast to most other digital *testimonios* in this selection, music is a continuous part of the soundtrack. Carlos' story also follows a clear topic line: It is about defining what being an (undocumented immigrant) means to his understanding of the myth of the American Dream.

The production quality is most clearly evident in the introductory ad to Carlos' digital *testimonio.* Apparently produced within a campaign called "I am America", this ad includes small photos of ethnically diverse people, which digitally dissolve into one, large U.S. flag. It appears as if Carlos is one of those people chosen to present 'his story' within this campaign, as his voice is one of the voices that the soundtrack plays while the photos then compose the American flag, repeating the name of the campaign, "I am America". The ending of the video clip is similar to the introduction ad, professionally produced within the campaign and also including voices and images. However, the running moving image of Carlos is digitally edited to 'join' the other photos 'in' the flag.

Without getting into much detail on the multimodal constellations at this point,[7] the meaning of the collage can easily be deduced from the first impression that the multimedia ensemble creates: Without the images and the voices, there would be no flag. But the images are not visible in this flag: rather, they blend into the colors and shape of the U.S. flag. In addition to that, the ethnic diversity of the people in the photos, implies, as Pallares and Flores-González state, that the current Movement is a "panethnic [...] movement" (xxiii). However, since they all become elements of the flag, they symbolize the assimilationist idea of the 'melting pot'. Mauk and Oakland explain: "In recent decades, debates on national identity have centered on questions of unity as against diversity (ethnic pluralism)" (10). The debate, here, includes the metaphors of the melting pot or the salad bowl, the former generally referring to "assimilation" and the latter to "integration" of immigrants in the United States (ibid). Therefore, the contrast between "absolute national unity" and "levels of partial blending" is frequently up for debate (ibid). Critical questions that arise from this context are, in particular, which of the two metaphors "captures the character of American society" and "who is to decide who is included or excluded from these mixtures" (55). Likewise, Campbell and Kean stress that consensus on the idea of the melting pot "in reality [...] never existed", however, there is "a persistent emphasis upon the 'melting pot' as a way of bringing people together into the American nation" (26). Essentially, "the model of the melting pot assumed that everyone could better themselves in American society, despite any ethnic distinctiveness, and improve their position through economic opportunity" (61).

Campbell and Kean's claim, in particular, points to the ideological frame in which the 'Weareamerica' campaign's ad places Carlos' digital *testimonio.* It not only brushes over ethnic differences but also shapes Carlos' words to work within the melting pot metaphor. In connection to the American Dream, Carlos argues that "this country has prided itself on" the possibility to "change this country for the better", that "we've seen that at the turn of this century we saw how immigrants ... em ... you know, changed this nation for the better of Irish, of Polish, of Italian descent". Then he provides the connecting link to himself and his family, arguing that he and his family "are no different than the immigrants from the past" (00:02:35–00:03:01). Consistent with the 'WeareAmerica' campaign, these are Carlos' final words in the narrative, before the image diminishes among very other little thumbnails of, presumably, digital narratives into a visual mix that creates the American flag – the mediatized American melting pot.

It is difficult to assess the exact meaning and message that this campaign intended to spread. When a local organizer from Chicago, Marcela Hernandez, was asked about the difference between more 'official' campaigns and autonomous productions, she answered that it was important to youth in the beginning of the Immigrant Rights Movement since 2006 to adhere to official campaigns because they had the resources to produce young people's *testimonios* in mainstream media. She explained her point as follows:

> I think a lot of the youth started organizing as part of the bigger immigration movement. But then we saw how, you know, non-profits or elected officials were shaping the story to what was gonna get them votes, to what was gonna get them, you know, what was gonna *appeal* to the mainstream of who you would call the mainstream folk, like the mainstream 'American'.
>
> (personal interview)

Perhaps Carlos' story had to be adjusted to the campaign's political logic which, as the introduction ad tells, followed assimilationist views rather than views favoring ethnic plurality. In any case, one needs to consider Carlos' narrative as a digital *testimonio* following a political logic that favored the legalization of undocumented immigrants in the United States and used new media affordances to shape crucial parts of this political message.

4.2. Illustrating dispossession, and the performative of static images

Stephanie Solis (1): illustrating dispossessed identity

Stephanie Solis' digital *testimonio* is among those two digital narratives which use the most pictures of all eight narratives,[8] demonstrating the techniques taught in the Center for Digital Storytelling. Storytellers are encouraged to use the multiple devices that digital storytelling offers, such as image, sound, writing, or verbal language from the off in combination with an animated picture show and music. During the narration of her core story of dispossession, Stephanie's use of photographs is most prominent. They perform the representational or illustrative function of photographs that Ryan stresses. The scholar identifies pictures' "principal narrative option" as the "illustrative mode", forming a "symbiotic relation with the verbal version" (*Moving Pictures* 139). To stress this symbiosis, the narrative generally uses a voice from the off when illustrative photographs are introduced. The narrating voice and the photographs engage in intermedial narration that produces meaning. The most prominent example can be found at the beginning of the narrative: Explaining in a voice from the off how her family lost many of their belongings, two pictures are slowly blended in: The first picture that is zoomed in slowly shows many stacked boxes in a bright and tidy storage place. The second picture shows a storage room with nothing at all in it. There is also very little light in this room. Daylight does not even reach all of the corners of the generally ill-conditioned room. The photo is darkened out really slowly when Stephanie talks about all of her baby photos being gone, and how that made her feel she didn't exist. The darkening of an already barely-lit room emphasizes the feeling of loss, particularly the loss of childhood. Both pictures are used as an illustration of what the storage room must have looked like, displayed in order to have the audience follow, and probably, connect to the narrative told by Stephanie's voice.

The order in which these two static images are blended in does more than represent the Solis family's loss of their belongings, however. Folded into the moving images of the video clip, they create an order of events that produces a small story of its own. As Schwanecke explains, "the successive organisation of pictures leads the recipient to make distinct conclusions", which "are based on the actual blending of spatial and temporal relations with presumed causal ones" (54). Montage, here, serves as a device to connect the different visual actions in pictures (the filling and the emptying of the room) and, thus, creates a storyline through the passing of story time (order) (cf. Hickethier 103). According to Steiner, "the insistence on temporality is part of every definition of *narrativity*, regardless of its philosophical orientation" (149). In this storyline, thus, the visual coherence is most important for the interpretation (ibid). Along the same lines, Ryan stresses the order established by the narrative timeline that essentially shapes the viewer's interpretation of the pictures (cf. *Moving Pictures* 141). Thus, the storage room metaphorically 'empties' – while a reverse order would also mean the opposite: the storage room would 'fill'.

This, first sequence of the digital narrative (00:00:11–00:01:10) also introduces the core story as a whole that Stephanie chooses to publish about herself in order to advocate the DREAM Act. The pictorial narrative created through the order in which these photos are shown, further, represents the literal act of dispossessing somebody. This small episode within Stephanie's narrative is further blended in a second time toward the middle of the digital *testimonio* in order to remind the viewer of this type of dispossession when Stephanie talks about her family's undocumented status and her perceived aporia (see: 00:02:23–00:02:30).

The digital *testimonio* utilizes a third photo to create a visual anchor for the story of dispossession. As Stephanie explains, the impact that the loss of her baby photos have had on her identity formation, she uses a form of multimodal narration, holding a photo into the visual frame of the camera, as if 'showing' it her imagined audience. Baetens and Bleyen call this function an "index", essentially "carving out a single moment of time in the real flux of life" (166). This function is very well-known and explored. However, the social and cultural context of the photograph is important for this narrative function (ibid; see also Wolf 136). The context is supplied not only through Stephanie's verbal narration but also her looks portrayed by the moving image. She holds in front of the camera a photo of her as a child, visually showing through facial expressions the emotional impact that this part of the narration has on her, looking sad and alert. Further, Stephanie directly involves her audience, as we feel personally addressed by this indexical value of the image.

Cultural identity is made up of identification with specific groups, which generally transmit "thoughts and behaviors from birth in the family and schools over the course of generations" (Jandt 7). Further, these groups provide a "shared system of symbols and meanings as well as norms for conduct" (ibid). Since Stephanie and her family moved to the United States when she was still an infant, as she explains to the viewer, those material things seem to have constantly served as reminders of her Philippine childhood; symbols that are innately connected to Stephanie's existence. The fact that the family was constantly on the move within the first years of building an existence in the United States, implies a sense of restlessness that Stephanie was very likely to have perceived during her childhood years. Apart from the geographic displacement, which was probably linked to the economic hardship of the family, being 'restless' can also impact identity formation, as the only symbolic reminders of Stephanie's Philippine roots were literally discarded. This struggle was clearly initiated by the parents. She describes her family also as being forever out of reach, just as Stephanie's identity in the United States may have been constantly 'on hold'.

The moving images are then replaced by the still image that Stephanie held in her hands seconds before and combined with her narration from the off. This shift in perspective brings her voice closer to the viewer, who is told that Stephanie did not remember what she looked like as a kid for a long time until this very image reminded her again. Through this move, the viewer him-/herself gets to have the visual 'experience' of 'remembering' what Stephanie looked like as a child. Since we do not know what she looked like before, the digital *testimonio* lets us take part in this 'epiphany'.

"Depending on the way in which photographs and literary language are combined, they illustrate, contextualise or contradict each other", according to Schwanecke (55). "The combination's effects", she adds, "may range from self-reference and metareference to various other forms of connotations and associations" (ibid). Likewise, Hickethier emphasizes that voice and image can be combined and contrastive – hence, create meaning (cf. 98). He points out that visual image always keeps an own meaning (cf. 104), expressing a sense of "Körperlichkeit" (corporeality) (cf. 105). Accordingly, as the image of a smiling, happy baby establishes a contrast to the serious background of the story that the viewer learned, the question comes up why such a happy baby was taken away from home to a nation that would likely dispossess her of her identity. The question is much more fundamental. How and why were Stephanie's parents convinced that it would be better for the family to move to the United States? In sum, while the digital *testimonio* does not offer a ready answer to this question, autobiographical story elements such as this photo open up a perspective to the story of undocumented immigrants that goes further than most the general knowledge of the immigration issue. First and foremost, they enable a personalized understanding for the matter.

Carlos Roa (3): plural performativity from the past

The use of photographs in Carlos' digital *testimonio* differs from Stephanie's in their narrative function. First of all, his pictures are left to 'tell a story' entirely on their own. Carlos does not explain, like Stephanie, what is depicted in the photos. The only reference that Carlos provides verbally are facts about his father and the legalization problem (discussed in Chapter 5) when a photo of a family gathering, foregrounding a middle-aged man, appears, and that he talks about his mother when the photo of her is blended in.

According to Ryan, Carlos' reticence to comment on the photos has an important consequence: Pictures, "left by themselves, lack the ability to articulate specific propositions and to explicitate causal relations" (Ryan, *Moving Pictures* 139). Therefore, the viewer understands that is it not important to understand what is happening in the photos. Rather, the photo's black-and-white mode signals that the memories associated with the photos are long passed. This fact is confirmed in case of Carlos' mother, who, as the viewer learns through written captions and in spoken word (hence, verbally and visually), died of breast cancer in 2006.

The use of the photos in Carlos' narrative, thus, performs another function. Not only do they personalize Carlos' account – providing visual proof for Carlos' immigration story – but they also add an emotive and humanizing dimension. Both parents are photographed not by themselves but in a group of people. The photograph of the father shows him at the end of a table with many small children and women (one of whom could be Carlos as a little boy). Playing with the heterosexual ideal of a 'family', this associative dimension of meaning, left by itself, relates to an ideational state of affairs: From this moment on, the photo of Carlos' father allows him to perform the caring family father who feeds many hungry children rather than the undocumented immigrant who crossed the Mexican-American border illegally. The photo, hence, constructs a gender performance that supports Carlos' verbal narrative in that he wishes to go to the military. His father thus implicitly unites with Carlos in his quest – his undocumented youth rights activism.

The photo of Carlos' mother works differently, emphasizing the emotive dimension of communication. For this, verbal contextualization, as implied earlier, is necessary. In 00:01:53–00:02:07, Carlos recounts that

> all she [his mother] wanted to do was to provide for [them], you know, provide for her family, as any other family in this country ... ehm ... and be able ... and she wanted us to realize, you know, our American Dream. She wanted to see her kids become professionals.

The latter sentence, in particular, connects his mother's dream to the concept of the *American* Dream that runs through the digital *testimonio* as a narrative red thread, therefore serving a textual function of the narrative, yet adding an emotional element: Carlos further recounts that his mother did not only strive for legalization of her children (and thus, what Carlos defines as the American Dream), but "fought *two* battles, you know – one of the being ... having breast cancer and the other, ehm ... you know, the fact that she was ... you know ... that her family was undocumented" (00:01:30–00:01:42). Being informed by the written captions that Carlos' mother 'lost her fight' against the cancer, the following logical connection to the struggle still left to fight in is that of legalization, which justifies Carlos' final words to fight in her memory. His activism (such as the Trail of Dreams, as introduced earlier) is, thus, legitimized by the death of his mother, meaning that all the action he takes as an activist are, from there on, done in 'somebody's honor' and to 'fulfill somebody's last wishes'.

The image, to sum up, triggers the textual connection to an emotional story and, at the same time, leads to Carlos' final words. Further, through the integration of photos of his parents, Carlos integrates other undocumented immigrants into his 'struggle' against dispossession: In combination with his words, the meaning of both of his parents' photos engages him in a sense of plural performativity; a story, says Athanasiou, that is "linked with the stories and claim of others" and a "collective demand [that] emerges from those singular histories" (157).

Notes

1 Further markers of conversational storytelling are, Ryan summarizes, for instance, "interruptions, requests for explanations, laughter, supportive vocalizations, and facial expression" (*Face-to-Face Narration* 41).
2 Stephanie Solis (1), Carlos Roa (3), Ivette Roman (7), and Luis Maldonado (8).
3 Writing, as Kress summarizes, needs completely different modes to visually express 'emphasis' such as bolding, size or spacing. So, for instance, "bolding in writing and loudness in speech are means of producing emphasis" (55).
4 The other personal stories recorded within that same action in Georgia that day and unloaded on a personal the YouTube account (not by him personally) do address the possibility of arrest in more detail, or even say that their story was to be put online in case they were arrested in the civil disobedience (which is likely to happen). This, David's video might just have been shortly before the act of civil disobedience was actually carried out on 5 April 2011, the same day that the video was also uploaded.
5 The association with poster-painting has its origin in the extensive craftsmanship that I also experienced during my research stay in Chicago in preparation for the National Coming Out of the Shadows Day in March 2014.
6 Stephanie Solis (1), Carlos Roa (3), and Luis Maldonado (8).
7 Since it can be said with certainty that this ad was not produced by Carlos, the analysis will of it will only go so far as it contextualizes Carlos' narrative in the Immigrant Rights Movement.
8 (along with Luis Maldonado's (8) narrative).

References

Abdollahi, Mohammad. DreamActivist. "My name is Mohammad and I am Undocumented." Online video clip. *YouTube*. YouTube, 19 Mar. 2010. Web. 22 Dec. 2014.

Baetens, Jan, and Mieke Bleyen. "Photo Narrative, Sequential Photography, Photonovels." *Intermediality and Storytelling*. Ed. Marina Grishakova and Marie-Laure Ryan. Berlin: De Gruyter, 2010. 165–182.

Benmayor, Rina. "Digital 'Testimonio' as a Signature Pedagogy for Latin@ Studies." *Equity & Excellence in Education: University of Massachusetts School of Education* 45.3 (2012): 507–524.

Beverley, John. *Testimonio: On the Politics of Truth*. Minneapolis: University of Minnesota Press, 2004.

Burgos-Debray, Elisabeth, ed. Introduction. *I, RIGOBERTA MENCHÚ: An Indian Woman in Guatemala*. By Rigoberta Menchú. London: Verso, 1984. xi–xxi.

Butler, Judith. *Excitable Speech: A Politics of the Performative*. New York: Routledge, 1997.

Butler, Judith, and Athena Athanasiou. *Dispossession: The Performative in the Political*. Cambridge: Polity Press, 2013.

Calderón, Mitzy. SUDDENmovementDotOrg. "I Am No Longer Hiding! I Am No Longer Afraid!" Online video clip. *YouTube*. YouTube, 13 Nov. 2010. Web. 22 Dec. 2014.

Campbell, Neil, and Alasdair Kean. *American Cultural Studies: An Introduction to American Culture*. 3rd ed. New York: Routledge, 2012.

Dunn, Anne. "Structures of Radio Drama." *Narrative and Media*. Ed. Helen Fulton et al. Cambridge: Cambridge University Press, 2005. 191–202.

Gugelberger, Georg M., ed. "Introduction: Institutionalization of Transgression: Testimonial Discourse and Beyond." *The Real Thing: Testimonial Discourse and Latin America*. Durham, NC: Duke University Press, 1996. 1–19.

Gutiérrez, Antonio. Personal interview. 25 March 2014.

Hennessy-Fiske, Molly. "More Minors Crossing Border Alone." Chicago Tribune, 4 Mar. 2014: 1.

Hernandez, Marcela. Personal interview. 27 March 2014.

Hickethier, Knut. "Erzählen mit Bildern: Für eine Narratologie der Audiovision." *Mediale Ordnungen: Erzählen, Archivieren, Beschreiben*. Ed. Corinna Müller and Irina Scheidgen. Marburg: Schüren Verlag, 2007. 91–106.

Jandt, Fred E. *An Introduction to Intercultural Communication: Identities in a Global Community*. 7th ed. Los Angeles, CA: SAGE, 2013.

Kalinak, Kathryn. *Film Music: A Very Short Introduction*. Oxford: Oxford University Press, 2010.

King, Kendall A., and Gemma Punti. "On the Margins: Undocumented Students' Narrated Experiences of (Il)legality." *Linguistics and Education* 23 (2012): 235–249.

Kress, Gunther. "What is Mode?" *The Routledge Handbook of Multimodal Analysis*. Ed. Carey Jewitt. London: Routledge, 2009. 54–67.

Lehtimäki, Markku. "The Failure of Art: Problems of Verbal and Visual Representation in *Let Us Now Praise Famous Men*." *Intermediality and Storytelling*. Ed. Marina Grishakova and Marie-Laure Ryan. Berlin: De Gruyter, 2010. 182–207.

Lexmann, Juraj. *Theory of Film Music*. Series of Slovak Academy of Sciences 2. Frankfurt am Main: Peter Lang, 2006.

Lim, Victor F. "Problematising 'Semiotic Resource'." *Perspectives on Multimodality*. Ed. Eija Ventola, Cassily Charles, and Martin Kaltenbacher. Document Design

Companion Series 6. Amsterdam: John Benjamins Publishing Company, 2004. 51–63.

Lozano, Pepe. "Immigrant Youth Arrested in Georgia after Civil Disobedience." *Peoplesworld*. n.p., 7 Apr. 2011. Web. 9 Mar. 2015.

Maldonado, Luis. Lagunas-Aguirre, Sheridan. "Luis Maldonado: A Brief Look into the Life of an Undocumented Immigrant." Online video clip. *YouTube*. YouTube, 20 Sept. 2013. Web. 9 Sept. 2014.

Mauk, David, and John Oakland. *American Civilization: An Introduction*. 5th ed. New York: Routledge, 2009.

Mueller, Benjamin. "To Help Unaccompanied Minors, New York City Posts Representatives at Immigration Court." *The New York Times*. 16 Sept. 2014. *The New York Times*. Web. 14 Oct. 2014.

Pallares, Amalia. *Family Activism: Immigrant Struggles and the Politics of Noncitizenship*. New Brunswick, Canada: Rutgers University Press, 2015.

———. "The Chicago Context." *Marcha! Latino Chicago and the Immigrant Rights Movement*. Ed. Amalia Pallares and Nilda Flores-González. Urbana, Chicago, and Springfield: University of Illinois Press, 2010. 37–61.

Pallares, Amalia, and Nilda Flores-González, eds. "Introduction." *Marcha! Latino Chicago and the Immigrant Rights Movement*. Urbana: University of Illinois Press, 2010. xv–xxix.

Pérez, William. *Americans by Heart: Undocumented Latino Students and the Promise of Higher Education*. New York: Teachers College Press, 2012.

Preston, Julia. "U.S. Setting Up Emergency Shelter in Texas as Youths Cross Border Alone." *The New York Times* 16 May 2014. *The New York Times*. Web. 20 May 2014.

Ramirez, David. Thedreamiscoming2011. "David Ramirez, Immigrant Youth Justice League." Online video clip. *YouTube*. YouTube, 5 Apr. 2011. Web. 22 Dec. 2014.

Randall, Margaret. "Reclaiming Voices: Notes on a New Female Practice in Journalism." *The Real Thing: Testimonial Discourse and Latin America*. Ed. Georg M. Gugelberger. Durham, NC: Duke University Press, 1996. 58–69.

Roa, Carlos. Cccvideovault. "Carlos: the Story of an Undocumented Student." Online video clip. *YouTube*. YouTube, 21 July 2010. Web. 22 Dec. 2014.

Roman, Ivette. MsKYYoung. "Maryland's Undocumented Immigrant Students – Ivette." Online video clip. *YouTube*. YouTube, 5 Jan. 2013. Web. 22 Dec. 2014.

Ryan, Marie-Laure, ed. "Part 1: Face-to-Face Narration." *Narrative across Media: The Languages of Storytelling*. Lincoln: University of Nebraska Press, 2004. 41–46.

———. "Part 3: Moving Pictures." *Narrative across Media: The Languages of Storytelling*. Lincoln: University of Nebraska Press, 2004. 195–201.

———. "Part 2: Still Pictures." *Narrative across Media: The Languages of Storytelling*. Lincoln: University of Nebraska Press, 2004. 139–144.

Schwanecke, Christine. *Intermedial Storytelling: Thematisation, Imitation and Incorporation of Photography in English and American Fiction at the Turn of the 21st Century*. Studies in English Literary and Cultural History 52. Trier: Wissenschaftlicher Verlag Trier, 2012.

Solis, Stephanie. UndergroundAtBrown. "Lost & Found (Story of a DREAM Act Student)." Online video clip. *YouTube*. YouTube, 12 May 2009. Web. 5 Nov. 2013.

Steiner, Wendy. "Pictorial Narrativity." *Narrative across Media*. Ed. Marie-Laure Ryan. Lincoln: University of Nebraska Press, 2004. 145–177.

Stöckl, Hartmut. "In Between Modes: Language and Image in Printed Media." *Perspectives on Multimodality*. Ed. Eija Ventola, Cassily Charles, and Martin Kaltenbacher. Document Design Companion Series 6. Amsterdam: John Benjamins Publishing Company, 2004. 9–30.

Velazquillo, Angelica. Mercy Sister. "An Undocumented Immigrant, Angelica, Tells Her Story." Online video clip. *YouTube*. YouTube, 2 Mar. 2012. Web. 22 Dec. 2014.

Wolf, Werner. "Pictorial Arts." *Storyworlds across Media*. Ed. Marie-Laure Ryan and Jan-Noël Thon. Frontiers of Narrative. Lincoln: University of Nebraska Press, 2014. 126–147.

8 Conclusions

1. Multimodal performances of dispossession

In his foreword to Peter Orner's *Underground America: Narratives of Undocumented Lives*, Luis Urrea wrote: "Undocumented immigrants have no way to tell you what they have experienced, or why, or who they are, or what they think" (1). While he, too, eventually used this provocative statement to conclude that personal narratives are the key to understanding the lives of undocumented immigrants in the United States, I use this claim here in order to contrast it with the results gathered in this study: Particularly striking is the fact that each and every aspect in Urrea's claim seems inaccurate with regard to the eight digital *testimonios* of undocumented youths published on YouTube and selected for this study. Not only can their videos potentially be viewed by people from all over the world who have access to the Internet, but the video format also provides multiple *ways* to express thoughts, feelings, and experiences.

In particular, the core story of dispossession, which consists of a central experience with dispossession in the narrators' lives caused by undocumented status, enables an understanding of situations of marginalization, oppression, and criminalization. Butler and Athanasiou's concept further establishes undocumented youths as relational beings who, in their inability to be self-sufficient, independent beings, are dispossessed of themselves through dispossessing powers – be it normative understandings of who can call him/herself an 'American', who can go to college, to the military, or which family members may stay in the United States and which cannot.

Through the performance of this sometimes traumatizing experience, however, other paths open up. As Butler stresses, dispossession materializes the 'political' when narrators retell it in their performance, which enacts the experience. Corporeal performances of dispossession in the digital *testimonios* have shown acts of injustice and powerlessness of those that, in the moment of the recording of the video, and whenever it is played again, dispossess themselves. The digital *testimonios* employ multimodality in their videos in order to perform dispossession according to different logics, as the following sections will summarize.

1.1. Enacting dispossession

First, undocumented youth narrators **imitate and perform dispossession**[1] by, for instance, metaphorically enacting the process of putting a 'post-it' onto the wall that reminds Stephanie Solis (1) of her inability to fully participate in activities that require a form of government identification; by **enacting the moment** Mohammad Abdollahi's (2) college acceptance letter was taken away from him by means of his own hand; or by using a metaphoric gesture that combined with the sound it creates, expresses the forcefulness of 'shooting down' Carlos Roa's dreams to go to college or the military. The enactment transfers the dispossessing power of that moment to the undocumented youth narrators themselves and, at the same time, appeals to the viewer's moral understanding and sense of agency 'for the cause', since the viewer is, through the performance in the visual moving image, turned into a witness of dispossession processes.

As the frame of the visual image focuses on the undocumented narrators' bodies, the youths further enact criminalization, for instance, through abstract pointing. Mitzy Calderón (6) sets herself off against 'others' – those who possess papers. The mostly plain background of the videos' settings eliminates other visual distractions. The setting and lighting of Mohammad Abdollahi's (2) video symbolically visualize his life 'in the shadows', reinforcing his own act of actively victimizing his body by pointing at it and claiming that he, as a human being, and an undocumented immigrant, 'is not good enough' to be accepted at a U.S. university, literally and symbolically pointing to a dehumanizing state of being. The audience on YouTube becomes a **witness** when it sees Luis' family's dispossession in very 'human' terms: Appearing in the video as a silent participant, Luis' nephew appears in the moving image along with Luis in scenes filmed outside of the apartment. Thus, Luis turns the viewer's attention to the recent rise in the numbers of undocumented immigrants deported in 2013 and the current campaigns against the criminalization of 'reentry'.

Through the visual moving image, particularly as it tracks changes in facial expression and bodily movement, undocumented youth perform dispossession as the narrative time of the video proceeds. Constant movement of his arms und upper body while sitting on the ground, in David Ramirez' (4) narrative, highlights the precarity and urgency that his undocumented status imposes on him, expressing the difficulty of his situation. This way, moving image illustrates dispossession as interminably mapped onto the bodies, as it catches 'changes' performed through the body. Stephanie Solis' (1) facial expressions, for instance, change from confident to sad as she begins to talk about her immigration status. The performance of visible emotions **displayed by the change** in facial expressions thus serves as an indicator of the current immigration status in the narratives. Dispossession, here, can be performed particularly well as a structure of feeling, expressed through the change in facial features.

Other medial variants of the visual channel, the 'visual static image', enacts dispossession through the logics of time as well: Through the blending-in of two photos that depict the same room but the first *with* items stored in it and the second *without* them, Stephanie Solis' (1), for instance, uses the 'illustrative mode' of photos to ***illustrate* dispossession** in Butler and Athanasiou's second sense of dispossession as a direct, material and non-material expression of loss.

Written language that is used only in some of the narratives as a variant to the spoken, contributes to **informing** the viewer of the narrator's dispossession. In two of the narratives, written language thus serves as a constant reminder of the dispossession through undocumented status by means of, for instance, the written words 'I am undocumented' printed on Mohammad Abdollahi's (2) t-shirt, or similar captions that appear in the visual moving image which depicts David Ramirez' (thus dispossessed) body (4).

The auditory channel in the eight digital *testimonios* likewise is able to enact dispossession, however, in a less direct sense. Speech, or rather the *absence* of it, is a means of performing the moment of dispossession and, in particular, the aporia described in David Ramirez' verbal metaphor of the feeling that undocumented status causes him to feel as if he was 'digging himself further into a hole'. David performs his dispossession, in this sense, as a **marker** of the limits of self-sufficiency that he expresses through explicit exhaling, pausing, and then stopping the recording altogether. Again not directly expressed through speech but by means of the core mode of (non-diegetic) music, Carlos Roa's digital *testimonio* utilizes classical instrumental music (piano and flute) to play a theme that serves as a harmonious 'leitmotif' for his deceased mother. The sadness of the music contrasts to his composed countenance while speaking of his mother. In turn, this contrast 'announces' a change in emotions, and thus, **highlights** Carlos' dispossession of fulfilling his mother's 'American Dream'.

Finally, film editing and montage is employed to enact and illustrate dispossession in the eight narratives. 'Zoom' primarily focuses on the narrators' faces as they recount or perform their dispossession through a **visible display of emotions**. Zooming *out*, in contrast, signalized to 'keep a distance', frames dispossession by de-emphasizing the narrators' centrality of the dispossessed body, and ends the narrative episode of the core story. The producers' freedom to determine narrative tone and topic advances the digital *testimonio*'s function as a political device in the Movement. Video editing through cuts, for instance, determines what the narrative is 'supposed to be about', cutting the moving image where 'everything *important* has been said', such as in Ivette Roman's (7) digital *testimonio.* Moving away from the undocumented status as a major force of dispossession, the video by means of cutting highlights the intersections of undocumented status with other forms of identity for which the narrator is dispossessed (in Ivette's case, sexual dispossession). This move de-emphasizes the dispossession of undocumented *students* at the time of the narrative's publishing in 2013, as the students, by then, have legal access to options such as the DACA or state versions of the DREAM Act, shifting the focus on other '**urgent**' **issues** in their narratives instead.

1.2. From dispossession to 'possession': performance as resistance

Performing dispossession, as the section above highlights, is not restricted to illustrating or enacting moments and states of dispossession. Rather, Butler and Athanasiou's understanding of dispossession as a form of political protest incorporates the possibility for undocumented youth to voice their **opposition and resistance** to the dispossession to which their families and communities are subjected. Their digital *testimonios* demonstrate an assumption of power that works beyond dominant ideological frameworks.

First, the narratives actively claim their belonging to U.S. citizenry and perform the 'possession' thereof. Stephanie Solis (1), for instance, by means of gesture shortly performs the pledge of allegiance and the waving of an American flag which constitutes a symbolic act ***performing* her legalization**; Carlos Roa's (3) metaphoric gestures perform an act of *personally* '**contributing**' to society; Angelica Velazquillo (5) shrugs her shoulders to illustrate that she has 'no choice' but to act and protest against the 'injustices her community is facing'; Mitzy Calderón (7), by means of an iconic gesture that connotes 'smallness', belittles the importance of a social security number as the precondition for '**belonging**'. While she does not belong legally, she expresses that she *does* belong by smiling and glancing up to the ceiling when she pronounces that at her alternative university, Freedom University in Georgia, all those excluded *belong*. Similarly, Angelica smiles and emphatically closes her eyes at the announcement of her degree in the introduction to her narrative. Through this, she expresses a sense of *legitimization* of the self and justification for why she is in the country illegally, emphasizing the 'worthiness' of undocumented immigrant students in the Movement.

Further, in Carlos Roa's (3) narrative, he induces **moral judgment** through a metaphoric gesture that visualizes the act of 'scolding' somebody. The difference that lies in the function of this gesture is not only an ideational one, however, but an interpersonal as well, since Carlos directly looks into the camera during this performance, and thus, expresses criticism at the 'general public' represented by the audience of YouTube for denying him his 'dreams'. The use of photos in the introduction to his narrative symbolizes the assimilationist idea of the 'melting pot', as images and voices of different ethnicities melt into a United States flag by means of digital editing of the moving image, following a political logic that favors the legalization of all undocumented immigrants in the United States, which Pallares stressed as a central underlying goal of the Movement and its marches since 2006.

The body of the dispossession, visualized by the moving image, further indicates resistances through posture, for instance. Through the spatial proportions of the framed visual image, undocumented youth establish a clear **hierarchy** between themselves and their wider audience, expressing a sense of personal agency through **elevated positions**, for instance. Likewise, facial expressions connote attitudes. While smiles are usually associated with happiness, in the digital narratives, smiles in combination with verbal language that expresses a contrasting sorrow or anger can become 'inappropriate' performative acts. Carlos Roa (3) performs this way when he **mocks** which immigrants in the course of immigration history of the United States obtain a personal claim to legalization. Narrating with humor and/or irony, in turn, creates power in online communities, transforming media logic and social shaping on YouTube into acts of political resistance.

Gestures and body movement further perform attitudes and opinions that interrogate the public treatment of undocumented immigrants in the United States, enacting to 'cheer' for the organization with a **triumphant hand gesture**; or, as Ivette Roman (7) does, emphasizing the intersectional struggle of her dispossession, being undocumented and a lesbian, while she **confirms her pronounced resistance** to fight against the discrimination she experiences by smiling and nodding at the sentence that she is 'a lesbian'. Judith Butler maintains that such a performance "suggests that certain cultural configurations of gender take the place of 'the real' and consolidate and augment their hegemony through that felicitous self-naturalization" (*Gender Trouble* 33).

In addition to the visual channel, the verbal speech act constitutes a crucial aspect to the ability of undocumented youth to express resistance and protest. Through the politics of the performative, "recalls, norms, names, signs, practices, and regulatory fictions can be invoked, cited anew, and challenged at once", Athanasiou summarizes (99). Consequently, undocumented youth assume the option of "**self-naming**" in their digital *testimonios*, 'outing' themselves to millions of potential viewers and exclaiming to be self-confident, 'unafraid', and 'unashamed' about this status (see, for instance, Mitzy Calderón (7) or Luis Maldonado (8)) – assuming the 'mottos' that the Movement produced in recent years to 'name' their campaigns and their struggle. Additionally, Carlos exclaims: 'I am America' in the introduction to his *testimonio*, expressing a crucial claim to legalization. This 're-naming' function of the speech act is predominantly, yet not confined to vocal speech: David Ramirez (4) uses written language (captions) to inscribe the motto of his campaign and Movement 'onto' his body.

The different modes of the voice further add an **activating effect** through the meaning that changes in the prosodic elements of rhythm, pitch, and volume produce. Undocumented youth narrators can **decriminalize** family members and actions of civil disobedience through a sharp rise in pitch; or express a sense of power through the use of rhythmic language and music. Luis Maldonado (8), for instance, metaphorically and literally prolongs his announced and **ever-continuing activism**. The drum beats, hence, symbolize ongoing acts of resistance.

1.3. Testimonial storytelling and collectivity on YouTube

Closely connected to the self-naming strategies mentioned in the section above, 'outing' as undocumented is the resistance to 'closetedness' that implies silences, not 'having a voice', and essentially being a voiceless 'subaltern' in Spivak's sense of the word. Undocumented youth, thus, actively put an end to their silences by literally **speaking their truth** in performative speech acts. Undocumented youth, thus, through their literal speaking out, become witnesses to their cause. It is the voice that is most important, bearing **witness** to ills that happen in the communities of the dispossessed. In fact, for two of the narratives in this selection, speech and moving image are the only devices the narrators require for their storytelling.

Through their oral storytelling, undocumented youth challenge ideas of truth and authenticity, as they blend their voice, visuals, name, biographical data, and photos. These strategies for performing the 'personal' through oral storytelling transform their digital *testimonios* into personalized accounts on YouTube. Yet, despite the personal detail and subjectivity, through this act of storytelling, they lay claim to 'a **voice for all**' immigrants dispossessed by their status. This claim works, in particular, through the close relation between their narratives and the genre of the *testimonio*, which becomes most discernible in the introductory sequences to their narratives that resemble *testimonios* such as that of Rigoberta Menchú. In these speech patterns, the narrators self-confidently perform a '**ritual**', stating their status, name, and age, and, at times, organizational affiliation.[2] This pattern, as it connects the youths across the widespread and diverse YouTube community, highlights a sense of belonging to the Movement, and a **collectiveness in the struggle** for the rights of the undocumented. It follows that the voice in combination with the visuals, the name, autobiographical data, and the declaration of undocumented status serve as an emphasis on community, but as an **individual signature** at the same time: a ritual that all undocumented youth can reproduce yet completely individualize in the spirit of individual output on platforms such as YouTube.

Adding an **interpersonal statement** in the form of "thank you" at the end of her narrative, Angelica, for instance, also transforms the viewer into a 'witness' to her cause, implying that she does not leave anyone else room to speak *for her* or interrupt her, while she establishes narrative contract with her viewer nevertheless. In contrast, captions, and a voice from the background in one of the narratives, show that the **production process** also may be a **communal** one. The **vocal intervention** by another person in Ivette Roman's *testimonio*, for instance, associates her with the caption in her video that contains the organizational logo of *Equality Maryland* – a campaign supporting undocumented youth LGBT immigrants. Likewise, written captions add another narrative perspective. In most cases, written captions *during* the video clip *describe* information on the narrators' diverse backgrounds and dispossessed identities. These reveal information that the undocumented narrator must have recounted in the process of 'in-depth interviewing' as one also encounters in the production of the traditional *testimonio*. In one case, a written caption also formulates the original interview question, which the narrator then answers. Using other perspectives contributes to the **simulation of a face-to-face *testimonio*** – an interaction and conversation with an interlocutor, which is, in most digital *testimonios*, replaced by the camera.

1.4. Mediatizing public space for YouTube: 'new form of politics'

The visual moving image in a clip on YouTube is certainly restricted in its actual space. The space depicted, however, does not have any limits. A few of the narratives in this selection have understood the device to 'occupy' spaces in their offline life that, through the performance of **resistant activities in that space**, serve as a form of political protest. In particular, the occupation of space offers options for **plural performativity**, in Butler and Athanasiou's sense of the word.

Therefore, some of the narratives form a '**public space**' for their undocumented body, materializing the dispossession in the performance and resisting it in the most literal sense. For this, the changes in setting as well as the concrete bodily movement and posture depict an **occupation** of public spaces. The **background settings** in which some of the videos are produced depict educational institutions, or community centers that hint at the existence of a **space for offline activism**. Moving images show Stephanie Solis (1), for instance, *in action*, giving a 'mock graduation speech,' and thus, inhabiting the space of her college campus, which, in the year of her publication, points to the need for a DREAM Act to enable undocumented youth to get higher education. In addition, having her viewer 'follow' her on public transportation and on campus has a similar effect in the narrative. Likewise, Luis Maldonado (8) performs his dispossession by **conquering 'real' spaces** as well: Throughout the digital narrative, the moving image depicts him walking at or sitting in front of the U.S.-Mexican border in Hidalgo, being 'contained' and 'restricted' by the presence of the border. As the camera depicts his feet, walking, the movement along the border symbolizes an **ongoing and active struggle**.

What is more, the still images (photographs) portray offline action, as the photo on Ivette Roman's (7) office wall explains. Luis Maldonado (8) uses photographs to portray himself, literally, 'in action' with or in front of a crowd of people that holds up posters or wears t-shirts that, through the use of written language, proclaim a 'belonging to' the Movement. Luis claims an active sense of belonging without having to verbally express it. Instead, the photos narrate this activism by themselves. In them, Luis unites with the crowd of activists and protesters in the performativity of resistance through the photos' **performativity of plurality** and **performativity in plurality**. Despite the fact that still images are said to be 'static' on all levels, Luis' photos depict the **dynamics** of the Movement – a movement in plurality.

2. Mediatization of politics – a voice to undocumented youth

Benmayor coined the term 'digital *testimonio*' as a mediated *testimonio* that amalgamates the tradition of the *testimonio* with digital storytelling on YouTube. This analysis of YouTube narratives of undocumented youth documents that digital ***testimonios* are mediatized** and, thus, an expression of the mediatization of politics that Esser and Strömbäck, most famously, proposed.

The mediatization of the storytelling through the use of multimodality as a major storytelling device has proven capable of transforming such a long-lasting tradition as that of the *testimonio*, fostering changes in practices that are part of mediatization processes. The mediatization of storytelling bears great potential for many more studies of such 'new' cultural phenomena that arose within the first decades of the new millennium. The frame of mediatization as a tool for understanding new media content such as digital *testimonios* of undocumented youth *within* and outside of their Movement, renegotiates issues such as personalization, participation, and agency.

With reference to mediatization theory, as the figure below shows, the *testimonio* is an 'open-ended' basis upon which the digital *testimonio* solidly forms. Like a sand glass, however, the media logic of YouTube 'raises' the digital *testimonio*, which gives it its own 'shape' – different from that of the *testimonio* (not an open-ended rectangle but a triangle), yet again different from the media logic (arrow) (Figure 8.1):

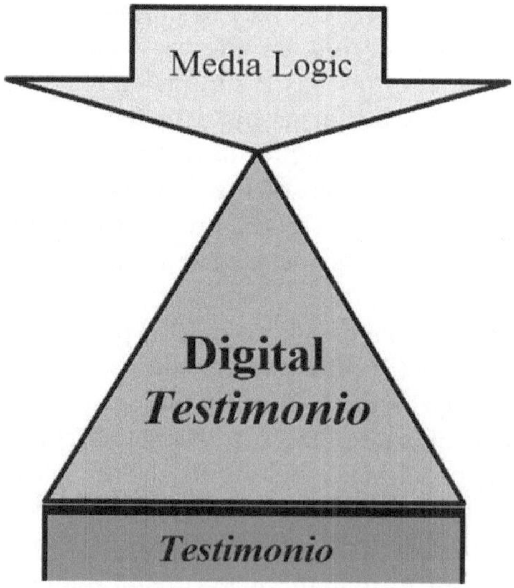

Figure 8.1 Digital *Testimonio* by S.Q.

One of the most basic implications that follows from this investigation is that, as Jäger et al. explain,

> with the pervasive expansion of computer technology and the development of networked communication towards the end of the 20th century, renewed shifts in cultural structures could be experienced leading to transformations in the various communicative cultures.
>
> (9)

The 'mediatization of politics', in this investigation, offered an understanding of the logic of the revived Immigrant Rights Movement as a unique vocalization of political protest led by undocumented youth. This voice inherently connects to the tradition of the *testimonio*, yet replaces its interlocutor and audience with the digital medium and community, while the visual space of the video serves as a major device for performing resistance. This resistance, however, is not confined to the public offline space but transforms the online 'space' to a site for activism as well. The integration of the Immigrant Rights Movement's politics into the spaces of the new medium, YouTube has proven that resistance against dispossession gains new perspectives that cannot only be confined to the offline sphere for activism. The resistance of undocumented youth manifests in the digital telling of their story, showing that it is not only in actual, physical revolutions that cultural weapons can be used. After all, storytelling of undocumented youth *is* politics. Thus, let us always be reminded of the fact that undocumented youth *possess* an agenda, and, with reference to 'his' Movement, in David Ramirez' words: "We're not cute. We're organized."[3]

Notes

1 All relevant concluding material will be highlighted in bold letters.
2 They do this consistently throughout the selection of narratives in this study, however, not every narrative mentions all aspects. Least conforming to this pattern are the narratives of Stephanie Solis (1) and Carlos Roa (3).
3 David Ramirez made this statement during his civil disobedience action in 2011, from which the *digital testimonio* analyzed in this study arose (Pallares 127).

References

Abdollahi, Mohammad. DreamActivist. "My name is Mohammad and I am Undocumented." Online video clip. *YouTube*. YouTube, 19 Mar. 2010. Web. 22 Dec. 2014.

Butler, Judith. *Gender Trouble: Feminism and the Subversion of Identity*. New York: Routledge, 1990.

Butler, Judith, and Athena Athanasiou. *Dispossession: The Performative in the Political*. Cambridge: Polity Press, 2013.

Calderón, Mitzy. SUDDENmovementDotOrg. "I Am No Longer Hiding! I Am No Longer Afraid!" Online video clip. *YouTube*. YouTube, 13 Nov. 2010. Web. 22 Dec. 2014.

Jäger, Ludwig, Erika Linz, and Irmela Schneider, eds. *Media, Culture, and Mediality: New Insights in the Current State of Research.* Bielefeld: Transcript Verlag, 2010.

Maldonado, Luis and Sheridan Lagunas-Aguirre. "Luis Maldonado: A Brief Look into the Life of an Undocumented Immigrant." Online video clip. *YouTube.* YouTube, 20 Sept. 2013. Web. 9 Sept. 2014.

Pallares, Amalia. *Family Activism: Immigrant Struggles and the Politics of Noncitizenship.* New Brunswick, Canada: Rutgers University Press, 2015.

Ramirez, David. Thedreamiscoming2011. "David Ramirez, Immigrant Youth Justice League." Online video clip. *YouTube.* YouTube, 5 Apr. 2011. Web. 22 Dec. 2014.

Roa, Carlos. Cccvideovault. "Carlos: the Story of an Undocumented Student." Online video clip. *YouTube.* YouTube, 21 July 2010. Web. 22 Dec. 2014.

Roman, Ivette. MsKYYoung. "Maryland's Undocumented Immigrant Students – Ivette." Online video clip. *YouTube.* YouTube, 5 Jan. 2013. Web. 22 Dec. 2014.

Solis, Stephanie. UndergroundAtBrown. "Lost & Found (Story of a DREAM Act Student)." Online video clip. *YouTube.* YouTube, 12 May 2009. Web. 5 Nov. 2013.

Urrea, Luis A. "Foreword." *Underground America: Narratives of Undocumented Lives.* Ed. Peter Orner. San Francisco, CA: McSweeney's Books, 2008. 375–379.

Velazquillo, Angelica. Mercy Sister. "An Undocumented Immigrant, Angelica, Tells Her Story." Online video clip. *YouTube.* YouTube, 2 Mar. 2012. Web. 22 Dec. 2014.

Index